THE PROFESSIONAL DESIGNER'S GUIDE TO GARDEN FURNISHINGS

THE PROFESSIONAL DESIGNER'S GUIDE TO GARDEN FURNISHINGS

Vanessa Gardner Nagel

APLD, NCIDQ

Timber Press // Portland London

Photography credits appear on page 297.

Published in 2013 by Timber Press, Inc.

The Haseltine Building
133 S.W. Second Avenue, Suite 450
Portland, Oregon 97204-3527
timberpress.com

2 The Quadrant
135 Salusbury Road
London NW6 6RJ
timberpress.co.uk

Printed in China
Book design by David Jacobson, ORT

Library of Congress Cataloging-in-Publication Data

Nagel, Vanessa Gardner.
The professional designer's guide to garden furnishings/Vanessa Gardner
Nagel.—1st ed.
    p. cm.
 Includes bibliographical references and index.
 ISBN 978-1-60469-293-8 (no)
 1. Garden ornaments and furniture. I. Title.
SB473.5.N34 2013
645'.8—dc23   2013001141

A catalog record for this book is also available from the British Library.

For
Thomas,
Annabella, and
Daniel,
may you always
be inspired
to follow
your heart.

Contents

PART 2: MATERIALS 86

TO THE TRADE 254

Acknowledgments

No author is an island. Without the help of my editors, Tom Fischer and Mindy Fitch, and the entire Timber Press crew who improved my words and designed this book, you would not be reading it now. I am immensely grateful to every manufacturer, vendor, fabricator, and artist who graciously contributed photographs and responded to a myriad of questions about their products. Special acknowledgment must go to Taylor Guess with Proteak for his inside story about teak, Cathryn Peters for her extensive knowledge of wicker, Roger Thomas for his enlightening information about glass, and Matt Goddard for his contagious appreciation of stone. Gratitude must especially extend to devoted friends and colleagues for helping to illustrate this book with their photographs. A special thanks to Laurel Young and Clark Jurgemeyer for taking on the task of reading text and providing helpful feedback, to J. J. DeSouza for her invaluable resources, and to Bonnie Bruce for reviewing sustainability information. I am ceaselessly indebted to my family for allowing me the extra time to write even when it means time away from them. Special thanks must also go to my ethereal writing muse, JoAnn Thomas, and to Julia Eggert, who pitched in with many hours to assure the book stayed on schedule. Finally to my dearest Michael, I owe appreciation beyond measure.

Facing:
Sexy garden candles atop a dining table provide a warm glow if the wine doesn't.

INTRODUCTION

Good garden furnishings, like good interior

furnishings, are an investment. Not everyone can afford the very best, but everyone should buy the very best they can afford. When I first turned my interior design skills inside out after a lengthy career and ventured into landscape design, I was surprised to find that many garden designers choose not to furnish a garden and stop at the plants. To me that is like an interior designer claiming that an interior is exclusively about the finishes. For obvious reasons interior designers don't stop at the carpet: people need places to sit, dine, sleep, and work. Even more, outdoor furnishings entice people to occupy a garden, thereby gaining a deeper experience of the magic of nature. So, after sitting outside on a fellow designer's deck one perfect summer evening—comfortable seating, candles lit, no mosquitoes, champagne with crème de cassis in hand—my belief was reinforced: outdoor furnishings are essential to a well-designed garden, too. Interior or exterior, design is about the total environment and making the best use of the space.

At the beginning of any garden design, you and your client will discuss many issues. One issue that deserves especially thorough discussion is how much value the client places on their garden. This will lead to discussion of the investment they will make, and the initial budget must not overlook garden furnishings. All the components of a garden should intertwine to create a design-consistent environment even if the style is eclectic. When you include garden furnishings as part of your conceptual plan presentation, yourclient will come to understand the entire concept, and furnishings will no longer be an afterthought.

This book aims to help you select appropriate outdoor furnishings for your clients by providing the tools needed to understand style, materials, products, and how the garden furnishings trade works.

Style—obviously an essential consideration—is the focus of the first section. If you want to choose the perfect furnishings, you must start with a solid foundation in design history. For this reason the style section begins with a short course on historical furnishing styles. Chapters on architecture, comfort, scale, and proportion round out the subject of style, and a chapter called "Preconceived Styles" discusses ubiquitous contemporary garden styles, which you may or may not want to use yourself, but which you do need to be aware of.

In the second section of the book I discuss materials, providing a lot of detail about how different materials are made, the history of how they came to be, and how they are fabricated. This is essential information for any designer serious about selecting the right material for specific garden furnishings and uses. I firmly believe you need to know your materials inside and out. Only then will you feel confident that your furnishings will not only look beautiful but will also hold up over time. For each material discussed, I also provide helpful information about evaluating sustainable practices of manufacturers and suppliers.

The final chapter, "To The Trade," covers what to expect when working with people in the furnishings trade and other trade-related issues. And last but not least, I include a list of garden furnishings resources to help you navigate the many companies producing everything from portable fire pits to planters, gazebos, garden furniture, and outdoor textiles.

If you incorporate furnishings into your garden designs, you will be able to ditch the days of returning to a project only to find ill-suited furnishings. Your clients will be happier because they will find value in their gardens as comfortable places to live. And since high-quality garden furnishings last longer, fewer furnishings will end up in landfills. All in all, a lot of benefits.

PART 1
STYLE

When it comes to selecting garden furnishings,

you can never ignore style—a broad term for the distinctive manner of creating something. Styles have names when they have very defined, easily identifiable characteristics. Designers may use only one style in a design. Alternatively they might create an eclectic mix of styles, which works beautifully so long as the designer pays attention to proportions and details. Consistency and harmony are essential. After all, if the line, form, and materials of a furnishing do not fit the theme of the garden, the furnishing will feel dissonant and out of place.

How did style become a factor in design? Where did it come from? Why is it important? What are stylistic influences, and how do we recognize them?

To begin with, it's important to recognize the connection between interior and exterior styles. As soon as people first put roofs over their heads, they established the idea of inside versus outside and began to treat those environments differently. Since indoor environments were protected from weather, interior furnishings could be made with a greater variety of materials and lasted longer. This led to interior styles being more highly developed than exterior styles.

Did ancient people take their interior furnishings outdoors in good weather? Did they create furnishings that could be left outdoors year-round? The truth is that we don't really know. What is certain is that exterior furnishing styles, like interior styles, were greatly affected by things like lifestyle and culture, geographic locale, and the availability of materials.

It would be difficult to pinpoint when exterior furnishings began to develop independently from interior furnishings, but some certainly did. Two examples are the Lutyens bench, designed in England in 1900, and the Adirondack chair, created in the US in 1903. Although outdoor furniture styles historically found much inspiration from interior styles, they were also influenced by the weather-resistant materials from which the furniture had to be made. For example, some styles developed specifically for outdoor teak furniture, like the Giverny bench. On the other hand, the development of plastics also led to some outdoor furniture increasingly and more easily mimicking indoor furniture. Contemporary incentives to recycle plastic have driven this idea even farther.

Clearly there is a strong (if not well-documented) connection between the development of interior and exterior furnishing styles. They

Facing:
Small garden, big lifestyle, with a beautiful array of outdoor furnishings.

are very much intertwined. However, contemporary designers are also challenging the traditional model that sees interiors and exteriors as separate environments. A desire to treat these spaces as one cohesive environment blurs the line between interior and exterior furnishings.

For these reasons I begin this section with a brief history of furniture style, including many pieces designed for interiors. Knowledge of stylistic history is an excellent starting point because it enables us, as designers, to achieve greater design consistency and deepen our understanding of detail and proportion.

Subsequent chapters focus on human scale, technology, architecture, culture, and lifestyle, which have always impacted the style of furnishings. From the double curve of an Egyptian stool to modern ergonomic forms, we design to work with human curves and proportions. Technology drives our capability to form and combine materials. Architecture responds to site and stimulates the design of furnishings that reside within it. Culture and lifestyle affect how we ornament our furnishings and their size, shape, and type. Contemporary "preconceived" garden styles (Asian, tropical, naturalistic, and so forth) are also discussed, since they tend to dominate garden designs.

With an understanding of these topics, you can feel confident that the garden furnishings you select will work with your designs and your clients' architecture.

History and Geography

Furnishings, including those made for outdoor spaces, have a very long history that spans the globe. The minute that humans found they needed a comfortable place to sit or something to store their stuff in, they began to furnish their surroundings. In ancient times, furniture was usually reserved for royalty and the upper classes, as typified by the oldest known monarchy, the Assyrians (3000 BC to 700 BC). Thrones and furnishings were made of wood and metal (including gold, silver, and bronze), possibly inlaid with ivory, and adorned with hand-carved animals' heads and feet. Seats began as backless stools and evolved into chairs with backs.

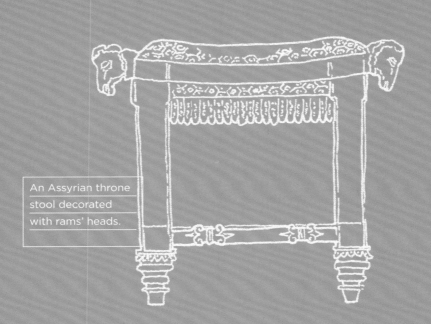

An Assyrian throne stool decorated with rams' heads.

Learning a bit of design history and exploring historical timelines can help us understand the relationships, events, and cultural interchanges that have impacted the design of furnishings. It is useful to note, for example, that during the European Renaissance, furnishings from the Ming dynasty (one of China's most notable design periods) were arriving from China, and for this reason the Ming period greatly influenced Renaissance artists and designers. Likewise, European exploration of Japan between 1500 and 1600 led to greater interest in Japanese exports. Edo period textiles, jewelry, and art were displayed at the 1862 International Exhibition in London, inspiring Western designers during the Arts and Crafts period.

This chapter explores the history of furnishing styles by focusing on the chair, one of the most basic pieces of furniture indoors or outside. As you consider iconic chair styles, from those of ancient Egypt and China all the way to contemporary designs, my hope is that you will better understand that historical events, geography, culture, the human body, technology, and materials all impact design—and continue to leave their imprint on furnishings, including those made specifically for outdoor use. This is essential information for garden designers. Garden furnishings do not develop in a vacuum, as the historical styles described in this chapter will validate.

Western furniture history timeline

Please note that unless an event occurred on a specific date, most dates listed are approximate. The evolution and dating of styles overlap and interweave through time.

Assyrian	3000 BC to 700 BC	Victorian	mid-1800s to early 1900s
Egyptian and Greek	3000 BC to 30 BC	Arts and Crafts	1860 to 1930s
Roman	753 BC to AD 565	Art Nouveau	1890 to 1920
Byzantine	330 to 1453	Art Deco	1920s to 1930s
Gothic	1000 to 1400	Bauhaus	1919 to 1933
Renaissance	1400 to 1600	Mid-century modern	1933 to 1970
Baroque	1600 to early 1700s	Postmodern	1960s to 1990s
Rococo	mid-1700s	Contextualist and contemporary	1990s to present
Neoclassical	late 1700s		
Directoire	1795 to 1799		
Regency and Empire	early to mid-1800s		

Egyptian (3000 BC to 30 BC)

Developing concurrently, and probably interactively, with the Assyrian style, Egyptian style began to relate the curvature of the human body to furniture. Simple stools sometimes had three legs, for added stability on uneven surfaces. Cross-legged stools with leather seats could be collapsed and moved at will. Egyptians also decorated their furniture with what they saw around them. Animal feet became the termination of a chair leg; hieroglyphics painted or etched onto a cabinet told a story about its owner or expressed religious beliefs. Lotus flowers, common to the region, found their way onto columns, and tabletops were engraved with games.

Greek (3000 BC to 30 BC)

Due to their proximity and interrelationships, the Greeks, Romans, and Egyptians all influenced each other's stylistic development. The Greeks developed a cross-legged stool similar to the Egyptians but also created the iconic klismos chair, which remains influential. The wooden chair's back was curved to support the sitter, while the legs splayed backward and forward to keep the chair from tipping over. The seat was made of strips of leather woven and attached to the wood frame, which held a cushion that formed to the body of the sitter. Other furnishings included beds and urns for storing food and water.

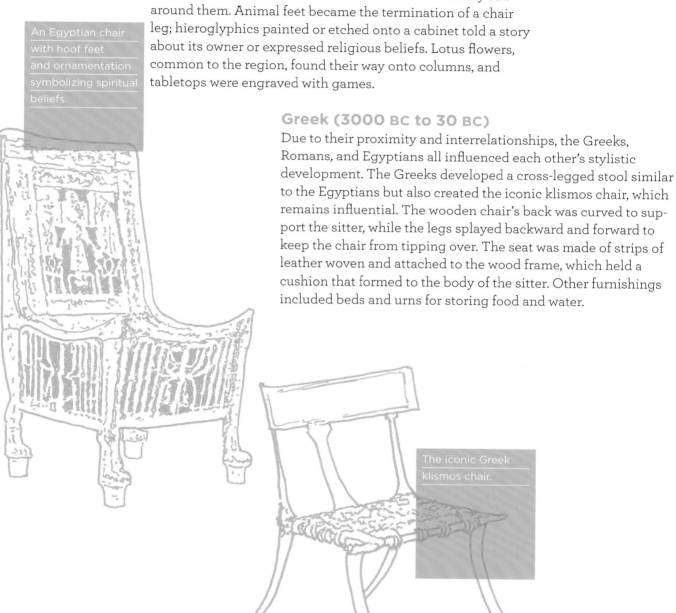

An Egyptian chair with hoof feet and ornamentation symbolizing spiritual beliefs.

The iconic Greek klismos chair.

Roman (753 BC to AD 565)

As the Romans conquered other countries and expanded outward, their culture impacted style in those conquered countries, and the culture of the conquered countries impacted Roman style. For example, the more politically involved Rome became with Egypt, the more infatuated Romans became with exotic Egyptian animals and other motifs. Romans preferred space and simplicity, so their minimalist furniture style left most of the ornamentation for their architectural surroundings. They did use sitting or sleeping pieces, including thrones for the wealthy and politically influential. The furnishings were rather bulky, incorporating popular motifs such as the gryphon. Other common embellishments included images of snakes, monkeys, and wolves.

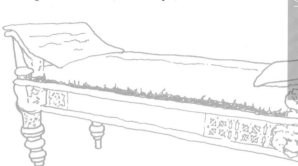

A simple Roman couch.

Byzantine (330 to 1453)

Much of what we know about style during the Byzantine era is due to the abundant mosaics that were produced. The empire of Greek conqueror Alexander the Great extended to areas that we now know as the Middle East. Eventually, Emperor Constantine moved the capitol of the Roman Empire from Rome to the city that would eventually be named for him, Constantinople. Islamic, Arabic, and Persian motifs and stylistic influences such as calligraphy, geometrical patterns, and the arabesque merged with Greco-Roman style. The considerable influence of Christianity also surfaced after Constantine declared Christianity to be a legal religion. Christian monastic life frequently influenced the Byzantine style. Some of the early Christian motifs included assorted flora and fauna.

Persistently changing political boundaries and technological progress allowed for new advances in architecture, which in turn influenced the style of furnishings. In 1453 the Moors retook Constantinople, and Islamic impact overtook Spain and Portugal. Ultimately Christian states overpowered the Moors, driving them from the Iberian Peninsula. The influence of religion during the austere Byzantine era gradually evolved into a style with more emotion, life, and eventually more interest in classical art: the Romanesque style (1000 to 1200), perhaps best known for its half-rounded arch. A flurry of church building projects led to greater creativity and increased technical innovation during this period.

Middle Ages and the Gothic Style (1000 to 1400)

Christianity was probably the strongest and most stable influence of the Gothic period, although royalty also had furnished castles or palaces. The rounded Romanesque arch evolved into the pointed Gothic arch, simultaneously influencing architecture and furnishings. Elements of style included linenfold paneling, elegant tracery, and the trefoil, a symbol of the Christian Trinity. The wood was primarily oak.

A Gothic church seat with linenfold paneling and a back carved with tracery.

Renaissance (1400 to 1600)

Revivals of Greco-Roman architecture became a defining trait of the Renaissance, although much of the Renaissance style continued to follow the Gothic style until the Baroque period. The Renaissance style spread to most areas of Europe, including Russia, and were adapted in varying degrees. Furnishings featured routinely used components (such as medallions and carved figures and flourishes), symmetry, and geometry, in addition to classical Roman style and proportion (which makes sense given that much of the Renaissance began in Italy).

Leonardo da Vinci played a key role in determining the Italian Renaissance style, by banning the Gothic principles previously established and introducing the classic simplicity of Greece and Rome. The Italians enjoyed furnishings of a more palatial character because the climate allowed a greater engagement with the outdoors. Heavy scroll and figure carving, inlaid ivory, and marble mosaic were popular. Iron, steel, and brass fittings were functional and artistic.

An English Renaissance chair with its stiff Gothic remnants.

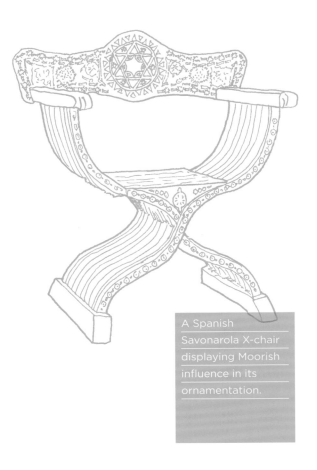

A Spanish Savonarola X-chair displaying Moorish influence in its ornamentation.

Italian furnishings had a considerable influence on the style of Louis XIII, with a little help from his Italian mother, Marie de' Medici. Scroll and shell carving were popular as ornamentation. Fancy and luxurious fabrics accompanied their furnishings. Griffins, birds, bouquets of flowers, fruits, and leaves were motifs, and some Arabian Arabesque style remained from Louis's predecessor. Ebony, imported from Africa and India, was a popular veneer with oak and pine. Chairs had seat coverings of imported cane, leather, or heavy fabric. Some of these trends continued into the Baroque period of Louis XIV.

Moorish design continued to influence Spanish Renaissance furnishings with its decorative carving, but the furnishings were influenced heavily by Italian design as well.

The Renaissance was slow to affect England and the Elizabethan style due to England's isolated location. Much of the style of Elizabethan furniture was disproportionate classicism, with clumsy workmanship, and some Gothic influence. Strapwork, a design that resembled interlaced bands or straps, was a popular motif, as was the Tudor rose. In the later Elizabethan period, scallop shells were favored. Massive and bulbous features on furnishings seemed to correspond with the larger-than-life monarchies of King Henry VIII and Queen Elizabeth I.

Baroque (1600 to early 1700s)

The Roman Catholic Church fostered the Baroque style as a response to Protestantism by using religious themes as ornamentation. The Church intended for cherubic angels ascending to heaven and other such exuberant motifs to influence their congregations and converts. Baroque furnishings tended to be beefy, muscular, considerably detailed pieces best suited to large residences, churches, or palaces. The style was intentionally dramatic, impressive, and status-seeking. The magnificent style of Louis XIV embodies the French Baroque style. Usually symmetrical, with rich veneers including marquetry, and Boulle work, this furniture style was also influenced by trade to the East. Lacquer and ornate floral patterns were added as items from China became better known. Trade also led to greater wealth, which meant that more people could afford richly detailed furnishings. The William and Mary style was popular in England during the Baroque period.

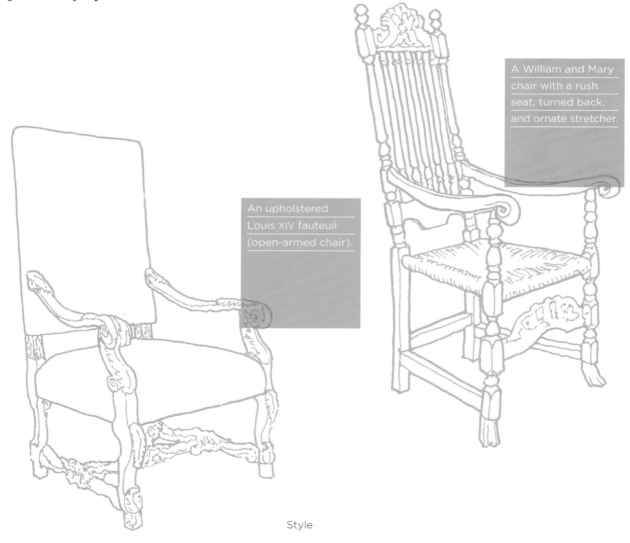

A William and Mary chair with a rush seat, turned back, and ornate stretcher.

An upholstered Louis XIV fauteuil (open-armed chair).

Rococo (mid-1700s)

Artists and craftspeople leaned toward asymmetry during the Rococo period and increased their level of embellishment, becoming more elaborate but more delicate in nature. The styles of Louis XV in France, and Queen Anne and Chippendale in England, also evolved into a more intimate scale, which is why we can so easily incorporate these styles into modern homes and gardens. The English styles tended toward

A curvaceous Louis XV chair with cabriole legs.

A Queen Anne chair with an urn-shaped back splat and spoon feet at the end of its cabriole legs.

more restraint, while the French took the style to fanciful heights.

With the death of Louis XIV, Louis XV was left with little treasury to continue the tradition of the grand salon. The boudoir became more important and affected not only the scale of furnishings but also the ornamentation, which became elegant and pretty. Love scenes ornamented screens. Fanciful, white-painted or gilded carvings of cupids, doves, and scrolls were the rage. Softer pastel colors were also popular in elegant upholstery. Continued trade with China led to lacquered furnishings. The cabriole leg, an ancient Chinese and Grecian animal leg interpretation, was consistent with this period.

Queen Anne designers initiated the use of the cabriole leg in England. Other features of the style are the shell motif, yoke-shaped top rails, urn-shaped back splats, and spoon or pad feet.

Thomas Chippendale distinguished his style with his use of shell motif, elaborate pierced splats, claw-and-ball feet, and cabriole legs (which later became straight legs as the Chinese style influenced him).

The yoke-back of this Chippendale chair displays some of the Chinese influence in Thomas Chippendale's designs. The claw-and-ball foot was popular at the end of the Rococo period and carried forward into the Neoclassical period.

Neoclassical (late 1700s)

Neoclassicism was a reaction to the Rococo style and was inspired partly by the unearthing of Pompeii and Herculaneum. Roman motifs, straighter lines, lighter scale, and formal symmetry developed into the styles of Louis XVI in France and Sheraton, Adam, and Hepplewhite in England. Shield and lyre backs became popular as classical motifs.

Typical motifs of the Louis XVI style were fluted legs with square tops and a rosette, classical urn shapes, mechanically derived curves, and the lighter scale of the Rococo style.

In England the three Adam brothers popularized the Adam style after their travels to Italy to observe the classical ruins. Working earlier than Sheraton or Hepplewhite, they were contemporaries of Chippendale and are considered early neo-classicists. Use of Roman decorative motifs (such as framed medallions, vases, urns and tripods, arabesque vine scrolls, sphinxes, griffins, and dancing nymphs) typifies their style, as do flat grotesque panels, pilasters, painted ornaments such as swags and ribbons, and complex pastel color schemes.

Named for Thomas Sheraton, the Sheraton style overlaps with the style of George Hepplewhite. Rounded, straight, tapered

This Louis XVI fauteuil displays a more symmetrical design, an oval back, and straight fluted legs.

A popular shield-back Hepplewhite chair with straight, tapered legs.

legs (versus the squared legs typified by Hepplewhite) were typical of the style. A simple spade foot, cylindrical foot, or tapered arrow foot would accompany the legs. The scale was more delicate than that of the Queen Anne period, and furnishings were painted or embellished with marquetry. Fans, urns, flowers, feathers, drapery swags, and lyres were also common motifs. Chair backs were more likely to be square, as opposed to the shield back popularized by Hepplewhite, and flow seamlessly into the chair arms. Hepplewhite's reeded or fluted legs and slightly more ornate style were accompanied by H-stretchers between the legs for reinforcement and round-fronted seats. Otherwise his furnishings were similar in ornamentation to Sheraton.

Directoire (1795 to 1799)

Following the French Revolution, the French shunned the elaborate styles of their former king and queen, and a simpler style known as Directoire became popular. Revolutionary themes were typical, such as crossed arrows in the back of a chair, and metal became a fashionable construction material. Although this period was short lived, the style remains popular due to its simplicity and scale, which fit comfortably into contemporary homes and gardens. The Directoire period quickly evolved into the Empire period in France. The Regency style became its popular equivalent in England.

Splayed legs and simpler patterns are typical of the Directoire period. The scroll arms display the transition to the Empire style.

Regency and Empire (early to mid-1800s)

During the early nineteenth century, designers took neoclassicism one step further. The English Regency style equated with the French Empire and German Biedermeier styles. As Napoléon marched around Europe, designers created furnishings with saberlike legs, simple, elegant lines, and considerable Greco-Roman, Egyptian, and Chinese influence. The Empire style used heavier woods with ornamentation from ancient Greek and Roman empire themes, the furniture often upholstered with chintz fabric (an elaborately floral cotton fabric).

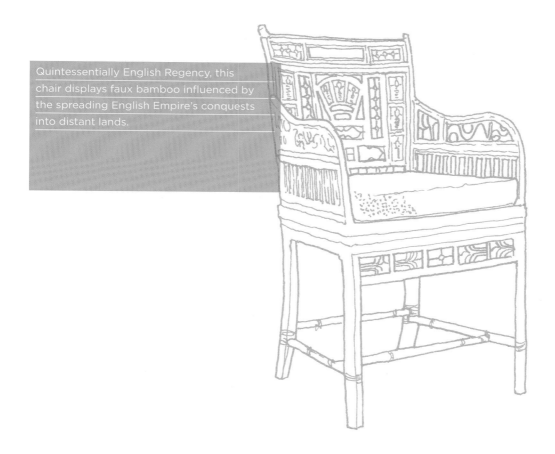

Quintessentially English Regency, this chair displays faux bamboo influenced by the spreading English Empire's conquests into distant lands.

In the Biedermeier style, a slight klismos leg is evident. Biedermeier was perhaps the simplest style of this era, often mixing light woods with black-painted accents, though not exclusively.

The Federal and Shaker styles developed in the United States as the new styles from Europe made their way across the Atlantic. The style known as Duncan Phyfe, named for a popular American cabinetmaker, encompassed both American Federal and English Regency traits. The Shaker style remains very popular due to its simplicity and scale.

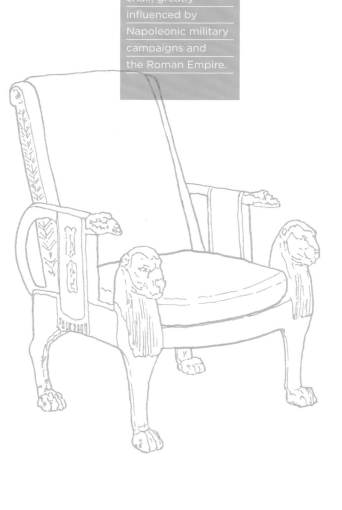

A French Empire chair, greatly influenced by Napoleonic military campaigns and the Roman Empire.

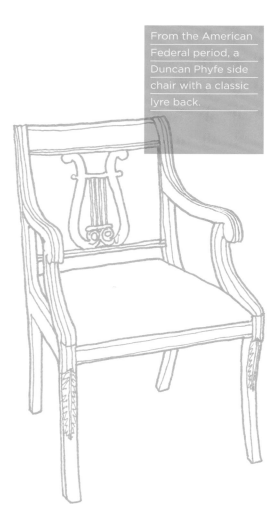

From the American Federal period, a Duncan Phyfe side chair with a classic lyre back.

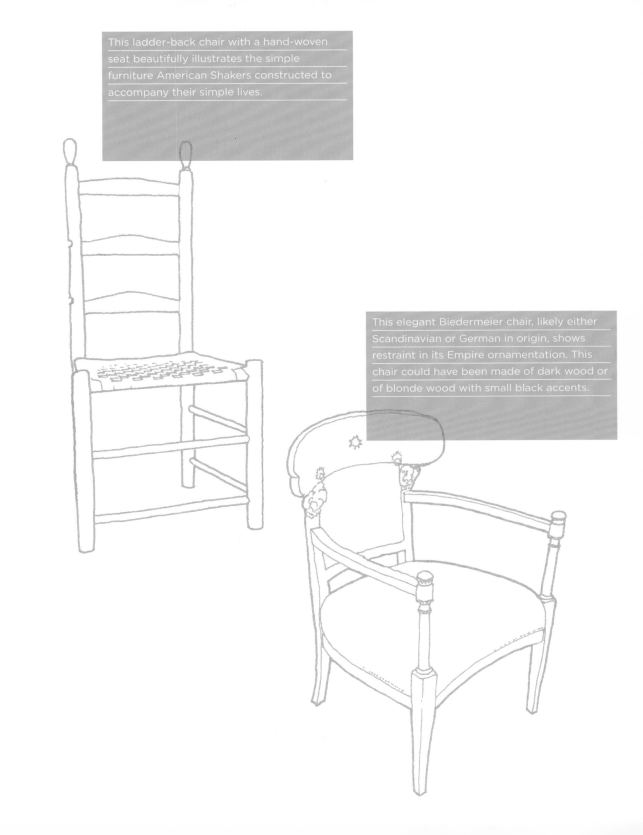

This ladder-back chair with a hand-woven seat beautifully illustrates the simple furniture American Shakers constructed to accompany their simple lives.

This elegant Biedermeier chair, likely either Scandinavian or German in origin, shows restraint in its Empire ornamentation. This chair could have been made of dark wood or of blonde wood with small black accents.

Victorian (mid-1800s to early 1900s)

During the reign of Queen Victoria, designers referenced history and created a hectic assortment of styles. They combined exaggerated Gothic ornamentation and Rococo curves with luxuriant upholstery. Chair legs shortened and seats deepened to accommodate the use of springs in upholstery seating. Today, one of the easiest ways to distinguish elegant Rococo from its exaggerated cousin, Rococo Revival, is by noting differences in scale and proportion. Machine-driven factories began to make furniture, leading to the Eastlake style with its often generous-to-a-fault use of turnings and machined decoration.

The Eastlake style helped usher in the Industrial Revolution with its mechanized ornamentation. This chair displays considerable restraint compared with some Eastlake furniture.

The Rococo Revival style stretched Louis XV to Victorian proportions.

Arts and Crafts (1860 to 1930s)

The Arts and Crafts movement originated in England partly as a response to the Great Exhibition of 1851. William Morris initiated the style to counter the stylistic artificiality and convoluted pieces he had seen, which ignored the innate qualities of the material. He and other contemporaries promoted traditional craftsmanship with simple forms (often romantic, medieval, or folk) as their inspiration. In the United States, Arts and Crafts was often called Craftsman. The style exemplified political reform of the day and a philosophy driven by the desire to establish craft guilds that rejected the grand

An upholstered William Morris Arts and Crafts chair.

An Adirondack chair.

classical style. It was important to use ordinary materials in a handcrafted, artistic manner. Ornamentation was secondary to materials and construction.

English architect Sir Edwin Lutyens designed the Lutyens bench, a stylistic blend of Arts and Crafts and classicism, during his collaboration with garden designer Gertrude Jekyll. This bench was originally called the Thakeham seat, named after the garden for which it was designed. It remains popular in gardens today. Frank Lloyd Wright, Greene and Greene, Julia Morgan, and Bernard Maybeck represented American Craftsman architecture, while Gustav Stickley promoted his furniture designs through his magazine *The Craftsman*.

Arts and Crafts is typified by simple construction without extraneous decoration and an emphasis on the materials. Flora and fauna patterns were part of the vernacular in the British countryside. Gothic Revival and medieval design influenced the bold forms and strong colors of Arts and Crafts furnishings, as did the Japanese presentation within the Great London Exhibition of 1862.

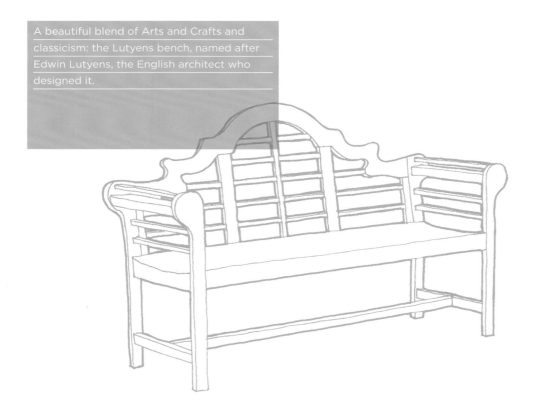

A beautiful blend of Arts and Crafts and classicism: the Lutyens bench, named after Edwin Lutyens, the English architect who designed it.

One now-ubiquitous piece of garden furniture originated during this time. In the town of Westport, New York, by the Adirondack Mountains, Thomas Lee discovered he had a shortage of comfortable chairs for his summer home by Lake Champlain. In 1903, through trial and error, he ultimately assembled a chair, tested and approved by his family. He shared the design with local carpenter Harry Bunnell, and in 1904, without Lee's knowledge, Bunnell requested a patent for what he called the Westport chair. He received that patent in 1905 and made history with what we recognize today as the Adirondack chair.

Art Nouveau (1890 to 1920)

Organic, plant-inspired motifs, curvilinear forms, undulating lines, and a sharp curve known as the whiplash all distinguish the Art Nouveau style. These pieces were usually more cheaply constructed than Arts and Crafts furniture, which relied solely on handmade technique. Designs by Louis Comfort Tiffany, Gustav Klimt, Charles Rennie Mackintosh, Antoni Gaudi, Michael Thonet, and René Lalique popularized the style. Along with Arts and Crafts, Art Nouveau was an important transition from neoclassicism to modernism.

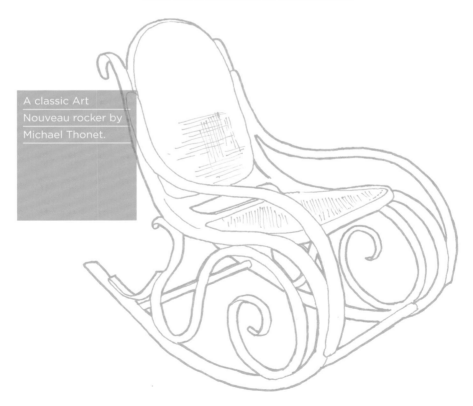

A classic Art Nouveau rocker by Michael Thonet.

Art Deco (1920s to 1930s)

As with previous styles, Art Deco found inspiration in historical designs. The style was influenced primarily by the 1925 Exposition Internationale des Arts Décoratifs et Industriels Modernes (International Exhibition of Modern Decorative and Industrial Arts), which also gave Art Deco its name. Designs incorporated bold colors, geometric shapes, and linear styling; motifs from the Egyptian style and from Mexican and African tribal art; and nature-inspired themes such as the sun, moon, and stars. Sleek wood, enamel, gleaming metals, and plastics were favored materials, and fabrics featured exotic animal or tropical patterns. Émile-Jacques Ruhlmann's furniture hid any form of joinery, suggesting pieces sculpted from a single piece of wood. René Lalique and Charles Rennie Mackintosh continued into this period as well, with their own expressions of Art Deco. German craftsman Ludwig Mies van der Rohe, best known for his modern designs, began his career as a stonecutter at this time.

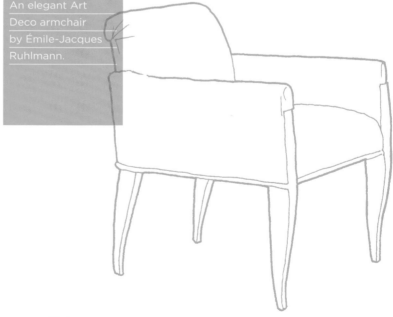

An elegant Art
Deco armchair
by Émile-Jacques
Ruhlmann.

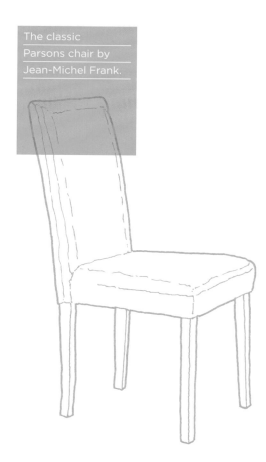

The classic Parsons chair by Jean-Michel Frank.

Modernism (1919 to 1970s)

The Bauhaus style was among the most influential elements of the modernist movement. It originated in the Bauhaus school, founded by Walter Gropius in Weimar, Germany, in 1919. One purpose of the Bauhaus (or International) style was to unify art, craft, and technology. Designers embraced the role of machines.

"Less is more," a motto adopted by Ludwig Mies van der Rohe, became associated with modernism and minimalism. In the world of furnishings, modernism challenged tradition. Marcel Breuer designed the Cesca and Wassily chairs, and Van der Rohe designed the Brno and Barcelona chairs. Charles and Ray Eames became known for their use of steel, molded plywood, and plastics. Gropius and Eames also influenced a young Italian designer, Harry Bertoia, who later designed sculptural, welded-wire furniture pieces known as the Bertoia Collection. Growing global access caused designers like Frank Lloyd Wright to blend modernism with African and Japanese styles. Eileen Gray's cantilevered table and Isamu Noguchi's sculptural coffee table are both famous designs from this period, as are Le Corbusier's LC armchairs. The Red and Blue chair designed by Gerrit Rietveld became an icon of the De Stijl movement (also known as neoplasticism), as did paintings by Piet Mondrian.

Designers from this period believed in pure abstraction—simple squares and rectangles, black, white, and primary colors. Charles Rennie Mackintosh, initially known for his Arts and Crafts style furniture, was later influenced by Bauhaus designs and developed a strongly geometric style that also influenced his fabrics. One of his most popular designs is the Hill House chair.

In 1910, Frank Alvah Parsons became the sole director of the New York School of Fine and Applied Art (later named Parsons School of Design in his honor). The development in 1921 of a satellite campus in Paris allowed Parsons to expand into France his design principle of pursuing beauty in ordinary things. This led to the design, by Paris instructor and interior designer Jean-Michel Frank, of the strikingly linear Parsons table in the 1930s, eventually accompanied by the Parsons chair.

The new modernism also influenced Scandinavian designers Arne Jacobsen, Alvar Aalto, and Hans Wegner, who contributed to the development of the style known as Danish or Swedish Modern. This style, most popular following World War II, was known for its use of woods like teak, clean lines, and comfort, as typified by Wegner's Cow Horn chair and Aalto's Paimio chair.

Mid-century modern is a recognizable style popularized from the 1930s to the 1970s. One example can be found in the streamlined, minimalist Eichler homes (named for developer Joseph Eichler) still so popular in California, built for middle-class families after World War II.

Gerrit Rietveld's Red and Blue chair.

The Cesca chair, designed by Baauhaus leader Marcel Breuer, combined traditional craftsmanship, in its wood and caning, with the contemporary technology of formed stainless steel.

Ludwig Mies van der Rohe's Barcelona chair.

Hans Wegner's iconic Wishbone chair was influenced by the shape of a Chinese ceremonial chair.

Alvar Aalto's Paimio chair.

Le Corbusier's LC3 chair combined a metal frame with upholstered cushions.

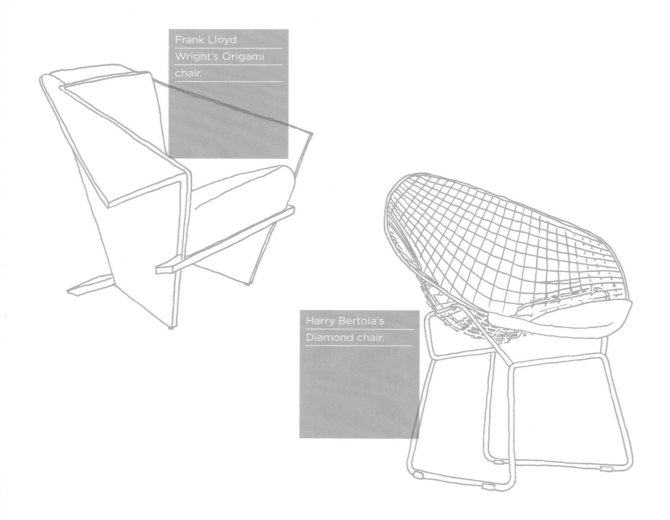

Frank Lloyd Wright's Origami chair.

Harry Bertoia's Diamond chair.

Postmodern to Contemporary (1960s to present)

Art Deco and Pop Art inspired postmodern designers, whose work has been described as vivacious, unconventional, and decorative. In its simplest explanation, this style was a reaction to the perceived severity of modernism. Postmodernism began with architecture but soon percolated into everyday furnishings. Italian architect and designer Ettore Sottsass cofounded the Memphis Group, known for its postmodern furnishings using glass, ceramic, and metal. Architect Michael Graves, who designed the postmodern Portland Building in the late 1980s, began designing household items such as his popular teakettle.

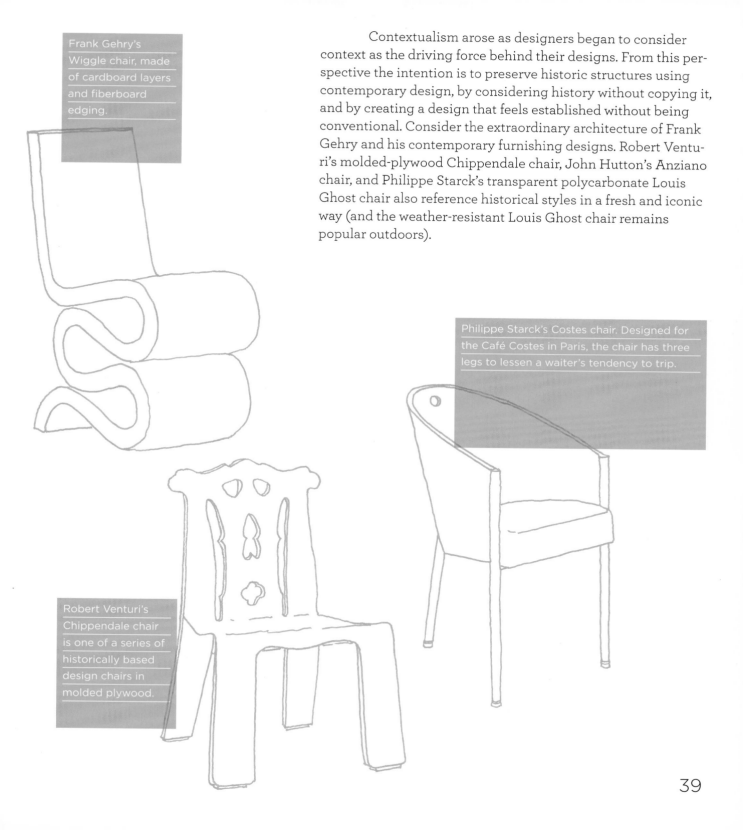

Contextualism arose as designers began to consider context as the driving force behind their designs. From this perspective the intention is to preserve historic structures using contemporary design, by considering history without copying it, and by creating a design that feels established without being conventional. Consider the extraordinary architecture of Frank Gehry and his contemporary furnishing designs. Robert Venturi's molded-plywood Chippendale chair, John Hutton's Anziano chair, and Philippe Starck's transparent polycarbonate Louis Ghost chair also reference historical styles in a fresh and iconic way (and the weather-resistant Louis Ghost chair remains popular outdoors).

The Anziano chair, designed by John Hutton for Donghia, reflects the influence of the early Greek klismos chair.

Philippe Starck's Louis Ghost chair. Do you see the ghost of Louis XVI?

Mario Bellini's minimalist Bellini chair, a one-piece injection molding of modified, fiberglass reinforced polypropylene.

Eastern furniture history timeline

Please note that unless an event occurred on a specific date, most dates listed are approximate. The evolution and dating of styles overlap and interweave through time.

Chinese

Chu Kingdom	circa 500 BC
Han dynasty	206 BC to AD 220
Northern and Southern dynasties (period of division)	220 to 581
Sui and Tang dynasties	581 to 907
Five Dynasties period	907 to 960
Song and Yuan dynasties	960 to 1368
Ming dynasty	1368 to 1644
Qing (Manchu) dynasty	1644 to 1912
Transformation period	1912 to 1949
Communist and socialist period	1949 to 1980s
Redevelopment	mid-1980s to present

Japanese

Ancient periods	300 BC to 1185
Feudal periods	1185 to 1603
Edo period	1603 to 1868
Meiji, Taishō, Shōwa periods	1868 to 1989

Korean

Silla period	57 BC to 936
Koryŏ period	936 to 1392
Chosŏn period	1392 to 1910
Colonial period	1910 to 1945
Division of Korea	1945 to present

Chinese

Very few examples of pre-sixteenth-century Chinese furnishings still exist. The floor mat, created for sitting, was the first Chinese furnishing. It developed as Buddhism entered China around 495 AD, bringing with it the idea of the Buddha sitting on a raised platform. These platforms evolved into honorary seats and, as people began to recline on them, into beds and daybeds. Taller versions became tables. The Chinese also adapted folding stools from nomadic tribes to the north and west (now Mongolia) and developed woven, hourglass-shaped stools. The earliest known furniture can be divided into three distinct construction forms: frame and panel, yoke and rack, and bamboo.

The style now recognized as Chinese began to appear during the Tang dynasty, as the ruling class began to use round- and yoke-back chairs. Later, during the Song dynasty, artisans further developed the style, adding joinery such as the miter, mortise and tenon, and dovetail. Antique furnishings peaked during the Ming dynasty, characterized by simple, smooth, flowing lines; plain, elegant ornamentation; and woods such as elm, camphor, beech, fir, cypress, walnut, pine, and oak. As trade bans lifted, a greater variety of wood arrived from other Asian ports, and denser wood led to more complex joinery and improved craftsmanship. Furniture aficionados generally agree that quality declined during the Qing dynasty, perhaps due to political unrest and diminished prosperity.

Typical Chinese furnishings include meditation chairs large enough to sit on with legs folded, tall yoke chairs with a bottom stretcher to rest the feet, daybeds, and opium beds where one can perform a variety of daily tasks, such as reading, lounging, and writing. The style is typified by thick lacquer finishes and detailed engravings and paintings of Taoist images such as mountains, dragons, clouds, birds, and flowers. Chinese furniture tends to be symmetrical, with typically bronze or brass hardware. Though antique furnishings were generally made with softwood, modern "classic" pieces are made with exotic hardwoods.

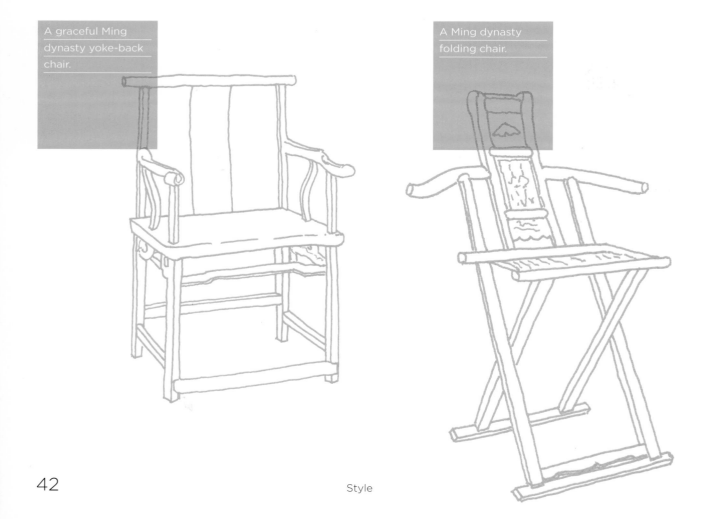

A graceful Ming dynasty yoke-back chair.

A Ming dynasty folding chair.

Japanese

Japanese furnishings were limited prior to the late 1800s. The austerity and spiritual values of Zen Buddhism, which had made its way from China during the thirteenth century, influenced design. Bare rooms were favored over those filled with furnishings. Like the Chinese, the Japanese used floor mats, but the mats were complemented with furnishings such as low tables and stackable storage components.

During the Edo period the Japanese developed *tansu,* beautiful storage boxes and cabinets steeped in ancient Japanese woodworking traditions. Tansu are made to match the function for which they are used, some storing kimonos or swords, others ceremonial tea utensils. Elaborate black ironwork, asymmetry, and simplicity typify tansu, as does the color of the wood, which tends to have a reddish cast.

Contemporary American craftspeople are increasingly interested in Japanese woodworking and building traditional tansu or tansu-inspired furniture because of its elegant simplicity.

Korean

Traditional Korean style is based primarily on uncontrived natural beauty. Furnishings were influenced by the Chinese as far back as the Han dynasty (206 BC to AD 220), although the Koreans did not use chairs or high tables. As with Japanese furnishings, Korean furnishings were primarily storage pieces using simple geometrical design. Furniture was typically symmetrical and featured silver-colored hardware and frequently enhancements of mother-of-pearl, tortoiseshell, and ox-horn. Bats and butterflies influenced the design of the hardware, and more ornamentation was used in northern Korea due to limited wood resources. Pieces from the Koryŏ and Chosŏn periods are highly valued for their simplicity and practicality.

Linking Furnishings to Architecture

It is no accident that architects have so frequently designed furnishings inspired by the elegance of their architecture. Architects and designers know that the most beautiful, psychologically comfortable environments are those with a high degree of design consistency. This is why it is so important to pay attention to adjacent buildings when selecting furnishings for a garden.

Facing:

Classic Bertoia chairs and a modern table complement a contemporary home.

Every beautifully designed building has a distinctive architectural language. If you can identify the building's broad vernacular, you can more easily identify the most appropriate style of furnishings for the garden. When reviewing architectural character, consider the following categories:

Geometry: Identify squares, half-circles, triangles, and other shapes, particularly on the roofline but also on walls, doors, windows, and elsewhere.

Symmetry: Is the design generally asymmetrical or symmetrical?

Structural ornamentation: Note columns, balustrades, and beams. Is there an obvious rhythm? Are there details in a support to the roof?

Attached ornamentation: This includes molding, framework, finials, and the like. Look at the doors, windows, and trim. Is there a pattern worth repeating or complementing? Are the details curvaceous or straight? Where are they located? What frames a window or door? Are there details in a frieze such as dentil or egg-and-dart molding? Is the style minimalist, without much ornamental detail at all?

Scale: Examine the scale of the home and its components. Are there significant ratios or noteworthy proportions to consider? For example, what is the ratio of the square footage of the windows compared to the size of the house?

Materials: What material predominates—wood, stone, brick, concrete, glass? Is the texture smooth or rough? Consider whether you want a material to blend in or be conspicuous through contrast.

Pattern: Consider light and shadow. Note the placement of elements on horizontal and vertical planes.

Function: What is the building's purpose? Is it a dwelling, office, garage?

Color: What color is the body of the house? What is the trim color? What are the accent colors? How much is one color used in relationship to another?

Each new furnishing for a garden deserves this appraisal against existing conditions (or a proposed remodel) to determine whether it will work. Would you really want to hang Tibetan prayer flags in the middle of a formal Italian garden? A pebble dropped into a pond creates a small ripple, while a boulder makes a big splash. Keep this in mind when determining how much a new furnishing will affect the look of your client's space.

The first architectural details I notice about this home are its symmetry, colors, and materials. Other details of note are the halfround vent, formal columns at the entry, pilasters at each corner (including the entry corners), formal door with half round glass transom above and sidelights at either side, window shutters, divided windows, clapboard siding, and the home's colors. Many of these features could influence the selection of garden furnishings.

Coordinating colors
and style with their
Victorian house,
the homeowners
constructed this
ornate arbor
accompanied by
colorful wicker
furniture (a popular
style during the
Victorian period).

Furniture

When trying to help outdoor furniture fit with the architecture of a space, your most crucial tasks are to find those little details that the furniture and architecture have in common, consider the scale of each, and evaluate the proportion of the furniture in relationship to the architecture. Since furniture can have considerable presence in a garden, make sure the style, quantity, mass, texture, and color work with the architecture and scale of the space. It may or may not be possible and desirable to choose furniture in a style that matches the surrounding architecture.

Vivid, bright colors give objects more weight and visibility, which may or may not work in your favor depending on the situation. If a seating area is fairly substantial, it will occupy more actual and visual space. Two lightweight café chairs with a small table will have much less impact in a large space unless they are a bold color. If your large seating area is a subdued color that matches its surroundings, its style will be less noticeable.

You wouldn't normally see these contemporary chairs lining an Italian street. Even so, their simple curves work well with the curves of the more ornate buildings.

Fabric

Because awnings are often attached to the house, they absolutely need to work with the architecture. Simple umbrellas and fabric screens can work with almost any architecture, but the minute you use a stylized finial, pattern, or trim, you need to consider the character of the home. This goes for hammocks as well, particularly the supporting structure. If a hammock stand is large and bulky, you can minimize its presence by selecting a color that fades into the background.

Situated in a corner of the back garden, this simple stand and hammock coordinate nicely with the style of the home and provide a welcome retreat after hard work in the garden.

Art

As with outdoor furniture, the effect of garden art depends on its size, finish, color, and general character. Really simple art goes with nearly anything. And it may be trite to say, but art is truly in the eye of the beholder. A small, simple bungalow could be the perfect place for a little cottage kitsch such as a garden gnome. If you want to escape the kitsch but keep the gnome, you can spray it with solid metallic paint to minimize the visual detail and retain only the form. If the house is mid-century modern, you might get away with a flock of pink flamingoes.

I recommend reviewing the big picture to decide whether any outlandish taste actually contributes to the overall theme. Indeed, this points to the importance of having a theme in the first place, which can act as a filter and decision-making tool. Naturally, the theme of a garden should complement the architecture of the home. If the architecture is very simple, as with a ranch house, you may be able to develop a theme about almost anything.

Lighting

Because you should see the effect of outdoor lighting rather than the objects emitting that light, matching electrical outdoor light fixtures to architecture should be a minimal issue. Keep lights simple and out of sight if they are anything other than bollards. If they are bollards (or path lights), match existing metal colors to allow them to blend in with their surroundings. Consider the garden's theme if using fixtures that have an obvious form, such as a flower.

Candlelight is another cup of tea. Since candles emit such soft, nonglaring light, we want to notice them, and for this reason candle holders are available in an enormous range of styles. Size may make a difference if the candle holder is large, grand, and ornate, less so if it is a simple glass hurricane lamp. The quantity of candles can also make a big statement. Years ago I attended an unforgettable dinner at an old hacienda in Guadalajara, Mexico. The interior courtyard had been transformed into an intimate dining area, elegantly appointed with elaborate floral and lemon centerpieces. Surrounding the courtyard, and accenting many architectural features such as railings and balustrades, were hundreds of tiny votive candles. The effect of the candles was hypnotic, and the most memorable part of an amazing experience.

Containers

Fortunately, planters come in a wide assortment of materials, styles, colors, and sizes, which normally make finding a suitable one relatively easy. As with anything else that goes into a garden, selecting the right planter for the architecture is crucial. Often designers default to contemporary pots, which due

Simple but colorful ornaments are perfectly in tune with the architecture of this outdoor shower.

The recessed light alongside this stone staircase is stylistically plain and will not conflict with the traditionally styled home.

Dining alfresco in the evening is made all the more charming with a garden chandelier.

to their simplicity may work quite well, but not always. Once again, seek out the architectural details. Does the pot have a lip? If not, it may be a contemporary pot. When the pot does have a lip, it might be curved or square, simple or ornate, small or large, and so on. The pot may have no texture or be heavily textured. It may have a design or pattern. Compare these details to those in the architectural environment. They need to act as a team.

English lead egg cup planters are in accord with the pool house beyond and complement the architecture.

One can't ignore the excellent coordination of this gorgeous planter with the home's architecture.

Arbors, Gazebos, and Other Structures

Any prefabricated or custom-fabricated structure such as an arbor or gazebo has a major impact within a garden and should pick up the character of the existing architecture and work with the scale of both home and garden. Review the details on existing buildings. Identify one or two key characteristics in the architecture to repeat in the garden structure. For example, create a highly ornamented, curvilinear wire gazebo to complement a Victorian-style house, or a clean, simply geometric gazebo to match a mid-century home.

A metal screen that can also act as a shade structure complements the existing architecture, adding additional texture and interest.

Heating Elements

Consider how the design of a fire pit, fireplace, or outdoor heater will work with the overall character and scale of your client's home and garden. If you are working with a considerably detailed house, something very simple should not have a major impact on the overall design. Look at the details. What does the new item have in common with the house? Perhaps it is not a new item at all but an old metal fireplace formerly used indoors. A contemporary design might look like an alien spacecraft in the garden of a traditional house if the design process skips a beat.

Outdoor heaters tend to be fairly contemporary and are often silver or black, although other colors have crept into the market. Silver items tend to reflect colors around them, so will disappear to some extent visually. Black can disappear against a dark background or be visually pervasive against a light background. The design of outdoor heaters blends easily with the clean lines of ranch homes and contemporary homes.

A curved-top pergola offers the option of extending fabric just beneath the structure to increase the amount of shade. The curved details suit the more traditional architecture of the house.

Since heaters, portable fire pits, and fireplaces tend to be metal, it makes sense to look at the metal on the exterior of the home. There may be black hardware on a gate that you could match for the sake of design consistency. If you need to contend with multiple hardware finishes, it becomes even more important to match an existing hardware. Don't add more!

The massive fireplace on this patio sets the tone for the style and scale of the furnishings.

A simple, modern fire pit provides a stylish way to get the smoke out of your eyes while blending in with the contemporary home. Its simplicity might allow it to be used with other styles, too.

With no surrounding architecture, one does
what one wishes with some consideration
perhaps—of the local architectural vernacular.
Colorful fabric provides a splash of color, too.

Sorting It Out

After reviewing your client's existing architecture, create a list of the outdoor furnishings they intend to keep, if this applies to them. Do the furnishings complement the home, or should you suggest they be sold or donated? Determine whether any items on the list will need to be refurbished—for example, could you have a metal item powder coated or an old wicker chair rewoven to extend its life? Create a second list, this time of garden furnishings your client needs or wants to add. Compare the two lists and identify what you still need for the garden—furniture, art, pots, umbrella, cushions, heating, lighting, arbor, pergola? Evaluate each piece against the architectural style of the home.

Armless Louis XV fauteuils, painted and upholstered with an accent color for added punch, pay homage to the historical quality of this house. However, the designers produced an eclectic look by adding a modern shade canopy and table.

Comfort, Scale, and Proportion

Remember how Goldilocks, in "Goldilocks and the Three Bears," went from room to room, discovering that just one of three items in each room was right for her? She tested each item, determining how comfortable it was and making sure the scale and proportion suited her. So, too, do we inherently seek comfort in our relationship with garden furnishings, both physically and visually. If garden furnishings are out of scale, lack the proper proportion, or are uncomfortable, they can dampen our enthusiasm to wander out into our gardens. Conversely, when furnishings are just right, they allow us longer and richer outdoor experiences (even if some of us frenetic gardeners too often let the opportunity pass).

Anthropometric measurements

Buttock-popliteal length
(from buttocks to back of knee), *sitting*

Buttock-knee length
(from buttocks to front of knee), *sitting*

Buttock-toe length
sitting

Buttock-leg length
sitting

Thigh clearance
sitting

Hip breadth
sitting

Elbow to elbow breadth

Elbow rest height
sitting

Sitting height

Popliteal height
(back of knee to bottom of foot)

Knee height

Elbow height
standing

Maximum body breadth
standing (shoulder to shoulder)

Maximum body depth
standing (chest to back of buttocks)

Vertical reach height
sitting

Vertical reach height
standing

Side arm reach
(center top of head to fingertips when arm is stretched fully to the side)

Thumb tip reach
(back of head to fingertips when arm is stretched fully to the front)

Eye height
standing

Eye height
sitting

Vertical grip reach
standing

Human Factors

We humans come into contact with so many objects that we have found it necessary to develop an entire science around fitting those objects to our bodies. This science, called ergonomics (or human factors), plays a significant role in the design of garden furnishings. When we use a chair, table, grill, arbor, or even a garden tool, we want to feel comfortable. Ergonomics uses anthropometry (the measurement of human beings) to understand how best to construct products in relationship to the size and scale of people.

Most people give little thought to how a chair relates to a table, unless the chair they happen to be sitting on is too high for the table, or the table is too low for their chair (a surprisingly common occurrence at restaurants!). Think about how awkward something feels when it isn't suited to you. A poorly designed furnishing can trip you up, cause you to fall or slide around, or just generally make you feel clumsy.

Style

Anthropometrists measure a wide variety of people in order to develop average measurements and ratios. They consider things like the length of the upper leg so that designers can create chairs suited to the depth of the average person or built-in benches of a suitable height. In this way anthropometry keeps furniture comfortable for most people. However, since there are a myriad of chair types and styles, with variable measurements, it's important to consider the measurements of each garden furnishing you plan to purchase for your client.

Sustainable recycled rubber chairs provide a well-proportioned, comfortable place to sit and enjoy the wild meadow.

A wide variety of measurements are taken to ensure well-designed garden furniture and other outdoor furnishings. How do all of these measurements affect our purchases? No single product requires the use of every measurement, but several measurements can affect something as simple as an outdoor umbrella. Think about the reach needed to put an umbrella into the center hole of a table or into an umbrella base, and then expand and adjust it. Or consider the process of replacing a lamp in a light fixture mounted on a wall. Could a person in a wheelchair reach the light to change it? What about the height of a counter—is it suited to the family member who does the most cooking on an outdoor grill?

It's never fun to order a table and chairs only to discover, first, that the arms on the chairs are too high to fit beneath the tabletop, and then that the chairs are too wide to fit comfortably around the table. While ergonomics plays a role in making furniture

comfortable, you play a role in assuring all the components fit together as well as a jigsaw puzzle.

There's a good reason people test-drive furniture before buying it. They want to be comfortable! If you need to get a sense of how comfortable a piece will be dimensionally, compare the measurements of the piece against the measurements of the individuals who will be using it. This is particularly important if it will be next to impossible to try out a piece in advance. The softness or hardness of a chair, bench, sofa, or stool are also important, as are the edges of pieces. Items should have at least eased (barely rounded) edges as often as possible; otherwise they should have a radius (fully rounded edge) or chamfer (beveled edge).

Scale and Proportion

Human scale certainly affects design, but what about the proportion and scale of an object in relationship to the garden? For example, what is the appropriate size of a planter in relationship to a patio garden surrounded by walls? Rules of thumb governing the size of an object within its space would be convenient. However, so much depends on how you plan to use the space. If you plan to fill it with a dining table and chairs and there is very little space left, one or two very narrow but tall pots might be appropriate. They will take up little floor space but provide enough scale and impact with their height. Conversely, if you plan to use only two large chairs and a small end table, there will be much more leftover space. The end table could be quite large, and if you were to add a potted plant, it too could be large to balance the chairs. When you consider scale, think balance.

The old concept of small things in a small space simply isn't true. A couple of large objects in a small space can work splendidly as long as they don't overpower the space, work from a practical point of view, and are in balance with the other objects in the space and with the space itself. For instance, a large, comfortable chair in a small outdoor room might work as the focal point of the area. To balance it you might need to add bold plants such as large-leaved bananas (as opposed to delicate plants with tiny flowers and leaves, which would be out of scale).

The scale of a large umbrella and table with plenty of seating fits comfortably in a generous outdoor setting.

A small pillow at the back of a chair can seem larger in scale in a bold color.

An overscaled blue chair at the entrance to Cornerstone Gardens in Sonoma, California, gives visitors a hint of the delight within.

Details

Publisher and author William Feather said, "Beware of the person who can't be bothered by details." Businessman Sanford Weill chimed in with, "Details create the big picture." Architect Ludwig Mies van der Rohe added, "God is in the details." Undeniably, details are important. A detail might be obvious or it might be subtle. The more obvious it is, the more it should relate to the larger object. Details on a chair might be the foot, the leg, where the leg and seat join, the seat, structural portions that support and tie the legs together, where the back joins the seat, where the arms join the chair, the configuration of the back, the splat or rails in the back, or the design within the back if it is solid. Details occur in many places and can make a big difference in the appearance and experience of an object.

Some objects relate better to each other when there is some connection between their details. If one object has a curlicue, a complementary object might have a similar curve or a curlicue of a different scale. Conversely, trying to relate curlicue to triangle presents a bigger challenge. And it isn't just shape. For example, what is the relationship between a pink flamingo, a Buddha, a Mickey Mouse, and a gnome? Not much. All have curves, but beyond that, think about each object independently. Do they represent similar moods? Not really. Do they come from

The Koi chair's fishscale pattern is a detail you can't miss. A colorful pillow would add comfort to this overscaled piece.

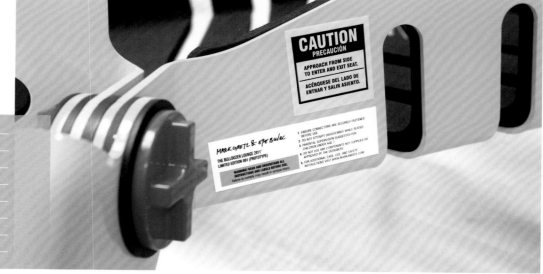

This detail of the Bulldozer Lounge chair demonstrates the degree to which designers must pay attention to every element of a furnishing.

CAUTION
PRECAUCIÓN
APPROACH FROM SIDE TO ENTER AND EXIT SEAT.
ACÉRQUESE DEL LADO DE ENTRAR Y SALIR ASIENTO.

MARK GOETZ & EFE BULUC
THE BULLDOZER LOUNGE 2011
LIMITED EDITION 001 (PROTOTYPE)
WARNING: READ AND UNDERSTAND ALL INSTRUCTIONS AND LABELS BEFORE USE.
Failure to comply may result in serious injury

1. ENSURE CONNECTORS ARE SECURELY FASTENED BEFORE USE.
2. DO NOT ATTEMPT DISASSEMBLY WHILE SEATED.
3. PARENTAL SUPERVISION SUGGESTED FOR CHILDREN UNDER AGE 7.
4. DO NOT USE ANY COMPONENTS NOT SUPPLIED OR APPROVED BY THE DESIGNERS.
5. FOR ADDITIONAL CARE, USE, AND SAFETY INSTRUCTIONS VISIT WWW.MARKAMENT.COM

similar places or share similar associations? No. Where are the details that could bring any two of these objects together in a harmonious way? It would take a lot of imagination to combine such disparate items, so don't waste your energy in this direction unless a client forces you to. Even then, lay out for them in a logical way why it is difficult to achieve a well-designed garden in this manner.

Finding the Common Thread

Many people find it difficult to combine furnishing styles. To begin with, look at overall form and scale. Let's say the first item is a bench. Is it big and boxy or demure and curvaceous? Big and boxy. What is it made of? Cast aluminum with orange upholstery. What are the details? They are crisp and angular. Now bring in the second item, asking yourself what the two items have in common with each other. Perhaps a matching piece could be slightly smaller, boxy, with rectilinear details, upholstery fabric with a splash of coordinating orange, and cast aluminum feet on a wood frame. Both pieces have something in common, but with some interesting variation—just like a good marriage!

Preconceived Styles

We began with historical styles and now move into various preconceived styles so ubiquitous in contemporary garden design. Common styles—tropical, Zen, English cottage, and so forth—stem from numerous, varied sources. Their main inspiration may come from plants or planting styles (as with naturalistic, woodland, and desert styles), geographical or cultural associations (Asian, Mediterranean, Moorish courtyard), modern fashion (contemporary, urban townhouse), or other origins. Some preconceived styles are just conventional interpretations of historical styles. This last category includes mid-century modern, Federal, and Victorian, all of which were discussed in "History and Geography" and have a place here as well.

Preconceived styles originate from an individual's or group's interpretation of designs they have seen, whether actually or virtually, or that a group has developed based on what each individual brings to the table. In some cases a style is literally reconstructed or adapted. For example, a Japanese designer might create a new Japanese-style garden merely by adapting a traditional design to a new site. This sort of style tends to be predictable. A homeowner's translation of the Japanese style for her own garden would be another example, but it could be much less predictable, depending on how much of her own unique personality she introduces. Ultimately, if a designer's rendition captures the essence of a Japanese garden but remains far from a literal interpretation, the preconceived style evolves into a reconceived style.

The point is that preconceived styles are someone else's ideas. They are used to maintain design consistency, which is important, but if taken literally these styles can feel inflexible or so constrained that you feel you must follow them to the letter without any further thought. Don't design on autopilot! If you understand the broad history of furnishing styles, as described in "History and Geography," you can use this information (in addition to your client's needs and dreams and the reality of their site) to select garden furnishings without knowing anything about preconceived styles.

That said, preconceived styles do have their place, and with that in mind, I present a selection of typical models. I leave it to you to determine how or whether you should use them.

High-quality design showrooms and stores offer a treasure chest of resources for all styles.

Asian

Asian style often conjures Zen and Japanese styles but is so much more, finding inspiration in Chinese, Balinese, Korean, Thai, and other Southeast Asian styles as well. Zen is Asian minimalist and uses materials in a way that represents a condensed vision of the world according to the Zen philosophy. Chinese garden style uses fewer plants and places more emphasis on architecture. Chinese and Korean styles also tend to be more symmetrical, while Japanese style emphasizes asymmetry. Japanese style uses more plants than Chinese style, but not as many plants as the other Asian styles, which tend to be more tropical.

Materials: Wood, bamboo, rattan, stone, ceramics with no glaze or subdued glazes, iron, bronze, brass

Typical plants: Bamboo, azalea, moss, pine, flowering cherry and plum

Furnishings: Oriental style, handcrafted, textiles with a high degree of texture or Asian pattern

Colors: Natural, muted, indigo

An elegant, Asian-style stone lantern hints to visitors the kind of garden they are about to enter.

Colonial and Federal

Colonial and Federal styles are strongly influenced by English (and sometimes German, Dutch, or French) and classical Greco-Roman design. Both styles tend to be formal, though Colonial is slightly less refined than Federal, and both make use of symmetry, including the use of pairs of items.

Materials: Cut stone; bluestone; blond or richly colored and polished woods; simple glass or crystal; polished brass; pewter; wrought or cast iron; striped, plaid, plain, or floral-patterned textiles with little sheen or texture, including leather; woven wicker; beautifully glazed ceramics with some chinoiserie (Chinese influenced)

Typical plants: Boxwood parterre, formal hedges of local broadleaf evergreen or deciduous shrubs, herbs, classic flowers and perennials such as roses and acanthus, fragrant plants, mown lawn (but consider drought-tolerant, low-maintenance alternatives)

Furnishings: Crisp, curvaceous or straight lines, formal, polished, with minimal textural contrast

Colors: Neutrals, muted jewel tones

In early spring, just after the formal hedges are clipped tight, drapes of blossoms highlight the gardens of Filoli, an estate with an eclectic design and strong Colonial influence.

Contemporary

This style refers to current, modern design, including use of technologically new or recycled materials, minimalism, uncluttered lines, and functional focus.

Materials: Stainless and powder-coated steel, synthetics, concrete, stone, glass, glazed ceramics, up-to-date textiles

Typical plants: Bold, muscular, structural or very finely textured plants to create distinct contrast with materials and furnishings

Furnishings: Minimalist, clean, in vogue

Colors: Cutting-edge, hip, trendy

Once a tennis court, this streamlined, contemporary water garden features a stainless steel and gilded bronze leaf sculpture.

Style

Country House

Country house refers to farmhouses, log houses, ranches, cabins, haciendas, and any other indigenous structures, but the style isn't necessarily rustic. What makes it different from the naturalistic style is its use of the local vernacular without necessarily fitting into the landscape.

Materials: Possibly indigenous, same as or complementary to the architecture; also, rustic-looking glass and ceramic, roughly to slightly textured or ethnically patterned textiles, wrought iron, galvanized or weathering steel, copper, medium-toned and natural-looking wood

Typical plants: Indigenous plants, annual food crops, annual and perennial flowers, fruiting trees and shrubs

Furnishings: Straightforward detailing, slightly curved to straight lines, simple, relatable forms

Colors: Neutrals, colors from natural dyes, barely muted primary and secondary colors

Made with local logs, this gazebo maintains a rural look for the wicker seating beneath within a certified organic garden.

Craftsman

Craftsman is the American cousin of English Arts and Crafts. Both styles are known for their low-pitched, multiplaned rooflines and exuberant rafter details, Oriental influence, handcrafted details, use of stone, triangular braced supports, trellised porches, wide and angled columns, and multilight windows.

Materials: Medium to dark woods, copper, bronze, colored glass, ceramic, stone

Typical plants: Plants with relaxed structure, richly colored flowers, ferns, and plants found in Japanese gardens

Furnishings: Adirondack chairs, gracefully handmade pieces with possible Japanese overtones

Colors: Rich, woodsy tones or muted pastels

A Craftsman-style home nestles into an artfully festive garden of fruits and vegetables.

Desert

A desert garden is one that functions on less water. It may be that the garden owner lives in an arid environment and has no choice but to make do, or it may be that minimal water usage is just an important part of the owner's approach. Desert gardens are often called xeric gardens, which celebrate drought-tolerant plants such as those found in desert oases, the American Southwest, and arid regions of Chile, South Africa, and other dry landscapes. Furnishings should include a shade structure; thick, heat-insulating, heat-reflecting walls; fountains and rills that use the minimally available water to good effect; and airy furniture that helps reduce perspiration. The layout should emphasize good air circulation, with sparser-than-usual plantings and visible gravelly soil.

Materials: Stone, gravel, antique glass, wrought iron and rusted steel, weathered wood, ceramic, lightweight fabric

Typical plants: Succulents, plants with gray-green or small leaves, grasses, palms

Furnishings: Casual, simple, with local details and patterns

Colors: Gray-greens, terra-cotta, slightly muted warm colors

A desert garden can occur in many locations around the world, with the design often drawn from local characteristics.

English Cottage

When we think of the quintessential cottage garden we imagine a half-timbered, thatched-roof English country home with rose-covered fabrics and arbors. This style, originally a reaction to more organized French gardens, allows for a semicasual garden with many perennials and strong evergreen structure. Crisscross and woven patterning are typical.

Materials: Darker woods, woven wicker, iron, stone, stucco, clear segmented glass perhaps with a few bubbles, textiles with floral patterns

Typical plants: Roses, perennials, broadleaf evergreen shrubs and conifers, deciduous shrubs and trees, native plants

Furnishings: Casual with a European country vibe, perhaps a little tongue in cheek, shabby-chic, antiques

Colors: Soft grays and warm creams, pastels, subdued jewel tones

A more low-maintenance version of an old-fashioned cottage garden surrounds an old stone English cottage.

Mediterranean

The Mediterranean style usually focuses on the southern regions of Europe and has evolved primarily due to the Mediterranean climate. Areas like California, South Africa, and Chile are sometimes described as having Mediterranean climates because they can successfully grow Mediterranean plants. Design elements include dark and rough-hewn wood, whitewashed surfaces, woven tapestries, generously sized furniture, long wood tables, courtyards, oil jars, tiled counters, carved wood furnishings, ornate hardware, and chandeliers.

Materials: Terra-cotta and Italian glazed ceramics and tiles, textiles with Provençal patterns, woven wicker, stone (particularly gravel), stucco, weathered glass, wrought iron, bronze

Typical plants: Mediterranean plants such as Italian cypress and French lavender, herbs, boxwood topiary and parterre

Furnishings: Formal but comfortable and relaxed

Colors: Whites and creams, bright primary and soft secondary or tertiary colors, particularly aquas and lavender

Views such as this one, across the northern Italian countryside, inspire Mediterranean gardens in similar climates around the world.

Mid-Century Modern

Mid-century modern covers the late 1940s through the early 1970s and was heavily influenced by Bauhaus and Scandinavian designers of the day. New materials and technologies drove these designers to remarkable experimentation. Many of their designs still look fresh and are used in contemporary designs. Look for organic and geometric forms, simplicity, and integration with nature.

Materials: Concrete, synthetics (including textiles), molded plastic, woven wire, polished stone and gravel, stainless steel, shiny glazed ceramics

Typical plants: Reeds and grasses, including mown lawn (but in place of water-guzzling turf grasses, consider drought-tolerant, low-maintenance alternatives); bold, structural plants that provide sharp contrast to the fine grasses

Furnishings: Fashioned by designers of the era, with clean lines and intriguing details

Colors: Oranges to rust to brown, aquas to turquoise to pastel blue, silver, black, charcoal, yellow-greens to gray-greens to dark greens

A mid-century home gets a new garden that updates its appearance but maintains the modern theme.

Moorish Courtyard

Moorish courtyard style is inspired by a wide geographic range of paradise gardens, including the Moorish gardens of North Africa and classics such as the Alhambra, Alcázar, and the Taj Mahal. This is a romantic style in every sense. Water is a primary component in the form of fountains and rills. Mosaics, geometric patterns, and arabesques are important features. Arches are typical architectural elements, including the classic horseshoe arch, the four-center arch (also known as the Tudor arch), and cusped arches.

Materials: Stone, ceramic tile, terra-cotta roof tile, teak, brass, copper

Typical plants: Palms, fruiting and flowering vines, pond plants, dwarf fruit trees, roses and other fragrant flowers, bulbs native to the Middle East (tulips, Crown Imperial fritillaries, dwarf iris, perhaps saffron crocus)

Furnishings: Flamboyant, complex, opulent with restraint, Egyptian influenced, with brocade or intricately patterned textiles

Colors: Jewel tones, metallics, exotic bird colors

Moorish design influences this Spanish courtyard within the Alcázar of Seville, Spain.

Naturalistic

This term should immediately elicit a question: naturalistic where? That is the point. This style is natural to the site of the garden in question, which could be anything from a desert to a sunny mountain meadow. The term itself implies a mimicking of nature, an acknowledgment that gardening is not nature itself. This style also includes lakeside or riverside gardens, in which case you would also consider the water element in your design. The focus is on the plants, not so much on the furnishings. The architecture should blend into the site.

Materials: Native wood, rough stone or river rock, unpolished or powder-coated metals, woven wicker, willow, reed, glass, recycled materials (including synthetics)

Typical plants: Native plants or plants that grow like natives (they thrive but are noninvasive)

Furnishings: Uncomplicated with clean lines

Colors: Earthy, natural colors with bright, floral accents

A new house and garden settle into wooded acreage by native and naturalistic plantings.

Shore

This style refers specifically to ocean shores. Inspiration for a seaside garden would include sea creatures, seagulls, seashells, glass floats, driftwood, lighthouses, sand dunes, sunsets and sunrises, and magnificent views of never-ending, pounding waves.

Materials: Sand, stone, weathered wood (particularly driftwood), synthetics, wicker, glass

Typical plants: Local conifers, grasses, herbs, salt- and drought-tolerant plants

Furnishings: Current, clean, crisp, casual

Colors: Light neutrals and naturals, blues, turquoises

As with any well-designed garden element located near a beach, this artful fish-cleaning station by renowned designer Maya Lin is able to withstand salt air, sandy soil, and blustery weather. The sink is made of polished basalt and rests on a weathered wood deck. A stainless steel cable guard rail surrounds the deck.

Tropical

Tropical style takes its inspiration from any tropical area of the world, not just Hawaii and the South Pacific—think Central America, tropical Africa and India, and Southeast Asia. This style is lush, warm, casual, and often combined with shore style, but it could also be influenced by a jungle or rainforest. Tropical designs tend to be a little rustic, unrefined, and romantic. Plants are used abundantly, with no visible bare earth.

Materials: Teak and other tropical woods (use eco-harvested woods), bamboo, woven materials such as thatch and wicker, bubbly glass, terra-cotta, softly glazed ceramics

Typical plants: Palms, bananas, cannas, and other plants with large, lush leaves; anything tropical or tropical-looking; plants with bodacious and fragrant flowers

Furnishings: Heavily ethnic, simple details with complex curves

Colors: Tropical fruit and flower colors; rich, deep greens; sumptuously saturated jewel tones of tropical bird colors

Massive leaves, lush growth, and vibrantly colored flowers create a tropical-style garden almost anywhere. In this garden, ethnically inspired sculptures emphasize the effect, looking as though they came from a lost jungle civilization.

Urban Townhouse

Urban settings tend to be somewhat small and constrained by surrounding buildings. These settings are usually very contemporary or historical. When they have a historical reference, the style becomes quite traditional, but when the setting is contemporary, so goes the style. That said, it is not unusual to see a sophisticated and eclectic mix with the urban townhouse style. Because the nature of a city is hustle and bustle, townhouse gardens often inspire respite and tranquility, perhaps with the use of trickling water or even adjacency to an urban lake. They can also incorporate elements of Asian, contemporary, traditional, tropical, and desert gardens. Materials are often inspired by adjacent buildings.

Materials: Concrete, steel, wrought iron, brick, brownstone, cut stone, glass, ceramic

Typical plants: Smog-resistant and low-maintenance plants, massed plantings of soft textures with bold accent plants

Furnishings: Scaled to suit a smaller, possibly enclosed garden; very chic, probably cutting edge in at least some respects, possibly eclectic

Colors: Sophisticated, muted secondary and tertiary pastels or shades, many shades of neutrals

A minimalist terrace garden by an urban lake extends the contemporary architectural style and adds comfort combined with a magnificent view amidst a bustling city.

Victorian

Victorian style is curvaceous, exuberant, and abundantly detailed. Many people consider it overly fussy and too busy. I have seen this style subdued with the use of monochromatic color schemes and minimally detailed contemporary furnishings. However, its true nature is anything but constrained. Depending on one's perspective, Victorian gardens can feel either cloyingly or charmingly sweet. Planting schemes are prodigious, audacious, and bold.

Materials: Heavily patterned, textured, and floral textiles; dark or white-painted, carved woods; cast iron, ceramic, wicker

Typical plants: An exuberant palette of many different plants, including tropical plants, in as many different colors as possible

Furnishings: Generously scaled and upholstered, curvaceous, intricately detailed, comfortable

Colors: Slightly muted; nearly any shade of red, green, or blue or combination thereof; whites and off-whites

An intricately detailed Victorian home has an exquisite garden to match—including the very Victorian use of a palm tree.

Woodland

Though the woodland style is sometimes lumped in with the naturalistic style, it has its own distinctive elements. You can find woodland gardens around the world, but all share a common feature: more shade than sun. Curvilinear paths wind through tall trees. There may be boulders among the natural detritus and possibly creeks, streams, and ravines. As in naturalistic gardens, furnishings are less of a focus and should not detract from the real star: lush plants.

Materials: Stone, gravel, rusted steel, weathered wood, unrefined ceramics in wildflower colors, rough and casual textiles and glass

Typical plants: Deciduous and evergreen trees, shade-tolerant native shrubs, woodland wildflowers, ferns, mosses

Furnishings: Very casual, simple with clean lines, textiles with leafy patterns and natural colors

Colors: Greens, warm browns, accent colors of local wildflowers

A rusty metal owl appears to swoop through this woodland garden nestled at the edge of a forest.

PART 2
MATERIALS

Materials might be the most important

consideration when selecting garden furnishings, since they affect not only style but also a host of other criteria.

In reviewing each material covered in these chapters, I considered the same questions I had to ask when I was a commercial interior designer for a global architectural and engineering firm. When we wrote specifications for our clients, we assessed each material thoroughly, including testing standards, fabrication, assembly, installation, and maintenance. This sort of attention to detail is essential, because when you understand where materials come from, how they get to a useful state, and how fabricators transform them into something functional or ornamental, you can more clearly imagine the possibilities. In short, it enhances your creativity.

Facing:
A Haitian artist recycled an old metal oil drum to create this whimsical garden art, which could be used for a panel in a gate or screen or simply attached to an exterior wall.

This section comprehensively reviews each type of material typically found on the market: wood, metal, textiles, wicker, ceramics, stone, glass, concrete, and synthetics. It should also give you an idea of how to evaluate less common materials on your own. Each chapter ends with a checklist to use when reviewing a material's suitability for a given project.

Throughout these chapters you will notice references to testing and standards. Excellent organizations have created standards through testing materials or for the sake of sustainability. It is helpful to be familiar with the most important organizations:

ISO (International Organization for Standardization) is a voluntary network of national standards institutes in 162 countries with one representative per country. It is the world's largest developer of international standards, having published more than 18,500 standards.

ASTM International (American Society for Testing and Materials) is a voluntary international organization that develops a consensus of technical standards that cover materials (such as textiles, metal products, petroleum products, paints, rubber, and plastics), products, systems, and services. They publish the *Annual Book of ASTM Standards.*

ANSI (American National Standards Institute) writes the rules and procedures for consensus standards developers. This organization does not concern itself with the technical content of the standard, only the process. ANSI also provides accrediting programs for the ISO in quality and environmental management and acts as the official representative to the ISO from the United States.

BIFMA (Business and Institutional Furniture Manufacturer's Association) is an ANSI-accredited standards developer, using the ANSI process to develop consensus standards. As its name indicates, this organization focuses on commercial furniture, including some products popular for outdoor use. Together, ANSI and BIFMA developed a sustainability standard called level, which provides independent third-party certification for commercial furniture. Level stringently measures a product's off-gassing and recycled content, corporate social responsibility, and other sustainability issues. Certified products receive a level conformance mark with a rating of 1, 2, or 3.

MBDC (McDonough Braungart Design Chemistry) is an international firm providing sustainability certification that verifies use of healthy, ecologically responsible design and materials. MBDC has consulted with clients as a third-party certifier since 1995 and was founded by world-renowned authors William McDonough and Michael Braungart (*Cradle to Cradle*).

LEED (Leadership in Energy and Environmental Design), an internationally recognized rating system developed by the US Green Building Council (USGBC), provides third-party certification for buildings, homes, and communities. Components of those environments, including furnishings, are evaluated on the basis of their overall sustainability, particularly in areas such as human and environmental health, sustainable site development, water, energy, and materials.

SITES (Sustainable Sites Initiative) was codeveloped by the American Society of Landscape Architects (ASLA), the Lady Bird Johnson Wildflower Center, and the United States Botanic Garden (USBG). Guidelines and performance benchmarks cover areas such as soils, vegetation, and human health, and materials and products are rated according to their ecological impact.

International Living Future Institute promotes the Living Building Challenge, a certification program that promotes responsibility and sustainability in the built environment. Standards focus on all issues of the environment, including materials, site, water, energy, health, equity, and beauty.

CITES (Convention on International Trade in Endangered Species of Wild Fauna and Flora) aims to ensure that international trade of wild animals and plants does not threaten their survival.

If you want to know which tests a product has undergone, look on the manufacturer's tag. If the information isn't on the tag, contact the manufacturer.

Each chapter in this section includes discussion about sustainable practices for that material, such as where the material comes from; current collecting, manufacturing, and fabricating practices; organizations that evaluate the material's level of sustainability; and potential recyclability. If you are not thinking about the health of our planet when recommending furnishings to your clients, you are missing an opportunity to make the world a better one.

While each material has its own sustainability issues (nothing is perfect!), certain broad questions should be applied to all of them. First, does the company that harvests, collects, or mines the natural resources used for this material or product belong to an independent third-party certification organization that monitors, regulates, or certifies its sustainable harvesting? If not, is there a comparable or competitive firm that does? If this does not apply, ask the manufacturer whether they are able to verify that the material is harvested, collected, or mined in a sustainable manner. Likewise, ask yourself whether the major raw material is a rapidly renewable resource. If applicable, is the material or product prepared for manufacture or finished in a sustainable manner (for example, using limited energy and water, with nontoxic finishes)? Finally, how local (close to the point of sale) is the material or product, and is it shipped by fuel-efficient transport to and from the manufacturer?

Wood

Everyone adores wood for its range of beautiful colors and grains, its warm appearance, and its degree of comfort when sat upon or touched. Wood crafters and fabricators also appreciate the ease with which most woods can be cut or carved into nearly any shape imaginable. Wood is the most available material for garden furnishings and requires the least amount of energy when it comes to construction, making it one of the most popular materials. It is also a sustainable choice.

With so many wood choices available, it is important to know the broad range of characteristics found among different woods. Trees grow in nearly every area of the world, and climatic diversity affects not only whether trees can grow but also how they grow. The inherent nature of each wood dictates its use and suitability for use in an outdoor setting. Knowing how to differentiate wood types is important if you want your garden furnishings to be long-lasting, an important sustainability criterion.

Genetics

Wood's physical features can be summed up as color, grain, degree of hardness (measured as specific gravity), strength, and intrinsic durability. Most visible characteristics are inherent in the wood itself, while grain direction and variation tend to be a result of how the wood leaves the sawmill.

Hardwood and Softwood

Generally, softwoods come from needle-leaved conifers such as pine or redwood, whereas hardwoods come from broad-leaved trees. However, this classification is not always a good indicator of a tree's actual softness or hardness. For example, balsa wood is very soft but is technically a hardwood, and yew is a softwood but is harder than most hardwoods. As a rule, softwoods are less dense than hardwoods. Density is an indicator of a wood's strength—the higher the density, the stronger the wood. However, denser woods are also more difficult to cut or machine, may have a higher degree of shrinking and swelling, and are considerably heavier.

Growth Rings

An old stump left over from a cleared forest displays the many growth rings that reveal its age. The bark and inner wood are more resistant to the mosses and decay mechanisms designed by nature to return this log to the soil.

Growth rings tell us more about a tree than its age. The greatest amount of sap and growth occur during the spring (early wood). It's a lighter color and a wider band. The narrow dark ring adjacent to this light ring represents summer growth (latewood). Tree rings vary with the type of wood. The end grain of a piece of lumber exhibits a portion of a tree's growth rings. While end grain may not be visible in a piece of garden furniture, it may be helpful to know what time of year the lumber was cut. Ask the manufacturer for this information if needed.

Winter-cut wood contains less sap and takes less time to dry. It is also less vulnerable to variations in humidity that can cause cupping, warping, and end or surface checking (cracking).

The difference between heartwood and sapwood is usually obvious because heartwood is generally noticeably darker and softwood lighter. But this is not always true, and not all woody plants form heartwood.

Heartwood is the older, interior wood of a tree, the result of a genetically programmed chemical transformation that renders the wood more decay resistant. Essentially, heartwood is dead and therefore unable to decay further. Considering that heartwood has been exposed to more potential threats, such as fire, insects, and weather, during the tree's lifetime, it is surprising that this dead wood is as strong as it is.

Sapwood is the young, living, outer wood of a tree, where the sap runs through. Young trees are entirely sapwood.

There can be considerable variation in the amount of heartwood and sapwood in any given tree depending on where it grows. A tree growing robustly in the open will form more sapwood than the same tree growing with sparser growth in a dense forest. Variation also exists within each tree. Sapwood will be

Materials

more plentiful at the tree's base and in its youngest parts, thinner in its oldest parts. Additionally, as anyone who has ever grown a tree can tell you, trees do not grow evenly year to year due to climatic variations.

Some trees form thin sapwood due to genetic influences, including sassafras, black locust, chestnut, Osage-orange, and mulberry. Others inherently grow thicker sapwood, such as hickory, maple, beech, pine, and ash. Trees that do not form heartwood tend to be tropical, although this is not true of all tropical trees. Tropical trees also produce chemical inhibitors in response to attack to increase their decay resistance.

Bamboo

Bamboo is the only monocot of substantial interest for garden furnishings. Members of the roughly one hundred genera of bamboo, all technically part of the grass family, are so strong that manufacturers and contractors use them as building and construction materials in areas of the world where bamboo is native.

Bamboo's hardness and strength come from its physical makeup. In addition to lignin (found in dicot wood), bamboo cells contain up to 5% silica. Bamboo adds girth not through annual concentric growth rings but through scattered, individually encased bundles of cells.

Because bamboo grows so rapidly, it is increasingly popular as an eco-friendly material for many uses beyond furniture, including textiles. Some vendors use it to create arbors and trellises, and it can even be stripped and woven in a manner similar to wicker. Without some sort of coating, however, bamboo has limited weather resistance. Opinions vary as to the best way to preserve bamboo. Much depends on where and how it grows and what type of bamboo it is.

Bamboo furniture is long-lasting outdoors only when finished with a waterproof preservative. This aging chair displays traditional Chinese joinery.

Characteristics

Each wood type has its own distinctive color. Woods with obvious differences between the heartwood and sapwood usually have a darker hardwood. However, a noticeable difference in color does not mean there is any discernible difference in the wood's inherent characteristics.

In woods that exhibit distinct, usually darker, bands of latewood, you can judge density by comparing the percentage of latewood to early wood. Woods with a higher percentage of latewood are denser and therefore harder and stronger. This is particularly true of conifers. Except for this fact, wood color is not an indicator of wood strength. If the wood shows abnormal discoloration it may be diseased and weakened. Discoloration may also result from physical injury, fungal rot, insect attacks, or other damage. Some specific staining, such as spalting (caused by fungal growth), can even be a sought-after trait, because it is visually appealing with little to no harm to the wood.

Weather resistance is a crucial criterion when selecting outdoor furnishings. Wood is a natural, biodegradable material, which seems counterproductive to its use in a garden. No one perfect characteristic can be applied to all woods to predict their durability, so knowing something about a wood before you recommend an outdoor furnishing made of it is crucial if you want a piece that lasts.

The primary (though imperfect) indicator of a wood's durability is the age it was when harvested. Wood that is harvested when young has less heartwood and therefore less decay resistance. Some managed plantations harvest younger trees, producing narrower wood boards for manufacturers. Since this issue affects the quality of wood furnishings, it is one reason for the wide variation in cost.

Teak is unquestionably the benchmark for outdoor woods because it has so many ideal qualities: strength, durability, easy workability, stability, and beautiful color. It is indigenous to portions of India, Myanmar, the Lao People's Democratic Republic, and Thailand, and has naturalized in Java and Indonesia. Teak plantations have been established throughout tropical areas around the world, including Southeast Asia, Africa, Latin America, Pacific Islands, and northern Australia. In the interest of serving North America and Europe, plantation businesses have also developed in

Facing:
In this seating area, the frame of the component sofa and table are weather resistant teak, which will turn gray with age.

Durable woods

This abbreviated list represents a selection of the most frequently encountered durable woods, all well suited for outdoor use and able to last twenty-five years or more as long as they are not in contact with soil (and assuming the wood is older growth, where this applies). Many species have more than one common name, often locally dubbed, which can be very confusing in the trade. For this reason woods are listed by botanical name. *Eucalyptus* includes more durable woods than can be listed here, so I have listed only the most commonly used species from that genus.

Wood resources vary as some woods become scarcer and sustainable plantations become established. Before purchasing a wood, always investigate to determine whether it is a threatened species and identify its status in international trade (see cites.org and iucnredlist.org). No vulnerable or endangered species are listed here, but some could be considered at low risk or find their way onto a CITES Appendix II or III. Some commonly available woods are listed on CITES as vulnerable or endangered species, including *Sequoia* (redwood), *Khaya* (African mahogany), and *Millettia* (wenge).

Botanical name	Common name	Native habitat
Acacia harpophylla	brigalow	Australia
Acacia melanoxylon	Australian blackwood	Tasmania, Australia
Albizia saman (syn. *Samanea saman*)	rain tree, monkeypod	Central and South America
Alnus rubra	red alder	western North America
Brosimum guianense	snakewood, letterwood	coastal regions of northeastern South America
Brosimum rubescens (syn. *B. paraense*)	bloodwood	tropical South America
Calocedrus decurrens	incense cedar	western North America
Castanospermum australe	black bean	Australia
Catalpa speciosa	catawba	midwestern United States

Botanical name	Common name	Native habitat
Chamaecyparis lawsoniana	Port Orford cedar	southwestern Oregon, north-western California
Chamaecyparis nootkatensis	yellow cedar	western North America
Chamaecyparis thyoides	Atlantic white cedar	eastern North America
Colophospermum mopane	mopane	southern Africa
Cupressus arizonica	Arizona cypress	southwestern North America
Dalbergia retusa	cocobolo	Central America
Dalbergia spruceana	Brazilian rosewood, Amazon rosewood	Brazil, Venezuela, Bolivia
Dalbergia stevensonii	Honduran rosewood	Belize
Diospyros celebica	Macassar ebony	Southeast Asia
Diospyros crassiflora	Gaboon ebony	western Africa
Dipteryx odorata	cumaru	northern South America
Dryobalanops aromatica	kapor	Malaysia, Indonesia, Southeast Asia
Eucalyptus grandis	blue gum	Australia
Eucalyptus marginata	jarrah	Australia
Eucalyptus urograndis (E. grandis x E. urophylla)	Lyptus	Brazil
Gmelina dalrympleana, G. leichhardtii, G. fasciculiflora	beech	Australia
Hymenaea courbaril	jatobá	southern Mexico, Central America, northern South America
Juglans hindsii (syn. J. californica)	California walnut	California
Juglans nigra	black walnut	eastern North America
Juniperus deppeana	alligator juniper	southwestern United States, northern Mexico
Juniperus virginiana	eastern red cedar	eastern North America
Lophostemon confertus (syn. Tristiana conferta)	brush box	Australia
Machaerium scleroxylon	pau ferro	tropical South America (mainly Brazil and Bolivia)

Botanical name	Common name	Native habitat
Maclura pomifera	Osage-orange	southern American Great Plains
Maclura tinctoria	Argentine Osage-orange	West Indies, Central and South America
Mansonia altissima	mansonia	tropical West Africa
Metopium brownei	chechen	Dominican Republic, Cuba, Jamaica, northern Guatemala, Belize, southern Mexico
Milicia excelsa (syn. *Chlorophora excelsa*)	iroko	Africa
Millettia stuhlmannii	panga panga	Congo, Kenya, Mozambique, Tanzania, Zimbabwe
Morus rubra	red mulberry	eastern North America
Myroxylon balsamum	Santos mahogany	Central and South America
Peltogyne ssp.	purpleheart	Central and South America
Prosopis africana	African mesquite	Africa
Prosopis glandulosa	honey mesquite	southwestern North America
Prosopis kuntzei	itin	Gran Chaco region of South America
Prosopis nigra	black mesquite	South America
Pterocarpus soyauxii	padauk	central Africa and tropical West Africa
Quercus alba	white oak	eastern North America
Quercus bicolor	swamp white oak	eastern and midwestern United States
Quercus ilex	holm oak	Mediterranean Basin
Quercus lyrata	overcup oak	eastern United States
Quercus macrocarpa	bur oak	eastern and midwestern United States
Quercus petraea	sessile oak	most of Europe to Asia Minor
Quercus prinus	chestnut oak	eastern United States
Quercus robur	English oak	Europe to Asia Minor and North Africa

Botanical name	Common name	Native habitat
Quercus stellata	post oak	eastern North America
Quercus virginiana	live oak, southern live oak, encino	southeastern United States
Robinia pseudoacacia	black locust	southeastern United States
Sassafras albidum	sassafras	eastern United States
Swartzia cubensis	Mexican ebony	southern Mexico, Central America, northern South America
Syncarpia glomulifera	turpentine	Australia
Tabebuia chrysantha	yellow ipê	northern South America
Tabebuia impetiginosa	pink ipê	Mexico, South America
Tabebuia roseo-alba	white ipê	Brazil, Argentina, Paraguay
Tabebuia serratifolia	yellow poui	Central and South America
Taxodium distichum	baldcypress (old growth)	southeastern United States
Taxus baccata	European yew	Europe, southwestern Asia
Taxus brevifolia	Pacific yew	American Pacific Northwest
Tectona grandis	teak (old growth)	India, Myanmar, Indonesia, Malaysia
Thuja occidentalis	arborvitae	northeastern North America
Thuja plicata	western red cedar	western North America
Toona calantas	calantas	Indonesia, Malaysia
Toona ciliata	Australian red cedar	Australia

areas of Mexico and Central America. Some plantation owners make an effort to grow teak more slowly to improve its durability, though teak is nearly as strong and durable when young, with mostly sapwood. In its native habitat it does not grow as a monoculture forest and seems to grow best among other less valuable trees. This typically does not happen on a plantation unless owners interplant teak among locally native plants.

A considerable number of eucalyptus are sufficiently durable for use as garden furnishings. Lyptus, a plantation-grown cross between *Eucalyptus grandis* and *E. urophylla*, is very strong and compares favorably to hard maple and oak. It also has a closed grain (with minute or nonexistent pores), which gives it a texturally even appearance.

One further note about durability: it does not necessarily equate to structural strength or density. Conversely, density may be an indicator of durability.

Sawn-lumber patterns

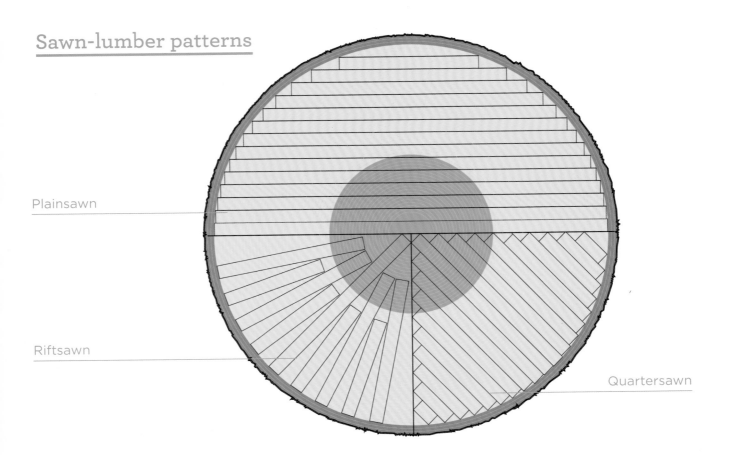

Plainsawn

Riftsawn

Quartersawn

Materials

Fabrication

Wood is acquired for use by either harvesting a tree or, better yet, finding some reclaimed wood. The manner in which wood is sawn at the mill, cut by the fabricator, and assembled varies greatly. Fabrication methods affect quality and therefore cost, and you really do get what you pay for.

The first task at the sawmill is to strip away the outer bark of a tree. This bark and other waste are used to make wood products such as particleboard. The stripped logs are then cut into quartersawn, riftsawn, or plainsawn lumber, each yielding a different look. Quartersawn and riftsawn are more even patterns than plainsawn, producing the most stable lumber, which shrinks more in thickness than width. Plainsawn wood is wider, and its production less expensive and less labor intensive, with less waste. Whatever wood pattern is selected may affect the ultimate success of a garden furnishing. Plainsawn wood is probably the most problematic because it has grain in several directions, which can cause the wood to dry unevenly and then warp. Shrinkage is also a bigger problem with plainsawn wood. However, if these issues are taken into consideration when the wood is purchased, cut, and assembled into a furnishing, there may be no further complications.

Veneers are not used outdoors because they delaminate from their plywood base. However, solid wood has its own set of problems.

Drying Wood

The way in which wood is seasoned or dried can make an enormous difference in its quality. Air-drying teak in the tropical climate in which it grows makes little sense, because tropical air is too humid. Yet you may discover manufacturers that tout on-site, air-dried teak. Wood is typically dried to a 12% moisture level during kiln-drying, an expensive seasoning process due to the energy it requires. Properly seasoned, Grade A wood dried to 12% will not crack, split, or shrink. Though more expensive, it is worth the cost.

Joinery

When wood is joined, the more surface area that is in contact between pieces, the better. Several ways of joining wood do not involve adhesives. For an arbor, gravity alone can keep a top piece nestled snuggly within a prepared groove. Tongue and groove, dovetail, and mortise and tenon are particularly noteworthy traditional joints. Fabricators also use dowels or biscuits to improve lesser joints, like butt or lap joints. A dowel is a small, round, linear piece that fits within two round holes in each piece of wood to connect the two pieces. A biscuit is an oval, thin piece of composite wood that fits into a narrow slot on each piece of wood, then swells to tighten the joint. For garden furniture, good joinery combined with a top-quality, water-resistant adhesive works best for creating a long-lasting bond.

The more surface area involved in a joint, the better the adhesion.

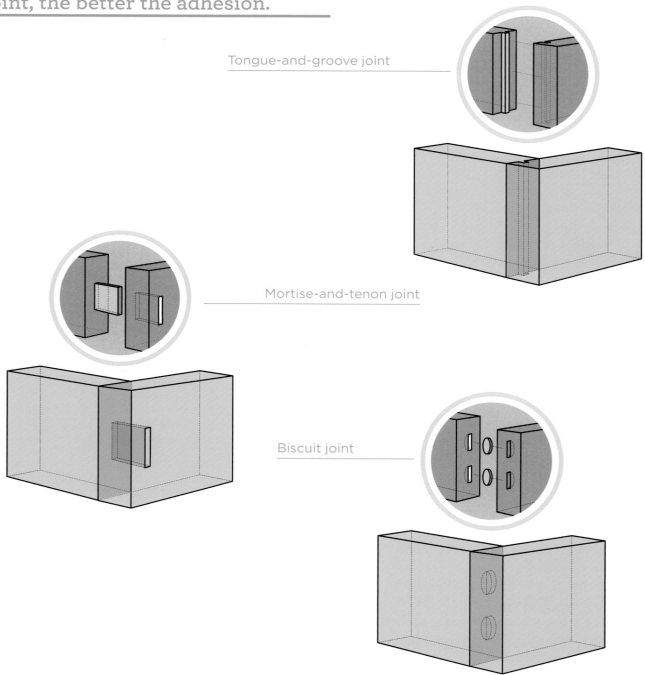

Tongue-and-groove joint

Mortise-and-tenon joint

Biscuit joint

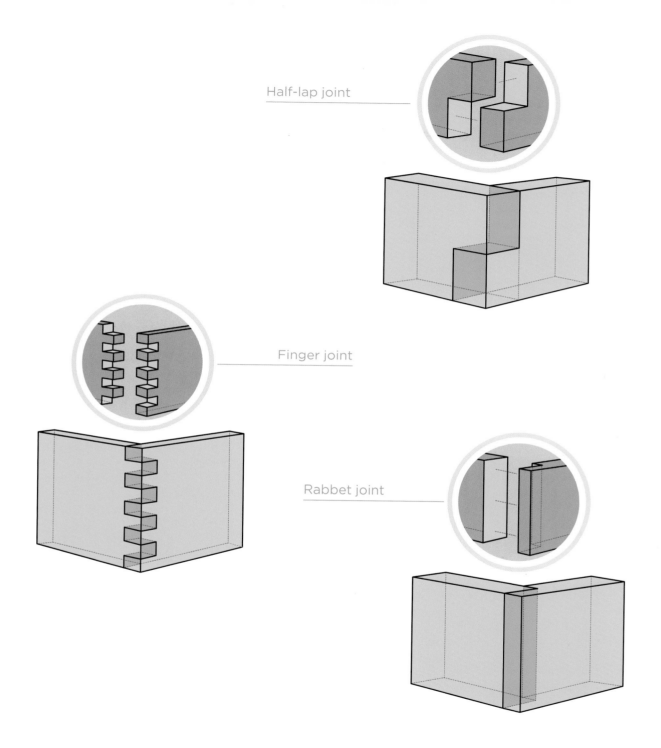

Half-lap joint

Finger joint

Rabbet joint

103

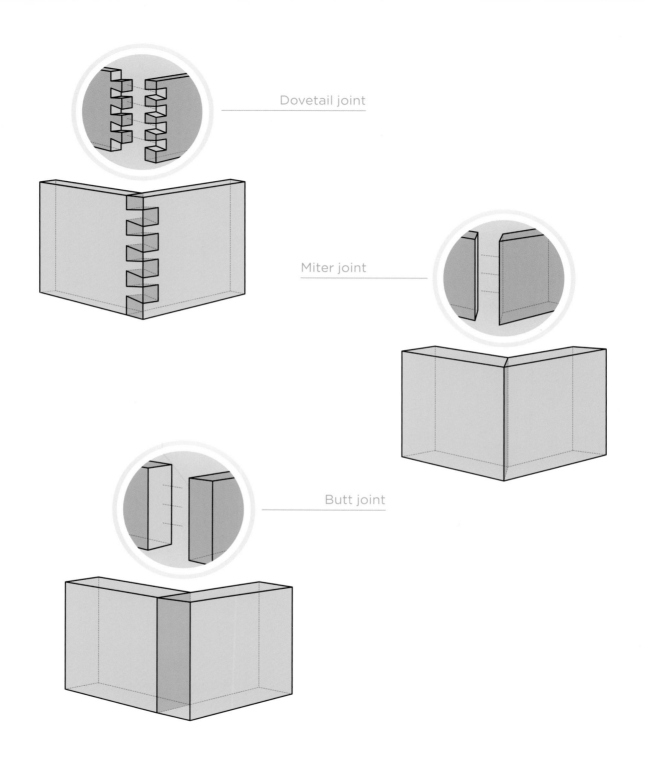

Dovetail joint

Miter joint

Butt joint

Wood is anisotropic, meaning it expands and contracts at different rates along the grain versus across the grain. When joining wood, fabricators must take this into consideration; otherwise, they risk a failed joint. When glued together, wood grain must align in the same direction or the joint will crack.

Adhesives

When you evaluate joinery, it is a good idea to also evaluate the adhesive used. Adhesives for garden furniture must be waterproof. Reputable retailers recommend high-quality, dependable adhesives, pointing out that lower-quality glues lead to eventual failure of a garden furnishing. This is good advice. Only a few adhesives work best with wood for outdoor use: polyurethane, resorcinol-formaldehyde resin, and epoxy.

Polyurethane, primarily known as Gorilla Glue in the United States, is a very strong, fast-curing, flexible, stainable glue. It requires clamping and works best with premoistened wood, drying to a light tan color.

Resorcinol-formaldehyde resin, a mix of a liquid resin and powdered catalyst, is extremely strong, durable under extreme conditions, and resistant to boiling water, salt water, and ultraviolet (UV) light. Because it is dark purple, there is little to no room for placement error. It is also toxic.

Epoxy is stronger than resorcinol, with a higher tolerance for placement error. It cures under a wide range of temperatures and moisture levels, does not require clamping, and has good gap-filling properties. It is resistant to UV light and salt water, and heat resistant to 350°F. Epoxy is also expensive, and overexposure may trigger an allergic reaction.

Superior wood joinery, such as this butterfly joint, can give a well designed piece of furniture a long life while adding beauty.

Finishing

Because there are so many different types of wood, each wood's merits and issues should be considered when determining the finish. Although many manufacturers say a wood can be left unfinished, it will last longer if finished. A finish can last for a long time or need regular reapplication, depending on its quality (and the quality of any primer that might be needed).

Wood that sits outside has to deal with weather: moisture from rain and humidity, drying sun, and wind that pummels it with tiny bits of debris and grit. It also has to withstand wood-chewing insects. To become both weather and pest resistant, outdoor wood typically requires some sort of preservative or protective coating.

The range of coatings is complicated and extensive, from transparent stains to enamel paints. All are meant only for objects that will not be in contact with soil. To

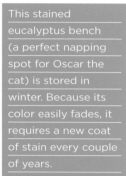

This stained eucalyptus bench (a perfect napping spot for Oscar the cat) is stored in winter. Because its color easily fades, it requires a new coat of stain every couple of years.

Materials

begin with, find out whether the wood you wish to finish has been impregnated with preservative or is inherently resinous. If you are finishing an unfinished piece, talk to a coating specialist at the paint store or an architectural representative to determine the most appropriate type of coating for the wood you have. It is also a good idea to read the Material Safety Data Sheet (MSDS) for any finish under consideration. The MSDS will describe its degree of sustainability and list any precautions needed during application.

Since wood is vulnerable outdoors, manufacturers frequently protect it with enamel paint. Though impervious, paint doesn't last forever and will need to be reapplied periodically. The type of wood will affect your choice of primer more than your choice of paint, because primers come into direct contact with the wood. Also, keep in mind that colors fade, especially vivid colors.

Paint is vulnerable to certain problems, depending on the type of weather the painted wood is exposed to, the variety of the wood, the type of paint, the paint's consistency and adherence, and the primer used. In certain circumstances paint may crack, blister, chalk (develop a fine white powder on the surface), peel, run (show visible drips), alligator (develop a cracking pattern), mildew, wrinkle, or check (develop long, shallow, evenly spaced cracks). Read care instructions and prevent these problems with any pieces you buy. If problems do occur, contact the manufacturer or fabricator for instructions on how to resolve the issue.

Stains are a little different from enamel paints and fall into two categories: penetrating (including water repellents) and film-forming (including semitransparent and opaque "stains"). A penetrating stain's absorption rate will vary depending on the type of stain and the wood's characteristics. Unlike film-forming stains, penetrating stains allow wood to breathe. Extensive preparation of the wood is not needed for penetrating stains, because these stains do not crack and peel.

Although clear penetrating finishes can protect wood, their surface life is limited. The solvent included in water repellents, water-repellent preservatives, and some stains can also allow the binder, preservatives, and water repellents to penetrate the wood, improving its longevity. Pigmented, semitransparent stains contain a limited amount of pigment and therefore provide some sun and UV protection. A vast range of stain colors are available, including custom matching. Pigmented penetrating options include oil-based, solvent-borne, semitransparent stains. The greater the level of transparency, the more visible the wood grain will be, and the more the wood color will affect the color of the stain.

Water-repellent preservatives (WRPs) such as marine or spar finishes are among the best available transparent, exterior, water-repellent wood finishes. They should have UV absorbers to help protect both the finish and the wood. They should also flex with the wood as it expands and contracts. WRPs can be oil- or water-based

Materials

and found with sheens varying from glossy to satin. (If they are water-based or latex stains, technically they are nonpenetrating stains.) WRPs need reapplication when the finish gets dull, possibly once per year. Some finishes advertise extensive longevity. Many of these finishes, even the ones that advertise lower VOCs (volatile organic compounds), also stipulate that they need to be applied in a controlled commercial environment with the appropriate gear to prevent inhalation or contact.

Film-forming stains have more pigment than pigmented penetrating stains. You will usually see them as latex-based semitransparent stains or latex or oil-based opaque stains. However, a nonpenetrating, film-forming stain is technically a paint and should be treated as such.

A semitransparent latex stain is transparent by virtue of its thin coat, which reduces its durability. Opaque latex-based stains have more solids and a thicker coat but don't hide wood imperfections as well as paint. They are also more mildew resistant and flexible than oil-based stains.

Silicate-Impregnated Wood

Silicate-impregnated (glass-impregnated) wood is not new. In nature it is produced over thousands of years, requiring not only silicate but also tons of pressure. The result is wood that has crystallized into stone, what we call petrified wood.

A similar material can be produced by soaking wood in water and sodium silicate. During the drying process the silicon is left bonded to the wood, resulting in a hard, strong, waterproof material that is resistant to fire, pests, and warping. Silicate-treated wood is a great alternative to wood preserved with arsenic, is only slightly more expensive than pressure-treated wood, and can be cut, painted, or stained as with other woods. It grays in the sun and is fully recyclable. It is also lighter than other treated woods and is fastener-friendly, meaning it will not corrode fasteners or cause them to move. TimberSIL pioneered commercial silicate-treated wood, first producing it in 2010.

Standards

Wood undergoes a wide range of testing, primarily to determine whether it will meet a set of criteria for a specific use. ANSI and ISO standards are often used as benchmarks.

Moisture content is a crucial test because it affects a number of other wood attributes, and because wood with high moisture content is more prone to decay. The goal is to dry wood to a level of 12% moisture. To find out whether the wood has reached this level, manufacturers or their testing agencies test it using moisture meters. These meters measure electrical resistance, which increases when moisture content decreases.

Computerized tests have been developed to determine a number of woods' mechanical properties. The specific gravity test is the most important test of wood strength. Two compression tests—parallel to grain and perpendicular to grain—also determine strength and hardness. The impact test determines deflection and stiffness. The shear strength test determines the strength of an adhesive bond between two pieces of wood. The hardness (Janka ball) test measures the wood's ability to resist denting. The cleavage test determines splitting resistance. And the abrasion test measures durability.

Knots and Other Defects

Knots reflect their complicated root cause: the many directions that a branch can grow out from a tree. As trees age, they lose branches. Trees respond to the death and eventual loss of a branch or growth bud by growing around it, but the inner heart of the tree may be full of knots (which is why knots may fall out of a board or panel of wood). Because their lower branches fall more easily, conifers tend to have more knots than hardwood trees. Since knots are more difficult to work with and can weaken the wood, the outer sapwood part of the tree may be stronger and easier to fabricate. A tree that grows in a dense forest is less likely to have as many knots since its branch growth is sparser. Although knots are desirable in certain types of wood for the sake of appearance, they are usually considered flaws.

The US Forestry Service grades logs for bark distortion, grub holes, bird pecks, bumps, adventitious branches, frost cracks, straight seams, splits, bark pockets, gum spots, and stains. Too many defects indicate an inferior grade of wood.

Care and Maintenance

Caring for outdoor wood will tend to put you in one of two camps: those who maintain a finish and those who prefer an unfinished, grayed appearance. Depending on the wood the latter can work quite well, but eventually it will break down, particularly in freezing weather or extreme heat. The trick to finishes is applying them properly and in a timely manner. This usually involves cleaning with mild soapy water, air-drying, and lightly sanding prior to refinishing.

Sustainability

Wood is a renewable resource but only when managed properly. Responsible sourcing is probably the biggest issue with wood.

The rainforests in the Amazon and in tropical Africa are our planet's lungs. We need to pay special attention to these gigantic carbon sinks. The Rainforest Alliance does this through certification, verification, and validation services.

There are two types of certification for wood: forest certification, which governs the forest operation for producing the raw material, and chain-of-custody (COC), which tracks manufacturers and companies that process the wood on its way to market. The Forest Stewardship Council (FSC) and Conservation International (CI) both monitor responsible forest management and COC. The Sustainable Forestry Initiative (SFI) develops forest management standards. The Programme for the Endorsement of Forest Certification (PEFC) is the largest certification program. It endorses national programs, is tailored to local conditions, and provides third-party certification, assessing sustainable benchmarks for consistency with international requirements. Some companies have issues with these forest management organizations, not because they don't believe in certification but because they want the procedures to be more transparent. They want assurances that certified wood lives up to its environmental promises.

Don't waste wood. Consider using products made with reclaimed wood or recycled wood fiber. This limits the number of trees that need to be harvested and the energy consumed for transport, and sends fewer items to the landfill.

Foresters focused on renewable practices are establishing slow-growth plantations closer to their markets to limit transport energy and cost, and to reduce habitat destruction in Southeast Asian tropical forests. Support them.

Remember that the more durable and better maintained the wood, the longer it will last. Evaluate finishes for their eco-friendliness and amount of VOCs. Most coating and paint manufacturers produce VOC-free alternatives.

Wood checklist

Is this wood suited to this use?

Evaluate any joinery. Will it hold up to this use?

How is the wood finished? Will it hold up to the weather?

Will weatherizing add or detract from its value?

What standards or tests has this wood met?

What maintenance will be required to keep this wood product in like-new condition?

Are there warranties from the manufacturer or retailer, and if so, what do they cover and for what period of time?

Metal

People have mined, melted, and formed metal since ancient times. In its liquid state, metal can take the form of almost any shape imaginable. Unlike most materials, metal can be remarkably thin and still exceedingly strong. It is no wonder this material is used in so many ways for garden furnishings. Metal objects as diverse as elegant fire pits, planters, and dramatic garden art become the glittering earrings and bracelets of a garden.

The metals most suitable for outdoor furnishings are aluminum, copper, zinc, and alloys such as steel, wrought iron, cast iron, brass, and bronze. The outdoor furnishings industry typically uses aluminum, stainless steel, cast iron, and wrought iron for art and heating, arbors and screens, plant containers, and light fixtures. Certain metals even become fibers for use in the textile industry.

Each metal type has its own distinguishing characteristic and when combined with other elements can create unique alloys. Alloys also exist within a given metal (for example, oxygen-free copper versus electrolytic tough pitch copper). Alloys are created to solve problems for a particular use. For example, many metals corrode when exposed to oxygen. Ferrous (iron-based) alloys rust, while other metals like copper and brass oxidize, turning shades of blue-green. Aluminum and zinc resist corrosion through passivation, which is the creation of corrosion-resistant oxide as the outer layer of the metal. Ordinary steel will passivate in alkaline environments, which is why rebar (reinforcing bar) works well in concrete. For ferrous metals, a process called Parkerizing or phosphating is a preferred method that forms a manganese phosphate or zinc phosphate shield. Black oxidizing, previously known as bluing or browning, is an older, less successful, but chemically similar coating. When different metals are placed next to each other, galvanic corrosion can develop.

A remarkable 95% copper awning creates unique shadows and a shady respite next to a pool deck.

Iron

Iron is the fourth most common element in the earth's crust and has a long history of use. Evidence of smelted iron exists from as long ago as 2700 BC in Mesopotamia and northern Syria. China produced cast iron in roughly 500 BC, and Europe caught up during the Middle Ages. By the time of the Industrial Revolution, numerous countries around the world were using iron.

Today it is easier to refine iron ore into pure iron. By eliminating impurities, refiners produce new types of iron. Gray iron, for example, has a higher content of silicon and boasts several advantages over the original white iron: it is less brittle, easier to finish, exhibits less shrinkage, and results in better casting.

Iron is generally found as iron oxide minerals such as magnetite and hematite. Because it does not form passivating oxide layers, the exterior of iron oxidizes to rust. This is why iron is usually powder coated or painted.

Although iron's greatest use is in the processing of steel, wrought iron is often used in the garden furnishings industry to cast ornately detailed furniture and beautiful containers or fashion objects.

An iron basin designed for use with wood will develop a rusted patina over time. Combined with granite, the two materials forge an artistic fire pit. The joinery allows for differing expansion and contraction rates of the two materials.

Steel

Of the many types of steel, all are alloys of mostly iron combined with varying percentages of carbon and other elements like manganese, chromium, and nickel. Many kinds of steel have been produced in response to a wide variety of needs. Several types are used outdoors, including carbon steel, galvanized steel, stainless steel, and weathering steel (known primarily by its trade name, Cor-Ten).

Carbon Steel

Ninety percent of steel produced is carbon steel, and this is primarily what steel artists use. Carbon steel has a low resistance to rusting compared with other grades of steel. Artists generally use hot-rolled (or black) steel, which is readily available, darker gray, and less expensive than cold-rolled steel. Cold-rolled steel can require a special order, increasing the cost and time required, but is more flexible and lighter in weight, with a higher yielding strength. It is used most frequently in the auto and appliance industries.

Galvanized Steel

Steel is galvanized when it has been coated with zinc to prevent rusting. It is not a coating in the same sense as paint, because the zinc alloys or merges with the steel at the point of contact, rendering it inseparable. Iron can also be galvanized.

Many products are galvanized through the hot-dip process. However, electrochemical and electrodeposition processes may also be used. Galvanized steel is used in many outdoor products because it is easy to work with, inexpensive, and long-lasting (though not impervious). Its dull gray color is not particularly attractive and may be its most notable detractor, but at least there is no discoloration over time. AK Steel produces aluminized steel, a similar material that uses aluminum rather than zinc.

Stainless Steel

Stainless steel is so named because it *stains less*. It is highly resistant to weather, but if not cleaned regularly can rust. How is this possible?

Rusty steel candleholders fit right in with the color of a custom-fabricated fire pit.

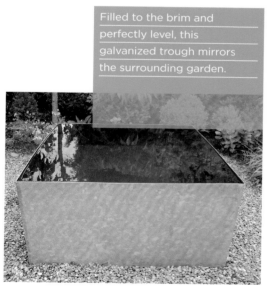

Filled to the brim and perfectly level, this galvanized trough mirrors the surrounding garden.

Stainless steel alloys differ from carbon steel because they have a minimum of 10.5% chromium. When chromium is added to steel, it reacts with oxygen to create an invisible, thin (but tough) protective layer over the iron. Because this passive film reacts with oxygen, even when it is scratched the chromium can reform it. Other elements that enhance stainless steel's rust-resistant properties are molybdenum, nickel, niobium, and titanium. Stainless steel is more susceptible to corrosion near the ocean, because more salt in the air means less oxygen. Some manufacturers recommend keeping their stainless steel products at least 25 miles from the ocean, or suggest a higher grade of stainless steel. Their goal is to make a smoother surface, less subject to pitting, because pitting decreases rust resistance. This is also why it is important to keep stainless steel clean. Cleaning removes dirt that can create or exacerbate pitting. Such pitting is often not noticed until you see rust.

Stainless steel is divided into three major classes: austenitic, martensitic, and ferritic. Most stainless steel (70%) falls into the austenitic category and by virtue of its properties is the only kind used for garden furnishings. This low-carbon steel contains

Stainless steel and teak are a perfect long-lasting combination for outdoor furniture.

Materials

anywhere from 10% to 30% chromium. Other elements are added, such as molybdenum, titanium, and particularly nickel. Through annealing, stainless steel also has nonmagnetic properties. Annealing involves heating and then cooling the steel to make it stronger, easier to form, and harder.

Stainless steel is categorized by series and types. Types in the 300 series are typically used to make garden furnishings. Type 304 (also known as A2 or 18/8) is the most commonly used stainless steel outside the United States. Type 304L contains less carbon, which makes it easier to weld but also decreases its strength. Type 304N is very similar to 304L, but nitrogen has been added to increase its tensile strength and its yield. Type 316 (also known as A4) is the next most commonly used grade. It contains chromium, nickel, and molybdenum (added to improve resistance to salt) and is often used for food processing. Manufacturers should list the type of stainless steel used in their product. If they do not list the alloy type and grade of stainless steel, they may list "CRES," meaning corrosion-resistant steel—not as precise a label, since corrosion-resistant steel isn't necessarily stainless steel.

Weathering Steel

Weathering steel, or Cor-Ten steel, is a group of steel alloys. The alloy materials allow the steel to rust over a period of time, and the rust forms a weather-protective coating. For garden furnishings, weathering steel often appears as art. Fasteners and joints made of this material should rust at the same rate as the metal they join. Creating a pocket for water to pool is not advised, as this will speed the rusting process where the water sits. Weathering steel must be a thick enough gauge to resist weathering by abrasion and debris. It is also susceptible to salt and therefore inappropriate for a salt air location.

By day a clever use of Cor-Ten steel makes a creative ornamental splash block.

At night the steel comes alive as light glows through transparent, barrel-shaped, colored-glass buttons—a dramatic display with or without rain.

United States Steel has introduced a new generation of Cor-Ten steel called Cor-Ten AZP. Its improved qualities include a type of galvanized coating matched to the color of aged Cor-Ten. It has a high recycled content, is recyclable, and will not create stormwater runoff staining. However, for most garden uses, standard weathering steel is sufficient.

It should be noted that during the rusting process, steel coloration will be uneven if the fabricator has not applied an oxidizing agent to speed things up. Also, be cautious when it comes to placement of any product made with weathering steel, as rain may carry some of the rust onto other surfaces.

Aluminum

Aluminum is the most prevalent element in the earth's crust. It occurs in mineral form commonly mixed with other minerals, predominantly bauxite. Because it is lightweight, soft, malleable, and durable, aluminum is a perfect material for garden furnishings. It is also nonmagnetic.

This set of table and chairs—aluminum with antique copper finish—has weathered many years outdoors in a tough environment.

Aluminum's inherent corrosion resistance may be the best reason to use it for garden furnishings. The surface of pure aluminum physically oxidizes, creating a thin layer of aluminum oxide, a natural barrier to corrosion. Unfortunately this isn't the case for aluminum alloys, but they can be passivated through anodizing, alclading, or chromate conversion coating. The most robust of these methods is anodizing, which involves adding a thick oxide coating that also provides excellent electrical insulation. Alclading involves metallurgically bonding a thin layer of pure aluminum to an aluminum alloy. Chromate conversion coating is typically used on tools.

Historically, obtaining aluminum from the earth has been a difficult process. It is presently obtained through electrolysis, which is expensive due to the considerable amount of electricity required. Aluminum is 100% recyclable, and recycling uses a fraction of the energy required to extract aluminum from ore.

Copper

Beautiful, orangey-red copper is waterproof, malleable, and soft, and it conducts heat and electricity. It is a component of numerous alloys. Copper oxidizes beautifully,

The peak and ridge caps atop this butterfly house are made of copper, which has darkened over the years due to oxidation and weather. Additional aging will bring aqua-blue oxidation.

Materials

creating a blue-green verdigris patina that is highly corrosion resistant. The largest copper statue in the world, the Statue of Liberty, was formed using repoussé and chasing. (Repoussé involves hammering a metal on its back side to create an image on the front. Chasing, also called embossing, is the opposite technique.) Copper frequently finds its way into contemporary gardens as light fixtures, art, arbors and trellises (often of copper pipe), rain chains, and planters.

Copper is 100% recyclable, using somewhat fewer steps than needed for the original extraction. In fact it has been estimated that about 80% of all the copper that has ever been mined is still in use, having been recycled repeatedly.

Usually copper is purchased in sheets by the square foot, or in linear feet as copper rod or copper pipe. The roofing industry measures it in inches per square foot. Due to increased demand, copper has become more expensive and more prone to theft.

Brass

Brass is an alloy of copper combined with zinc in proportions that vary to suit the application. It is commonly used for door hardware and light fixtures because its

In the spirit of authenticity, spiritually minded gardeners included bronze Tibetan prayer wheels near their home's entry.

subdued golden finish is resistant to tarnishing. Its salt-air tolerance also makes it an ideal metal at the seashore. This soft metal is often used in situations to prevent sparks that might occur with another metal. It can have a yellow cast to it or be quite copper colored; the greater the copper content, the more likely brass will look like copper.

Bronze

Bronze is an alloy with a high content of copper and a small percentage of tin, although minor variations are available that exclude tin. Bronze is less brittle than iron but softer and weaker than steel. Copper-based alloys such as bronze have a lower melting point and are therefore easier to cast than iron or steel. Bronze also resists corrosion (particularly salt water corrosion) better than steel. Many outdoor sculptures are made of bronze. Hardware and lighting for outdoor use may suggest a "bronze finish," but the metal may not actually be bronze.

A little girl in the form of a cast bronze sculpture peeks over hostas.

Forming Metal

In their preliminary stages, metals are melted and formed into blocks called ingots. Once in this state, they can be forged, cast, or extruded into sheets, angles, flat bars, rods, pipes, and many other shapes, depending on what is required. Forging shapes metal by impact or pressure and varying degrees of heat. Casting involves pouring molten metal into a mold in the shape of the final product. With extrusion, heated metal is pushed through a die pattern—so if the pattern is a circle, for example, the result would be a round rod.

Forging

Forging is more costly than casting or extruding but yields a stronger product because it aligns the grain (crystalline structure) of the metal. The most common types are drop forging (similar to blacksmithing), open- or closed-die forging, automatic hot forging, precision forging, and press forging. Most of these methods prevent metal from being lost during the process.

Forging temperatures vary depending on the metal, which in the marketplace translates to costs that vary depending on the product. If a manufacturer produces a high volume but uses a more expensive method, the product may still be competitive with that of another manufacturer who generates a lower volume with a less costly method. There could be a quality difference between the two products that would be more obvious if one was more expensive than the other.

Old-fashioned blacksmithing is a rare art compared to the ubiquitous use of welded iron. The smith forms the malleable red-hot steel until it reaches the desired form. This is real wrought iron!

Casting

Casting involves either an expendable mold, which may only be used minimally, often only once, or a nonexpendable mold, which is longer-lasting. A variety of means and methods are used to assemble a mold, introduce metal into the mold, cool the metal, and finish the piece. This partly accounts for the range of costs and qualities for a cast piece.

You will most commonly encounter casting in the form of cast iron, but you may encounter other materials as well, particularly for garden art. I once took a sculpture class in which we created a carved foam piece of art, packed it in fine sand inside a garbage can, melted aluminum (which has a low melting point), and poured the aluminum through a foam cone connected to our piece. The aluminum took the shape of the carved piece as well as a portion of the pouring cone because the melting point of the foam was lower than that of the aluminum. Gases and flames escaped through a second cone attached to the piece. This lost-foam method was a very dramatic process! The lost-wax method is similar, except that the shape is made of wax, and the metal used is usually bronze.

Casting often leaves a seam. In the case of my aluminum project, parts of aluminum cones remained attached, which we had to cut off before we could sand and burnish the piece. In this case, there was not the degree of control that there would be in a manufacturing process. This meant that during the solidification process, "imperfections" occurred. In an art piece, such flaws may be acceptable and may in fact add to the textural quality. In a piece of furniture or a planter, however, they are generally not acceptable. If you know a piece has been cast and you do not see any seaming, it is either because the casting process was extremely precise or because the manufacturer machined the piece, as part of finishing, to remove visual seams. Either way the piece will be more expensive.

Because the solidification process requires a fair amount of control to cool a piece (meaning more time), and because metals can shrink appreciably during the cooling process (meaning greater use of material), the casting process can be more expensive, with the final cost depending on the metal. Aluminum has a high solidification shrinkage rate, which is why we had to continue pouring molten aluminum into our mold, using more than required just for the piece itself. Manufacturers may create oversized molds, creating patternmaker's allowances, which control the eventual size, distortion, and imperfections of a piece. Copper and its alloys, zinc, tin, and white cast iron have slightly lower solidification shrinkage rates than aluminum, but ductile cast iron has a considerably lower solidification shrinkage rate, making it a better material for casting.

Extrusion

Through the process of extrusion, manufacturers are able to work brittle metals, create complex cross-sections, and produce excellent surface finishes. This is the method that produces metal rods, pipes, and other lineal materials. Hot extrusion requires more costly equipment and upkeep, but the heat makes the metal easier to work with. Cold extrusion occurs at or near room temperature and produces a stronger metal with a better finish. Aluminum, zinc, lead, copper, tin, and steel are often extruded. The process is economical to a point, and beyond that manufacturers use roll forming. Visible defects such as cracking or surface lines may be found in extruded pieces.

Joining Metal

Once metal is formed, components that will make up a final piece need to be joined. Metal can be joined through welding, soldering, riveting, seaming, gluing, or hot fusion. Pieces can also be joined through mechanical methods using bolts, nuts, and screws, or machined methods involving tabs and slots or dovetailing.

Welding

The most common joinery method may be welding, which involves melting an area on two pieces, then adding a filler metal to create a pool of molten metal. Once joined, the

Artisans crafted this modern table by welding functional antique grillwork to a new metal base.

hot pool is allowed to cool to become a strong joint. Several methods of welding are used—arc welding, gas welding, TIG (tungsten inert gas) welding, fillet welding, plug welding, skip welding, and flash welding—and each can affect joinery appearance and strength. Knowing how to evaluate welding will assure that you obtain a quality piece that will last a long time.

A good weld has uniform and fine bead ripples and a uniform bead profile (height and width). The size of the weld should be appropriate to the stresses that will be placed on it. It should be neither too small nor too large. There should be no visible defects such as porosity (visible gas pores), cracks, or craters. Also look for the appropriate use of a spot weld, linear weld, or circumference weld.

Soldering

Soldering (or sweating) is similar to welding in that it melts a filler metal that joins the two pieces, but it does not melt the original two pieces as part of the process, because the filler metal has a lower melting point. The filler metal is known as the solder. What makes soldering different from hot gluing is the ability of the solder to alloy with the two pieces at the joint. There are three types of soldering, each requiring higher

An artist solders two sections of copper pipe.

Materials

temperatures but gaining in strength. Soft soldering uses tin or lead as the solder and should only be used for nonstructural purposes. Silver soldering, which uses silver or silver alloys as the solder, is stronger and requires more heat. Brazing, which uses a brass alloy, is the strongest form of soldering and requires the most heat (it also requires eye protection due to the bright light of the torch). This method may be used to repair cast-iron furnishings.

Flux is an additional material used in soldering. It facilitates the soldering process by eliminating oxidation, which would inhibit the joint from occurring. Some fluxes also provide some cleaning ability prior to the solder. Impurities must be removed from the solder area to assure a good joint.

Copper is one of the easiest metals to solder, with mild steel and iron being slightly more difficult and stainless steel and aluminum being difficult. An experienced fabricator will usually use an acetylene or propylene torch rather than propane because they produce a hotter flame, which allows the fabricator to solder more joints in a given period of time. (Aluminum soldering is an exception and can use propane heat.) Only after a joint is properly cleaned, fitted, and fluxed will the fabricator apply the flame. Previously soldered joints can be resoldered, but the original solder must be removed and the metal thoroughly cleaned beforehand.

It is important to know the characteristics of a well-soldered joint. The solder should be uniformly smooth, bright, and shiny (although lead-free solders can have a duller appearance). There should be no surface bubbles (an indication of flux or air trapped below the surface, which would weaken the joint). The soldering should be appropriately sized for the piece and joint. The joint should have a slightly concave surface, indicating that excessive heat and solder were not used, which could weaken it, and must be strong enough for the intended use. Finally, the joint should be fully connected to the base material without gaps.

Riveting

A rivet is a mechanical fastener that consists of two parts, a top (head) and a bottom (buck-tail). During installation, a rivet is placed in a hole connecting two metals. Then it is struck, causing the buck-tail to expand and hold the rivet in place permanently.

A variety of rivets are used, such as solid rivets, blind rivets, drive rivets, and semitubular rivets. If you decide to use rivets, make sure to determine the aesthetic outcome, because they are visible. They can create a very interesting pattern while acting as a fastener at the same time. Work with your metal fabricator to determine which type of rivet should be used, what material they should be made of, and where they will be placed. If you use a contrasting material, such as copper rivets on stainless steel, they will be even more noticeable. Rivets are often effective in situations where other fasteners are impractical, as when a high amount of heat could damage materials to be attached.

Seaming

We often see standing seam metal roofs, which use seams to connect the metal panels together. Seaming involves overlapping the two edges and then mechanically folding them over to crimp the panels together. This is usually only practical if you are attaching metal sheets to one another.

Finishing

A finish will make or break the performance and appearance of a metal, and a finish can only succeed with proper preparation. Thorough cleaning is everything when it comes to preparing metal surfaces. Without it, don't expect a finish to adhere or perform properly. Surface preparations range from complex multistage chemical cleaning to acid washes to abrasive blasting. Once the surface has been prepared, a finish can be applied, principally through plating, chemical conversion, etching, anodizing, painting and coating, or mechanical processes.

Plating

Manufacturers or fabricators plate metal for ornamental reasons, to prevent corrosion, or to provide a better wearing surface. A variety of plating methods exist, not all of which are suitable for all metals. Plating involves either a plating bath or an electrical current, or a combination of the two. Two common types of plating are electroplating, which is a combination process, and hot-dip plating, which is a plating bath method used for galvanization. Examples from the garden include galvanized pots or tanks used as pots (produced with hot-dip plating) and nickel-plated items such as frames for mounting wind socks.

Chemical Conversion

Metal coloring, chromate conversion, phosphate coating, and passivating are all examples of chemical conversion coatings. Metal coloring involves oxidizing the metal surface to alter its appearance, as when a blue-green appears on copper. Phosphate coatings occur when steel, iron, or zinc-plated steel is dipped into a dilute phosphate solution. Chromate conversion is among the most toxic forms of coatings, which is why it is used so much less now than in the past.

Etching

Etching agents either alter the surface aesthetic of a metal or can etch a design into the metal's surface. Etching usually involves a chemical and possibly masking if a pattern or design is applied. Copper is the preferred metal for etching, but steel is also popular even though its line quality is not quite as good. It has become very popular to etch photographs onto metal, a process that can be used to make fabulous screens or garden art.

Photochemical etching can be done on any metal with a minimum thickness that depends on the metal used. A photoresist material may be applied to any area not intended to be etched. A photosensitive material (possibly a photopolymer) is applied to the areas to be etched, the metal is exposed to light, and chemical residues are washed off.

Nontoxic etching uses acrylic polymers as a base and ferric chloride as the etching agent (because it will not produce toxic fumes). Washing soda solutions remove the polymers rather than toxic solvents. There is also a patented etching system that uses electricity to etch metal.

Anodizing

The most commonly anodized metal is aluminum. An electrolytic process, anodizing helps prevent corrosion and improves appearance and the surface's ability to accept another finish. Common aluminum anodizing uses chromic acid, sulfuric acid, and boric-sulfuric processes. Once anodized, the metal is sealed with something like chromic acid or hot water.

Painting and Coating

Finishers spray liquid paint and powder coatings onto a metal and allow the finish to cure. UV powders and liquids use UV light to cure the finish. Powder coating is one of the strongest and most durable metal finishes. However, it should not be used in a salt-air environment.

Repeated aubergine powder-coated arbors are easy to maintain and add a dash of color to each side of a reflecting pool.

On this whimsical glass and stainless steel fence, the artist buffed the circles to reduce the shininess of the otherwise sparkling stainless steel.

Physical vapor deposition (PVD) is a method that applies ultra-thin coating layers. Atoms of a finish are removed from a source and deposited onto a metal substrate. Afterward the source is converted to a vapor through heat and ion bombardment.

Mechanical

Three mechanical methods are used to finish metal: blast finishing, mass finishing, and polishing. Blast finishing removes surface imperfections to create a smooth matte finish. Mass finishing covers a large quantity of small parts, such as components used for assembling furnishings. It involves agitation within a solution containing water plus finishing and abrasive compounds. Polishing entails minimal rotational abrasion and buffing to remove surface defects.

Standards

Gauge (thickness) is different from metal to metal, and the lower the gauge the thicker the metal. For example, gauge 8 translates to 0.165 inch for stainless steel, 0.1285 inch for aluminum, and 0.125 inch for copper. To give you an idea of the difference between gauges, 16-gauge copper is 0.050 inch thick, while 24-gauge copper is 0.020 inch thick. Some materials are not available in all thicknesses. It is also useful to remember that the lower the gauge, the higher the cost and weight of the metal.

Metallurgical testing labs test metals for their chemical makeup and physical characteristics, including strength, porosity, thickness, and corrosive tendencies. They may also test alloys to determine whether the percentage of metals is accurate for the alloy. Indeed, they will also test materials to be recycled to assure that metals are properly directed for that purpose. Testing also implies that a threshold must be met; if the threshold is not met, the tested item fails. Laboratories become accredited by organizations such as ASTM for their testing proficiency.

Care and Maintenance

Generally speaking, most materials need to be kept clean for the best wearability, but metal maintenance varies according to the metal. There is conflicting information about the best way to clean metals that develop a patina, like copper, brass, and bronze. Some experts recommend applying a clear lacquer finish to prevent any oxidation (patina), which over time can eat through the metal, while others recommend allowing a patina to develop. It's always prudent to follow the manufacturer's maintenance instructions, especially if there is already a clear, protective finish. Rusting steel can pretty much be left alone, but stainless steel needs to be kept clean with mild soapy water and then dried. This prevents the surface from pitting due to environmental dust and dirt, which could ultimately expose the steel to rusting. Since this is particularly an issue in salt-air environments, make sure to use the appropriate type of stainless steel in seaside gardens. Aluminum, galvanized steel, powder-coated steel, and metals with clear finishes also need little if any care, perhaps just occasional hosing after a mild soapy sponge bath.

Sustainability

Metals are mined materials and therefore inherently involve scarring the surface of the earth. The mining industry can't bring sites back to their original pristine conditions, but what do they do to mitigate problems and restore habitat once mining operations have ceased? How sensitive are mining companies to the environment during all phases of operations?

Metals are not a renewable resource. Although they are a natural material, an extensive amount of energy is required to

At least two different gauges of metal rod were used to make these chairs: a thick gauge for the frame, a thin gauge for the woven portion. Structurally the chair requires a minimum gauge to support the average person.

transform them into useable goods. Smelting and other refinery processes should be monitored to assure no release of toxins and minimal use of energy and water. Some smelting processes can be toxic as the company extracts the metal from the mined dirt or ore.

Some mining companies continue to dump billions of tons of toxic heavy metals into rivers and oceans, particularly in the world's poorest countries. Certain metals can bioaccumulate in plants and animals, causing an increase in toxicity (as happens with tuna). Copper and brass involve the use of environmentally toxic sulfur dioxide and sulfuric acid during mining.

Consider the ethics, safety, and labor issues involved with mining. For more on mining operations and the environment, consult MiningWatch Canada, Sierra Club, or Worldwatch Institute.

Metal checklist

Is this metal suited to this use?

Evaluate any joinery. Will it hold up to this use?

If the piece is structural, will it remain structurally sound?

How is the metal finished? Will it hold up to the weather?

Is the product's finish appropriate for the type of metal to which it has been applied?

Will oxidation add or detract from the metal's value?

What standards or tests has this metal met?

What maintenance will be required to keep this metal product in like-new condition?

Are there warranties from the manufacturer or retailer, and if so, what do they cover and for what period of time?

Textiles

Textile technology began thousands of years ago when people first twisted flax fibers together to make linen string. Times have changed! Contemporary technology and a thirst for outdoor living have driven the textile industry to develop exponentially the range of outdoor textiles. A glorious array of fabrics are now widely available, none taking back seat to those used for interiors. Because there is such an assortment, it is more important than ever to know your textiles in order to match fabric to purpose.

Facing:
Pillows in a stylized botanical print bring extra visual texture to a cozy arbor with a seat to view the garden.

Using Textiles Outdoors

The use of outdoor fabric expands as textile technology evolves. Outdoor fabric was once used primarily for exterior umbrellas and cushions, but contemporary textiles, assembly methods, and cushion technology now allow nearly anything available for indoor fabric to be used outdoors.

Upholstery has come a long way from loose cushions: designers can now find fully upholstered furniture made for the great outdoors. Likewise, sun shades are more than just umbrellas and may include fabric stretched between anchored poles, or folding lengths of fabric on a cable system that can be adjusted or removed as needed. Hammocks may be traditional knotted-rope items or solid pieces of fabric.

Made for the outdoors, this fully upholstered seating area is as comfortable as anything indoors, but much easier to care for.

As softer outdoor fabrics come onto the market, draperies are increasingly popular for privacy screening. Even sheer fabrics are available for use in the garden. By stretching fabric across a frame, you can create a screen, provided specific attention is paid to how the fabric is attached to the frame. Tacking fabric to a wood frame will probably eventually tear the fabric due to wind stress at the point of attachment. Creating a pocket hem into which a frame is inserted will likely wear much better.

Garden standouts, Cuscino cushion chairs are covered in outdoor fabric and easily portable.

Fabric draped over a frame is used to shade an outdoor seating platform.

Quite a few manufacturers make outdoor area rugs, which have come a long way too: some are fully durable even in cool, rainy weather. They store easily as well. I usually roll mine and store them vertically indoors over the winter once they have been cleaned. This keeps them free of moisture and prevents creases. Of course, always check the manufacturer's recommendations for where an area rug should be used and stored. Some rugs are limited to outdoor areas beneath a roof.

An outdoor rug adds a little panache and creates a sense of unity between several pieces of furniture while also establishing an area's boundary.

The Basics

Textiles are complicated. They are both art and science, and the technology continues to change. Before you get *fiber* tangled with *yarn*, you need some information to unravel what can feel like a stubborn knot.

Though once applied only to woven fabrics, the term *textile* now covers fibers, yarns, and fabrics as well as products incorporating those materials. All fabrics are textiles, but not all textiles are fabrics. *Textile* can apply to an outdoor area rug, synthetic lawn, or even a pair of vinyl or rubber boots.

Fabric refers to any combination of fibers, yarns, or solutions constructed to form a flat, flexible material. A *fiber* is a slender and lengthy, natural or synthetic thread, threadlike structure, or filament that can usually be spun into a yarn. *Yarn* means two or more fibers twisted together and suitable for use in creating fabric.

A *staple fiber* is a comparatively short fiber, measured in inches or centimeters. It includes natural fibers such as cotton, wool, and flax but excludes silk or long synthetic filament fibers. *Filament* refers to a long fiber, measured in yards or meters. This includes silk and all synthetic fibers.

Greige means unfinished, as in greige goods (or gray goods). And *finish* is defined as any process that enhances the aesthetics or performance of greige goods.

Textiles are developed from natural or synthetic resources. Natural fibers include plant-based (cellulosic) or animal (protein) fibers. Before the dangers of asbestos were known, asbestos was used to create mineral-based fibers. Synthetic fibers were invented just after the turn of the twentieth century, beginning with cellulosic-based fibers. Petroleum-based fibers followed and now make up more than half of the textile market. Though metallic-based fibers are also available, they are seldom used to make fabric.

Standard fabric from furniture manufacturer Emu, made of synthetic filament yarn, wraps cushions and pillows on this sofa, making it a weather-resistant place to sit outdoors.

Performance Characteristics

Each type of fiber performs according to its own composition. In order to understand the differences between fibers, it is helpful to understand their attributes. The basic properties of fabric are used to compare, evaluate, and test fibers.

Intrinsic Characteristics

Textiles used for upholstery (or for any situation where the fabric may be rubbed) need to be abrasion resistant. Considerable friction occurs between an upholstery fabric and a person sitting on that fabric. If a fabric doesn't perform well in those conditions, fiber breaks and the material wears quickly. Nylon, olefin, and polyester are notably abrasion-resistant fibers.

Some fabrics, like cotton, get stronger when wet, while fabrics like wool and rayon weaken. So absorbency can be important in an environment that includes substantial rain or frequent morning dew. Some fibers are both moisture resistant and adsorbent, which can be an advantage outdoors. Wicking is another characteristic of some fibers; linen, for example, can transfer moisture away from a substrate through itself, which is why it is often used for summer clothing. Density is intertwined with

Hard surfaces are softened by a confluence of outdoor fabrics on modern butterfly chairs, nearby upholstered seating, and an overhead shade structure. The textiles used for seating must be abrasion resistant.

specific gravity, and both relate to fabric weight. A few fabrics, like olefin, are so lightweight that they float on water. Having such a low density makes it possible to create a textile with fewer raw materials. It also makes the material less expensive. Unless weight is required, it is advantageous in most cases to have a more lightweight fabric. Among other benefits, lightweights are less expensive to ship, may offer more warmth with less weight, and are easier to hang as draperies. Many synthetic fibers fill this niche.

If a fiber stretches and cannot return to its original shape, it is not dimensionally stable or has poor elasticity or elastic recovery. Textiles made from fibers like this will sag and lose their shape permanently, unlike elastomeric fibers, which bounce back. Shrinkage is also an issue related to dimensional stability, and heat may be related to altering the length or width of a fiber as well. Linen, olefin, and polyester are very dimensionally stable fibers, while wool is not.

Fibers that can carry an electrical charge are considered electrical conductors. Without this, a textile builds up electricity, which is then experienced as a shock. Perhaps you have noticed static electricity when removing a synthetic item from the dryer. Linen and cotton are good conductors of electricity and will not shock you.

Softer fabrics with good resiliency drape and wrap better than stiffer fabrics, and are less likely to set a crease when folded. Good drapability is particularly

This range of coordinating fabrics would add a giant dash of fun to a garden. One is a combination of polyester and acrylic, while the rest are 100% acrylic or 100% solution-dyed acrylic, which means that they won't all be equally successful in certain conditions.

important in curtains, which are increasingly seen in gardens as manufacturers improve fabrics for outdoor use. Contemporary sheer outdoor drapery fabrics make outdoor privacy elegant.

When people first see a fabric, they instinctively want to reach out and touch it. It may feel soft and cozy or scratchy and irritating. This feeling is referred to as the hand of the fabric. Obviously it is important that a textile be comfortable to touch. Fibers such as cotton, silk, rayon, bamboo, and many synthetic fibers usually offer a comfortable hand.

Loft in a fiber is measured by compressing a fiber and evaluating its ability to spring back to its original thickness. A fiber with a strong crimp would have good loft or bounce.

You've probably had a sweater that drove you crazy because of all the little fuzzy balls that formed on its surface. This is pilling. Staple fibers are prone to it, and that includes filament fibers cut to the size of staple fibers. However, synthetic filament fibers are stronger and have greater tenacity to cling to the surface than natural fibers do. Fabric shavers work well to remove pilling.

A fabric hammock needs fibers with high tensile strength.

Synthetic fabrics are thermoplastic and can be affected (melting, stiffening, or hardening) when exposed to even a few turns in a too-hot dryer. They should not be affected by ambient outdoor temperatures, however. Natural fibers are more heat resistant, although protein fibers can be scorched if they get too hot.

Resilience is the ability of a fiber to return to its original size after being stretched, twisted, or otherwise contorted. Nylon and wool have excellent resiliency and do not wrinkle easily. Wadding a bit of fabric in your hand at the store, releasing it, and then watching it for a minute will give you an idea of its resilience.

Shrinkage refers to the degree a fabric retains its original size and shape when cleaned (or repeatedly wetted and dried outdoors). Fabric shrinkage usually relates to moisture and heat, which is why cleaning will often trigger it. Fibers with good dimensional stability are less inclined to shrink.

Tensile strength is an indicator of durability and tendency to sag or pill. It is measured by testing how quickly a fiber breaks when stretched to its limits. The strength of a fiber under tension is an important attribute of a strong fabric. Pilling is the result of tenacious fibers that are too strong to break, more problematic with man-made staple-length fibers.

Wrinkle recovery is the ability of a fabric to recover from folding, bending, or twisting. Fibers with good resilience recover well from wrinkling.

Other Influences

Chemical resistance is an important characteristic, though the name can be misleading. The term *chemical* covers just about any artificially prepared compound, including things like vinegar, ketchup, coffee, and bleach—the likely culprits when it comes to splattering a lovely outdoor textile, as opposed to anything experimented with in a lab. Chemical resistance is obviously a big advantage near outdoor dining areas but is also beneficial when removing something like mildew from a bleach-resistant fiber. Many synthetic fibers are chemical resistant. Vegetative fibers like linen and cotton are somewhat resistant to alkalis, while protein fibers such as wool and silk have some resistance to acids.

Outdoor textiles are exposed to the sun and occasionally need cleaning. If a textile is white, colorfastness isn't a problem. If it is red, however, it may be more susceptible to fading. If you want the color to remain the same as when you bought it, choose a colorfast fiber. Any type of solution-dyed fiber (in which the dye was added to the fiber before the fiber was extruded) is very colorfast, while piece-dyed goods (in which a piece of fabric was dyed in a vat) might be problematic in the sun. You can't always tell the difference by physical examination, but if you can't find a tag or other information, you can try a little test. If you can access a seam, clip a small sliver of fabric from it and dab on a small dot of bleach. If the textile is colorfast, the bleach should have no effect.

Dye jobs are a critical consideration. Imagine lounging in your garden on your marvelous, vividly colored outdoor cushions. Everything is oh-so-perfect until you walk away with orange streaks on the back of your white pants. Definitely not marvelous! This is a symptom of a dye job gone wrong and a condition known as crocking. Depending on the dye method and fiber, the dye could transfer in either wet or dry conditions with just a little chafing. Use a spare piece of white fabric and a sample of the fabric to test for crocking. Solution-dyed fibers and yarn-dyed fibers (meaning the dye was applied to the yarn before the cloth was woven or knitted) have the most

One hundred percent solution-dyed acrylic fibers in coordinating colors and patterns.

Materials

resistance to crocking. When dyed according to a dye manufacturer's specifications, any fabric should also be crock resistant.

Because fire can spread quickly when aided by fabric, flammability is an important issue, even outdoors. Some fibers ignite quickly, while others resist flame. Still others melt, drip, or release potentially toxic gases. Flammability is a special concern for draperies and cushions to be placed near outdoor fireplaces, fire pits, or torch lights. Don't forget those very hot halogen lamps in outdoor light fixtures! While it is always important to keep fabric away from fire, use something flame resistant if there is any chance of a nearby spark. Modacrylic and acrylic are both inherently flame resistant, and the latter is appropriate for outdoor use.

Another important criteria for outdoor fabric is resistance to light, particularly UV light from the sun and other light sources, since nonresistant fabrics will rot or fade over time. Light-resistant fibers include acrylic, glass, and polyester. (Note that fibers that do not change color with UV exposure are lightfast, while fibers that do not change color for any reason are colorfast.)

Organism resistance refers to a fiber's ability to resist mold, mildew, insects, and other organisms. Synthetic fibers have the best resistance to fungi and pests, which have the intelligence to eat natural substances instead of petrochemicals.

The poorer your air quality, the more susceptible some fibers (especially natural fibers) will be to damage from pollution. Such pollution primarily contains organic and inorganic particulates, so keeping the fabric clean and dry will mitigate the issue. However, if ignored, the damage could be similar to sun rot or fading.

A double-decker umbrella has twice as much reason to be made with lightfast fabric.

Natural Fibers: Animal, Vegetable, Not Mineral

Natural fabrics biodegrade. This is good from one perspective, since you won't find them in a landfill, but it also means they could eventually join the compost pile if left outdoors for extended periods. Still, the many excellent qualities of these fibers are the industry's model for the conception of synthetic fibers. Hemp, for example, is strong, resilient, dimensionally stable, and highly resistant to light and abrasion.

Natural fibers

Fiber	Light resistance	Resiliency	Fire resistance	Abrasion resistance	Strength	Dimensional stability
Cotton	Low	Low	Low	Moderate	Moderate	Moderate
Wool	Low	High	Moderate	Moderate	High	Low
Linen	High	Low	Low	High	High	Moderate
Silk	Low	Moderate	Moderate	Moderate	Moderate	High
Coir	Moderate	Low	Low	High	High	Moderate
Hemp	High	Moderate	Low	High	High	High

Wool includes fibers from sheep, goats, alpacas, and other wool-producing animals. Note that bamboo and rayon fabrics are not included, as both are manufactured, regenerated, cellulosic fabrics. Cotton becomes rayon, and bamboo is still called bamboo.

Manufactured, regenerated fibers include rayon, acetate, lyocell, and bamboo. All are cellulosic-based. Because these fibers do not have durable properties for use outdoors, all are best used indoors or as apparel.

Synthetic Fibers

Synthetic fibers are manufactured when liquid polymers ooze through a shower-head-like structure called a spinneret. They are petroleum-based products and will not biodegrade. Herein lies the dilemma: we want to be comfortable outdoors with textiles that hold up to the elements, but we also want to be environmentally responsible.

Some common characteristics of synthetic fibers are heat sensitivity, resistance to (most) chemicals, good to high strength, oleophilic (oil-attracting) properties, low moisture absorbency, electrostatic properties, and resistance to moths, rot, and fungi. Their properties, either inherent or modified, determine how they are used.

The first synthetic fiber was nylon. In chemical terms, nylon is a polyamide, which is chemically related to the natural protein fibers, silk and wool. At first nylon was produced as a long, smooth, round monofilament fiber. But as scientists discovered they could more closely mimic natural fibers through various methods, properties such as texture, luster, and drapability improved. Nylon is an extremely durable fiber that is categorized as either high- or regular-tenacity, with the latter used in the furnishings industry. Nylon has good abrasion resistance, resilience, shrink resistance (due to heat setting), and pilling and stain resistance, making it perfect for carpets and synthetic lawn. However, nylon can degrade with sunlight, so when used outdoors it requires UV-resistant modifications. Because nylon has low absorbency, it is not comfortable to sit on, but in its UV-modified form it makes great material for an umbrella. Because it is lightweight, nylon is economical to ship. A variety of nylons are available, with differences in cross-sectional shape, dyeability, texture (or heat-set crimp), and factors such as antimicrobial, sunlight-resistant, or antistatic properties.

This synthetic lawn is 100% recycled material. The pile fiber is monofilament polyethylene. The thatch layer is 4000-denier nylon of mixed colors to resemble real thatch. A secondary backing enhances stability and strength and maximizes drainage.

Polyester

Polyester was introduced into the United States in 1950 by DuPont with the trade name Dacron. Polyester has good wet and dry resilience, dimensional stability, sunlight resistance, abrasion resistance, and overall better aesthetics than nylon, and it is very strong. Because of its low absorbency and ability to blend with other fibers, polyester works well blended with fibers such as cotton, which has good absorbency but doesn't share polyester's resilience. Polyester is lightweight and dries quickly. It is also prone to static buildup within the heat-sensitive fibers, but alterations in its cross-section help trap more moisture to alleviate this problem. Because polyester has such high resiliency, it offers great wrinkle resistance when blended with other fibers, meaning no ironing. Fiberfill used for outdoor cushions and padding is often polyester (for example, Polyfill). Industrial-strength polyester is also found outdoors in garden hoses, sails, and landscape fabric.

Olefin

Production of olefin began in Italy in 1957 and came to the United States in 1960. Resistant to abrasion, inexpensive, strong, chemically inert, thermoplastic, and static resistant, olefin fibers are made from both polypropylene and polyethylene. Olefins can be found as film yarns in addition to monofilament, multifilament, and staple fibers. When olefin fibers are crimped and modified, the process eliminates olefin's intrinsically waxy hand. Contemporary olefins do not look like their earlier cousins, whose appearance matched their artificiality. Solution-dyed olefins are also normally inexpensive, which makes them very appealing considering their other good qualities: strength, durability, resiliency, light weight, abrasion resistance, and chemical resistance. However, oily stains are difficult to remove, and since olefin is heat sensitive it should always be air-dried. Olefin fabrics are often used as geotextiles to prevent erosion and protect crops from pests and weeds. In fact, olefin has many uses indoors and out.

Acrylic

Acrylonitrile, the substance from which acrylic fibers are produced, was first synthesized in Germany in 1893. It was later named acrylic and combined with other chemicals such as homopolymer and copolymer. Acrylic fibers come in many cross-sectional shapes that generate a variety of properties, such as resiliency, softness, and improved dyeability. Acrylic fabrics are also lightweight, warm, and nonallergenic, and selected fibers show good chemical resistance. Acrylics are not as durable as olefin, polyester, or nylon but are comparable to cotton or wool. Upholstery fabrics made from acrylic yarns are reasonably abrasion resistant and more comfortable for sitting because the yarns have an irregular surface that alters the fabric's moisture absorption characteristics. Acrylic is often used outdoors for wool-like upholstery (either flat-woven or velvety pile), weather-resistant draperies, and sun-resistant awnings.

Modacrylic

Modacrylics (modified acrylics), introduced into the United States in 1949, have a larger proportion of other polymers than acrylics. Widely used in protective clothing and contract furnishings, they were the first flame-retardant, self-extinguishing fibers, a characteristic that also distinguishes them from acrylic, a similar material. Modacrylics are less durable than acrylics, but not appreciably, and are about as strong as wool.

Pick a color, any color. Have a good designer's workroom make a custom umbrella for an existing frame from this array of 100% solution-dyed acrylic fabrics.

Properties of top five synthetic fibers

Fiber	Light resistance	Resiliency	Fire resistance	Abrasion resistance	Strength	Dimensional stability
Nylon	Low (without modifications)	High	Melts	High	High	High
Polyester	High	High (wet or dry)	Melts	High	High	High
Olefin	Low (without modifications)	High	Melts	High	High	High
Acrylic	High	Moderate	Melts	Moderate	Moderate	Moderate
Modacrylic	High	Moderate	Retardant	Moderate	Low	Moderate

The elastic recovery of modacrylic is better than acrylic, and modacrylic is moderately resilient and dimensionally stable. Modacrylics are used minimally outdoors in comparison to other synthetic fibers but may be found as tent structures.

Other Fibers

A few other fibers that are suited to particular uses are worth mentioning. Neoprene is a synthetic rubber, and although wetsuits are probably its biggest claim to fame, it has also been used on furniture. Neoprene is resistant to chemicals but can be damaged by sunlight, perspiration, oil, and aging. Fibers with elastic characteristics such as spandex and elastoester may be used for tight-fitting textiles on furnishings but are otherwise used primarily as apparel.

Glass fibers are incombustible, which makes them desirable for the draperies of large buildings if they do not require opening and closing very often and are kept away from drafts that could abrade or bend the fibers. These hairlike fibers are heavy, brittle, and nonabsorbent but resistant to sunlight and soiling.

Although ancient cultures used gold and silver as yarns, metallic fibers became easier to use when coated with a transparent film, like Lurex, to reduce tarnishing. In the 1960s stainless steel fibers were developed primarily for the aerospace industry. More recently, aluminum yarns have become popular as decoration. Metallic yarns can reduce the electrostatic properties of synthetic yarns, but they are heavy and brittle, and once creased, they never recover.

Better known as vinyl, vinyon is a copolymer composed of at least 86% vinyl chloride and 14% vinyl acetate. Flame-retardant and very heat sensitive, it is also unaffected by moisture or pests and is a poor conductor of electricity. It can be used for umbrellas, upholstery protectors, and numerous other applications.

Saran is a copolymer that also includes vinyl chloride. It weathers well and is dimensionally stable, durable, and chemically resistant. Often used as a film, saran may be found in outdoor furnishings, although if light-colored objects are exposed to sunlight, they will darken.

Teflon is the most common fluoropolymer. Gore-Tex is a trade name for fabrics with a thin coating of Teflon. Because of its wind and rain resistance, Gore-Tex is used in outdoor wear, but it is not typically used in outdoor furnishings.

Leather

If you think leather belongs outdoors only as a jacket, think again. Outdoor leather makes a luxurious, durable material for garden furnishings.

Leather in the United States tends to be a byproduct of farm animals raised for other uses. Because leather is a natural hide, sizes and textures range considerably. Leather also has a high degree of variability due to the type of animal and things like scars and wrinkles. *Grain* describes the markings on the hide. Leather from an animal's legs or belly is thinner and coarser, so the best-quality leather comes from the back and sides.

Outdoor leather makes the upholstery of a patio sofa not only more luxurious but also waterproof.

Before a hide can be used it must be tanned to make it pliable and resistant to rot and water. The type of tanning process depends on the use of the leather. One process uses microscopic fluorochemical molecules that penetrate the hide, practically eliminating wrinkling and shrinking. This leaves the hide waterproof, washable or dry-cleanable, and soft, resulting in a leather or suede that is excellent for use outdoors.

Leather can undergo an array of finishing methods, which may improve irregularities and bleaching to whiten the hide before it is dyed. Hides can also be split into thinner layers to improve pliability. *Top grain* refers to the top layer of a split hide. It is the most expensive but wears the best. A hide that has not been split is referred to as *full grain*.

A rainbow of outdoor leathers.

Fabrication

Not every fiber type will have all the properties you want for a specific use. To resolve this issue, manufacturers can either add a finish or blend one fiber with another to enhance the properties of one or both fibers. Blending involves turning fibers into yarns and weaving, knitting, or in some way interlocking the yarns to create a textile.

Fibers to Yarns

Yarns begin as separate fibers. How these fibers are processed and turned into yarns determines their innumerable characteristics and combinations. Fibers can be fat or skinny depending upon the thickness or denier of a yarn, which is measured by the number of filaments. Yarns can be monofilaments or single fibers, such as fishing line. Short, staple fibers are twisted to make long yarns. Filament fibers are twisted to create filament yarns. Fibers are not necessarily identical when twisted together to become a yarn, which is usually done to improve the overall properties of the yarn. The characteristics of the yarn's twist also play a large part in the final textile's appearance and performance. Even monofilament yarns are twisted to alter their appearance. Extremely fine multifilament yarns are twisted slightly to make them easier to handle.

The amount of twist, the direction of the twist, and the characteristics of each fiber result in labels like bouclé (uneven yarn), slub (yarn with thick and thin sections), and chenille (velvety tufted yarn).

Weaving

Weaving presumes the use of a loom, and different types of looms produce a variety of weaves. For outdoor use, it's pretty simple. Warp yarns are installed on the loom and run the length of the fabric. They are usually the strongest yarns. Weft or filling yarns run crosswise or perpendicular to the warp yarns (over and under every other warp yarn to create a simple woven pattern). The selvage is the self-finished edge of a fabric. Two selvages, one on either side, run the length of a fabric. Selvages vary depending on the loom type, and some even contain woven or printed information. As yarns are woven, they are knotted to create a continuous length to finish the weaving of a fabric. Knots are typically placed on the back side of a fabric. Different weaves or patterns change the number of yarns per inch and the ratio of warp yarns to weft yarns. Computer-driven looms have greater detail capability. Plain, dobby, twill, basket, satin, and Jacquard are all examples of woven patterns.

Bias and *grain* are key terms related to woven fabrics. The bias is the diagonal of a piece of fabric. It can stretch. Pillow or cushion fabricators cut fabric on the bias for decorative edging, because it makes it easier to ease the edging around the pillows. Otherwise you want your fabric "on the grain." Grain refers to the direction of threads in a woven fabric. Lengthwise grain is the warp direction and runs the length of the

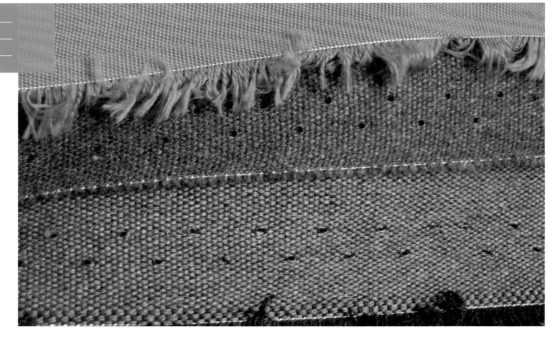

fabric. Crosswise grain is the weft direction and runs the width of the fabric, selvage to selvage. Draperies, upholstery, and sun shades must be cut on grain (which typically means lengthwise, as this has the most dimensional stability) to prevent the fabric from stretching.

Fabric width varies depending on the width of the loom on which the fabric was created. Standard contract-grade fabric is usually 54 inches but is sometimes 60 inches wide. While American fabric made for home sewing generally ranges from 36 inches to 45 inches wide, specialty fabrics from other countries may be narrower. Fabrics like muslin, nonwoven interfacing, and certain types of outdoor fabrics are used for a variety of mockups or backing and may come extra wide (96 inches, for example).

Looping: Knitting or Crochet

Knit and crocheted constructions are designed to stretch, and stretchiness is occasionally appropriate for outdoor use. Avoid these fabrics if you are looking for something to cover outdoor cushions, but consider them for sunshades.

Films

Films are created through a fairly complicated process that involves each of the following to some degree: a hot revolving drum, polymer solution, a warm area, narrow slits, and extrusion. (And you thought films were for Saturday night entertainment.)

Solutions are very similar to those used to create fibers for yarns and weaving. Films by themselves are not necessarily very strong and usually require a backing to improve their strength. They are sheets rather than yarns. Films have several classifications and a few similar properties, like being impermeable to air and water, inexpensive, and soil resistant although somewhat resilient. Impermeability is improved by punching selected films with thousands of tiny pinholes, which lets through air and fog but not rain. Films are made of vinyl or urethane. In cold weather you want the urethane film because it stays soft and pliable (like a blanket), while the vinyl film becomes brittle (think icicle). Practically speaking, films can be used for umbrellas, tablecloths, upholstery, shower curtains, wetsuits, rain apparel and, yes, perhaps an overhead sun shade?

Knotting

Because knotting can be done with any fiber, it is possible that a lacy fabric could find its way into the garden. These fabrics can be hand- or machine-knotted into beautifully multifaceted patterns. Did I mention macramé? This originally mid-twentieth-century trend is now used in some quite sophisticated furniture. Consider how it might be combined with metal wire and glass beads for an outdoor lantern or even a screen.

The Unbeweaveable wingback chair and ottoman are made by weaving a hand-knotted polypropylene rope to a bent stainless steel frame. An added benefit: great drainage.

Dyeing Processes

Dyeing is the art of adding color to fibers, yarns, and fabrics. It involves different types of dyes and a variety of methods. A high degree of variation means that some fabrics will be colorfast while others easily fade.

Solution Dyeing

When a synthetic fiber is in its liquid state, before it is extruded into a fiber, dye can be added to color it. This is solution dyeing. Fabrics that are made of 100% solution-dyed yarns are very colorfast and the best for outdoor use.

Fiber, Yarn, and Skein Dyeing

Fiber dyeing is a common way of coloring natural fibers, although a few synthetic fibers are colored this way, too. One advantage of dyeing fibers before they become yarns is that different colors can then be twisted into a multicolored yarn.

After fibers in the greige are twisted together to make a yarn, they can be dyed into a single colored yarn. However, if the fibers are different, they may take dyes

Red is an intense color and is often subject to fading. This seating is placed in a shaded grove, which will help reduce loss of color, particularly if the fabric was fiber-dyed.

differently, so a single dye bath can yield a monochromatic yarn with a variety of color intensity. Fabrics woven with yarn colored this way are known as heather fabrics. Yarns wound together (similar to how yarn is sold in stores) are called a skein. It is a common practice to dye yarns grouped as skeins.

Space Dyeing

In space dyeing, intermittent segments of a yarn are dyed with a color. This is often done with several colors so that the end result is a rainbow-colored yarn. Space-dyed yarns woven or knitted together can create very interesting patterns.

Ikat is a unique type of yarn dyeing that could be described as a type of space dyeing. Warp or weft yarns are bunched, tied, and dyed prior to weaving distinctly identifiable ikat patterns. Typically this technique is used on cottons and silks and is not colorfast.

Piece, Vat, and Union Dyeing

What piece, vat, and union dyeing have in common is that the dyeing process occurs within a vat using greige goods or fabrics that have been woven with undyed yarns. Textiles are dyed with a single dye, creating a solid color. Vat dyeing is just what it sounds like, whether the items being dyed are pieces, yarns, or fibers, whereas piece dyeing specifically involves large pieces of fabric. Union dyeing is a technique that allows chemically different yarns (for example, a protein-based yarn like wool and a plant-based one like cotton) to be dyed in the same vat for a uniform dye. This works when the chemical structure of one of the yarns is altered to dye similarly to the other yarn.

Printing

It is usually easy to tell a printed fabric from a woven-pattern fabric because the back side will be considerably lighter than the front. Printing involves applying colorfast pigments, rather than dye, to create a decorative pattern. There are three primary printing methods: direct, discharge, and resist. Few printed fabrics are suitable for limited outdoor use.

Direct printing is the most commonly used method. A paste may be made using gum or alginates (derived from seaweed) as a thickener. Most pastes do not require a thickening agent, as the primary materials are thick enough to use when combined. It is important for the agents other than the pigment to wash out following the printing process. Those agents must not absorb the pigment themselves but improve penetration of the pigment into the fabric. When a pattern is applied to an already dyed fabric, it is known as overprinting.

Discharge printing is used less often and requires that an entire piece be colored with a dye that is sensitive to removal by a chemical. The piece is printed with a chemical that removes the dye in the printed area. A subsequent printing may apply another color over the area where the color was removed.

Resist printing uses a resist paste (which resists dyeing). After a piece is imprinted with the paste, the piece is dyed and the paste removed, leaving a pattern in the darker background.

The pattern on this drapery fabric is clearly woven, not printed. When the reverse side is exactly opposite the front side, a weaving method created the effect.

Materials

Printing Techniques

Some prints are created by hand. Block printing, for example, involves carving a pattern into a block of wood or linoleum, placing dye on the block's surface, and then placing the block onto the fabric. Since every color requires a separate block, block printing is tedious, costly, and primarily used in crafts. Batik printing involves wax applied to fabric in the areas that the designer does not want to dye. When the wax is removed the pattern becomes visible. Tie-dye is a creative version of piece dyeing by hand. Fabric is knotted, tied, and dyed to create a starburst effect of colors on the fabric.

Many mechanical techniques are used as well. Digital printing entails an inkjet print head placing microscopic droplets of dye onto the fabric. Blotch printing directly prints the background color and design onto a white fabric, usually in one operation. Electrostatic printing spreads a dye-resin mixture onto a screen with the design and passes the fabric into an electrostatic field beneath the screen; the electrostatic field pulls the dye-resin mixture through the patterned area and onto the fabric. Warp printing uses warp yarns with a printed design before the fabric is woven. These yarns produce a hazed effect, and resulting fabrics appear wavy or shadowy. Airbrush painting uses a mechanized airbrush to spray dye to create a patterned fabric. Screen printing uses either cylindrical or flat screens made of polyester, vinyon, metal, silk, or nylon threads. The dyed paste is poured on the printing screen, then forced through the open areas onto the fabric. Stencil printing is a resist method in which metal or wood covers part of the design to prevent that part from taking the dye. Roller printing is mechanized block printing: an engraved pattern on a copper roller imprints the pattern on the fabric as it rolls through a machine. Duplex printing is similar to roller printing except that the pattern is applied to both sides of the fabric. Heat-transfer printing is a dry or wet process in which the fabric is pressed against a dye-patterned paper using a heated cylinder or water vapor. Photo printing involves applying a light-sensitive chemical to a fabric and then transferring a photograph onto it.

Textile Design

A myriad of recognizable patterns can be found in textile design. They may be realistic, stylized, inspired by another age or period, or perhaps derived from a particular geographic location. It's also not unusual to find outdoor fabrics with botanically inspired designs.

When selecting a textile pattern, consider the overall design of the garden. Would an African pattern be appropriate for a Zen garden? The scale of the pattern is also important, and a scale appropriate for a garden will typically differ from what might be used indoors. When blending patterns together, it's important to vary scale. Patterns that use the same scale tend to battle for attention when paired, rather than complementing each other.

An important criterion to remember when selecting fabric for a project is pattern repeat. Pattern repeat is the lengthwise distance from one distinctive point in a fabric pattern to the same point in the next repeat of the pattern. If the pattern is ¼-inch check, then the repeat horizontally and vertically will be ¼ inch, which is negligible in terms of requiring additional fabric to match the pattern at seams. If, however, the pattern is fairly large, you might have a 20-inch repeat vertically (lengthwise) and a 12-inch repeat horizontally (crosswise). This would require additional fabric to match patterns and thereby avoid an abrupt pattern interruption at a seam. You will usually see the pattern repeat noted on the fabric card attached to a fabric sample from a vendor.

A bold, botanically inspired pattern in several colorways.

Outdoor fabrics in coordinating, multiscaled patterns and colors.

Materials

Defects

Sometimes on the front or right surface of a fabric you will see a knot that tied two lengths of yarns together during the weaving process. This is a defect, since knots should occur on the back or wrong side of the fabric. That said, occasionally a designer prefers the back side of a fabric to the front. If so, the designer should ask a fabric representative whether it would be practical to use the back side of the fabric in their design and request that knots occur on the other side if this is approved by the fabric mill. If it is a simple woven fabric and the yarns are the same, this usually entails simply assuring that the knots occur on the reverse side. However, if it is a complex weave with yarns floating over several warp yarns on the back and different types of yarns, it may not be practical to use the back side. It is also important to note that using the back side of a fabric will not necessarily assure the same wearability as using the front side.

Uneven dyeing is another flaw (unless it is intentional or characteristic of the yarn type, but manufacturers usually offer disclaimers in those cases). Slubs in the yarn, streaks, holes, inconsistent width, stains, and uneven tension across the width of the fabric are also visible defects. Uneven tension will cause difficulty in sewing the fabric and result in poor drapability.

Latent defects cannot be seen until the fabric is used or cleaned. Shrinkage or stretching are examples in cases where the manufacturer claims that the fabric is dimensionally stable.

Finishing

Most fabrics on the market have had some sort of finish applied to them. Finishes are selected based on the fabric's intended use and are categorized by their impact on appearance or performance. When you order fabric, the mill sometimes sends it to a finishing company to apply a finish before sending it along to you . As a designer, you can often control the finishes needed. Much depends on the fabric manufacturer's expanse of operations. Sunbrella, for example, owns all or nearly all of its operations, from fiber creation to vendor delivery. In some cases fabric vendors pay for companies like Sunbrella, Outdura, or Bella-Dura to make their designs into fabrics that the fabric vendors can then sell. Conversely, these same companies sometimes create designs that they sell to a range of fabric vendors (also known as jobbers).

Appearance

Embossing, burn-out, napping, and caustic treatments are all used to alter the appearance of fabrics, including some made for outdoor use.

Embossing entails calendaring or pressing fabric between two heated rollers and then cooling the fabric.

Burn-out polyester has potential for drapery or screening, although it is less likely to be used outdoors. Yarns of the burn-out pattern are treated to make them susceptible to a chemical that will dissolve them, leaving a semitransparent pattern on the fabric.

Napping is a finish that literally leaves a nap or pile on the surface of fabric. Outdoor velvet is such a material. It has been woven to leave a pile, which is then cut in the finishing process. Nap has direction, a little like the fur of an animal, and this should be considered when applying it to furniture or using it as a drape. The smooth direction should be down in the drape and toward the front when upholstering a seat.

Caustic treatments may be used to improve soil-release qualities in some man-made fibers.

This fabric has alternating raised gros point stripes. The hand of gros point differs considerably from velvet. It feels coarser. Napped and very resilient, this fabric results from a warp-looped weaving method. It is nondirectional, so cannot be brushed into a different direction, with larger loops than a frieze.

How cool is outdoor velvet? Water just beads up on this luxurious napped fabric. Remember that napped fabrics have "direction" which may require additional yardage.

The nap of chenille results from weaving warp thread in groups, which allows for great pattern diversity.

Performance

Many finishes are used to enhance the performance of a textile, particularly if the textile does not have a necessary inherent characteristic. For instance, a Teflon finish may be applied to improve a fabric's ability to resist staining. Finishes for outdoor fabrics enhance abrasion resistance, water repellence, flame retardance, heat reflectance, UV resistance, soil repellence or releasing, wrinkle resistance, and antibacterial, antimildew, antirot, antislip, or antistatic properties. Many of these finishes are very effective, while some may have a limited life, depending on the extremes to which they may be exposed. Pay close attention to the details when researching fabrics. If you discover that a fabric may not perform as it is, can a finish be applied to it that will enhance its performance? This is something that needs to be investigated on a case-by-case basis.

Sewing

All fabric requires at least a little sewing, and many different effects can be created with a fabric simply by how it is sewn or pieced together with thread. Any good designer who works with fabric needs at least a basic working knowledge of sewing, even if only to have an intelligent conversation with the owner of a designer's workroom.

Terminology

Before you can discuss construction, it helps to know a few of the most important terms.

To *ease* a fabric is to pull a longer piece of it into a smaller area of fabric without any gathering or puckering. This often occurs around the corner of a cushion or pillow, because gathering or puckering in that area could be very unattractive.

To *hem* is to finish a raw edge of fabric by doubling back and stitching down, which prevents fraying and unraveling. Any edge not joined in a seam will require a hem. Hems should always occur on grain.

Railroading means running the length of a fabric side to side rather than front to back as is usually done. The fabric direction (run) can make a big difference in the amount of fabric used and will affect overall appearance and possibly performance since more wear will occur on the weft yarns.

Seam allowance refers to the area between the stitching and the raw, cut edge of the fabric. The usual seam allowance is ⅝ inch, but this might vary if something beyond a simple seam is created.

Working with Fabric

Joining two pieces of fabric implies a seam. Knowing when to select one kind of seam over the other is important, since the seam can make a difference in the overall effect of a piece and enhance a style or garden design. A simple seam involves putting the right sides of two fabric pieces together and sewing near the edges. When the fabric is turned to the right side, the sewn seam is on the wrong side and invisible (unless the fabric is transparent, in which case your fabricator might use a type of self-bound seam).

Beyond a simple seam, a variety of other seams apply to different situations. The type of seam used will depend on the fabric's construction, weight, required performance, and application. Think about how different the seams on a pair of jeans can look from those on a pair of khakis. Fabricators make jeans to perform under greater stress, so the seams are often self-enclosed and double-stitched to add strength and resistance to unraveling. This would also be true for an overhead sun shade that gets tugged by wind.

Gathering fabric allows it to drape beautifully or fit around things it might not otherwise fit. Shirring, pleating, and smocking are three methods of gathering fabric,

Seam types

Turned-and-stitched: The edges are turned under and stitched, similar to a hem.

Pinked: The raw edges are cut with pinking shears to reduce unraveling

Stitched-and-pinked: A combination of pinking and stitching are used close to the pinked edge.

Zigzagged: The raw edges are sewn with a zigzag stitch to reduce unraveling.

Bias-bound: The edges are wrapped with a narrow width of bias-cut fabric.

Flat-felled: A self-enclosed seam, formed on the right side of a fabric, in which one edge is trimmed, the other edge is folded over the trimmed edge, and both are sewn flat to the fabric. Durable and therefore often used for sportswear.

French: A self-enclosed classic seam for sheers in which the edge is stitched once on the right side and once on the wrong side, with a finished width of preferably ¼ inch.

Mock French: Similar to the French seam but typically used when a French seam is difficult to execute, as in a curve.

Self-bound: A self-enclosed seam in which one edge is trimmed while the other edge is folded and wrapped around the raw edge and sewn to the seam, not to the rest of the fabric. Best used for lightweight fabrics that don't unravel easily.

Overlock-stitch: A stitch pattern that combines straight and zigzag stitching, often created by an overlock machine.

Double-stitched: Having two lines of stitching, usually with one straight and the other either straight or zigzag.

Cording defines the edge of a pillow.

and all have a very different appearance. Simple shirring can create a ruffle (when only one edge is shirred) or a blousy effect (when both edges are shirred, gathering the fabric in between). Ruffles are a flourish usually better suited to Victorian and country house styles. Pleating comes in several styles, with box pleats being fairly common in creating tailored outdoor cushions. Smocking is generally done over a broad area and is tedious to execute but looks fairly simple. Depending on the fabric and the scale of the pattern (which can vary), smocking could be suitable for a number of different garden styles, but keep in mind that it does create space to catch water.

Cording can be used on outdoor cushions, pillows, upholstery, or even the edge of a tablecloth. A simple cord is wrapped in a matching or accent fabric and sewn firmly in place as part of the seam or as a hem. Fringe made of suitable outdoor yarn is also available for outdoor textiles and could be used on pillows or drapery or wherever your imagination takes you.

Appliqué can also be applied in garden furnishings as long as the thread is suitable for outdoor use (since more thread is used than in other techniques, selecting an appropriate thread is especially critical). Appliqué involves applying a cut piece of fabric in a pattern—for example, a circle—onto a second piece of fabric. The applied piece requires hemming around the edge to keep it from unraveling.

Many decorative stitches are available should you choose to go that direction, although for outdoor use they should be limited for the sake of durability. Some are hand stitches, as in blanket, overcast, or whip stitching. Hundreds of decorative stitches are available by machine, some of which may also perform the role of hemming. If you decide to use decorative stitches, make sure they cannot be snagged and that the thread used is weather resistant.

Standards

As a garden designer you need to know that the fabrics you work with will meet certain standards of performance. This requires learning a bit about the tests that assure those standards are met. The tests may not apply to outdoor fabrics in a residential setting, but they do provide helpful information about each fabric's characteristics.

Materials

Abrasion Resistance

The most common test for abrasion resistance is the Wyzenbeek test, which involves equipment rubbing the fabric back and forth. The results are read as "double rubs." Thirty thousand double rubs is entirely adequate for the average residential project, but if you are designing for a commercial project, the minimum for high usage is 100,000 double rubs.

The more rigorous Tabor test is less frequently used and involves rotating fabric with special equipment. This test requires a very tough fiber and construction to pass (nylon fabric usually passes). It is often used to test fabrics for auditorium seating.

The Martindale test (or "rub test") is used more frequently outside the United States and involves a combination of rubbing back and forth and in rotation. It is measured in thousands of rubs, with counts roughly equivalent to the Wyzenbeek test.

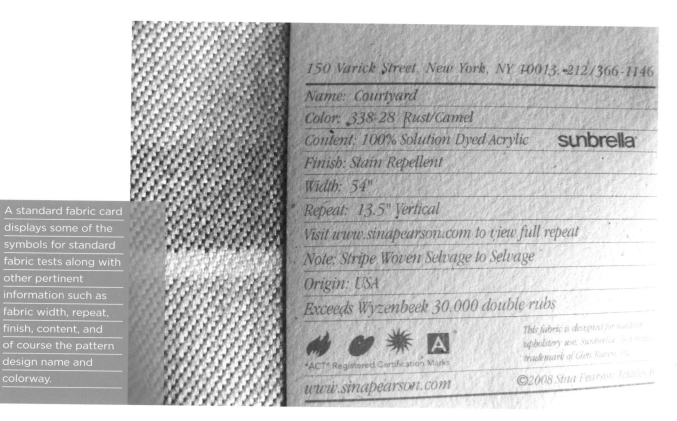

A standard fabric card displays some of the symbols for standard fabric tests along with other pertinent information such as fabric width, repeat, finish, content, and of course the pattern design name and colorway.

150 Varick Street, New York, NY 10013 · 212/366-1146

Name: Courtyard

Color: 338-28 Rust/Camel

Content: 100% Solution Dyed Acrylic

sunbrella

Finish: Stain Repellent

Width: 54"

Repeat: 13.5" Vertical

Visit www.sinapearson.com to view full repeat

Note: Stripe Woven Selvage to Selvage

Origin: USA

Exceeds Wyzenbeek 30,000 double rubs

This fabric is designed for indoor upholstery use. Sunbrella is a trademark of Glen Raven, Inc.

*ACT® Registered Certification Marks

www.sinapearson.com

©2008 Sina Pearson Textiles Inc.

Flame Resistance

An array of flammability tests for fabrics are used in every conceivable way. Testing for flammability may also include flame and smoke spread and fire resistance.

You will frequently see reference to the California Technical Bulletin 117, Section E, because it is a law with very strict requirements. The ACT (Association for Contract Textiles) exposes fabrics to a precise source of ignition to measure their performance. If the fabric is labeled Class I, it has passed the test. Quite a few other states beyond California accept this test.

NFPA 701-99 may eventually supersede the California Technical Bulletin 117. Two flame propagation test methods are used for fabrics that can be used as draperies, tablecloths, sunshades, awnings, banners, or even tents. The methods include testing fabric in its "as-new" state and again after being cleaned per the vendor's recommended cleaning method. Materials that meet the test requirements receive a "pass."

The ASTM E84, or tunnel test, uses 24-foot-long "adhered" and "nonadhered" samples, which are placed on the ceiling of the test tunnel and then exposed to a high-intensity flame at the first 4½ feet. The distance the flame spreads and the amount of time it burns are used to calculate a "flame spread index." This test is also used to determine a "smoke developed" value. Both values are compared to the characteristics of cement board and red oak materials to create the code classes: Class A (flame spread index of 25 or less, smoke developed value of 450 or less), Class B (flame spread index of 26 to 75, smoke developed value of 450 or less), and Class C (flame spread index of 76 to 200, smoke developed value of 450 or less). This test is only valid if the textile is used in a sprinklered occupancy, but you will find the test frequently listed on the cards attached to fabric samples.

Colorfastness to Light

The American Association of Textile Chemists and Colorists (AATCC) is the primary testing agency for colorfastness to light. Their test specifically analyzes a material's degree of resistance to the fading effects of light and is the ACT standard. For outdoor purposes, AATCC tests fabric upholstery, wrapped panels, and drapery. There are two testing grades, 1 or 3, which indicate

Acrylic fibers that are 100% solution-dyed should be relatively unaffected by sunlight.

either a carbon arc lamp or a xenon lamp source. The fabrics are exposed to either lamp under specified conditions. Colorfastness of a specimen is evaluated by comparing the color change of the exposed portion to a masked, unexposed portion using the AATCC Gray Scale for Color Change or as measured by a color instrument. The grades are 5 (no fading), 4 (slight fading), and 1 (high degree of fading).

Crocking

The test for crocking (performed by ACT) involves rubbing a fabric's surface under wet and dry conditions and measuring the transfer of dye from the fabric. Crocking is highly unusual in fabrics made for outdoor use, since most are solution-dyed. However, fabric that someone is wearing may crock onto an outdoor textile—something to consider when selecting white upholstery for garden furniture. And do consider crocking if you are not using solution-dyed fabrics. If a fabric has not been tested, you can evaluate it yourself by vigorously rubbing it onto a piece of white fabric both with and without water.

Physical Properties

ASTM tests a fabric's physical properties, including resistance to pilling, seam slippage, and tearing (or tensile strength).

The brush pill test involves rubbing the surface of a test fabric with nylon bristles for a specified length of time and then counting the number of pill balls. The fabric is rated from Class 1 (severe pilling) to Class 5 (no pilling). Class 3 is usually the minimum.

The grab test entails holding a fabric with two clamps, one that is stationary and one that moves away, so that tension increases until the fabric breaks or ruptures. Both warp and weft directions are tested. The rating is determined by the number of pounds required to break or rupture a fabric—50 pounds is the minimum for upholstery, 35 pounds for wrapped panels.

In the seam slippage test, a standard thread is used to sew a seam with specific stitches per inch and a standard seam allowance. This seam is used to measure the fabric's ability to resist seam slippage. The sewn fabric is clamped at opposite sides of the seam. Each of the two clamps is pulled away from the other, creating tension at the sewn seam to the point of separation at a specified distance. Both warp and weft directions are tested. The number of pounds needed to split the seam due to yarn slippage determines the rating. The minimum for upholstery and drapery is 25 pounds.

Care and Maintenance

Regular cleaning is fundamental to the endurance of outdoor fabric. The most crucial element is soil removal, since soil can abrade fabric and act as food for microorganisms, but many other things dirty outdoor fabrics as well—pollen, bird and critter excrement, berry juices, food and beverages, grass stains, and so on. Cleaning methods vary depending on the type of fiber and what causes the soiling. A stain usually falls into the category of greasy or nongreasy, which can determine how it might be removed.

Texilene is a proprietary, 100% solution-dyed, acrylic fiber used for sun shades and furnishings. It is shiny and has a hand somewhat different from other outdoor fabrics. The knitted cloth shown here is extra-heavy-duty, fire-rated HDPE (high density polyethylene) designed for large tension membrane structures and shade sails. It has been tested for breaking force and tension, tear resistance, and bursting force—all important tests for fabric used as a shade sail. It is also 12½ feet wide, considerably wider than most commercial-grade fabric.

Cleaning a fabric involves some method of removing the soil or stain and then, if needed, drying the fabric. Some fabrics can be washed in a washing machine, while others must be washed by hand. It is often important to pay attention to the temperature of the water, particularly for man-made fabrics. The same is true for drying and ironing temperatures. Occasionally fabric merely needs to be wiped clean with a damp cloth or sponge. Fabrics made of solution-dyed fibers can be bleached, which is a good way to remove mold or mildew. Dry cleaning is not usually required of outdoor fabrics, but leather should be professionally cleaned. Always pay attention to the manufacturer's recommendations for cleaning and storage. All fabrics should be stored in the driest place possible.

Sustainability

With fabric, sustainability begins with biodegradability. If a fabric is biodegradable, how often will it need to be replaced? Compare it with other fabrics that last longer for the cost. Recyclability is another issue. Find out whether the manufacturer will take back fabric at the end of its useful life for recycling.

Manufacturers of synthetic fabrics, like manufacturers of other synthetic products, have issues with respect to resource use and energy consumption. If the fabric is a synthetic recyclable textile, consider whether and how it can be recycled. For additional information, see the synthetics chapter.

Textiles checklist

Is this fiber suited to outdoor use?

Are the methods of fabric construction, dyeing, and sewing suitable for outdoor use?

Have any finishes been applied for the sake of use outdoors? Will they hold up to the weather? How long will they last?

Will this fabric perform in the conditions you expect?

What standards or tests has this fabric met?

What type of maintenance or storage will be required to give the fabric its longest life?

Are there warranties from the manufacturer, and if so, what do they cover and for what period of time?

Can this fabric be recycled?

Wicker

The term *wicker* applies to all woven furnishings independent of the type of material used, including synthetic "all-weather" wicker (also discussed in the "Synthetics" chapter) and rattan. Note that rattan is a material, while wicker is a process. When furniture is called rattan, it usually uses rattan peel or reed in addition to steam-bent rattan framework. Full-round or split-round materials processed from rattan reed are used to make wicker, which also integrates twists, curls, rolled arms, and loops.

People who weave wicker furniture ready their materials at their peak of growth and before the start of the rainy season. They then strip off the leaves and place the stems where they can dry completely. The most common natural materials used to create wicker are rattan and willow (in fact *wicker* evolved from the Swedish *vikker*, meaning "willow"). Bamboo, rush, and sea grass are less commonly used and should be confined to indoors or a covered area, or used outdoors only on dry summer days in the shade. Having said that, bamboo is often used outdoors regardless, in which case its life should be extended with a protective finish. Paper-based materials like Danish cording or fiber rush should not be used outdoors.

Woven rattan reed chairs obtained from Ikea and stained red-orange add punch to an outdoor deck during the summer. The stain penetrates the reed, which paint is unable to do. These chairs are set out only in summer, in a shady area, and are covered when it rains.

Natural materials biodegrade over time and will not last if kept outdoors all year long. Although people do use natural wicker materials outdoors, experts recommend either keeping them under cover or applying a finish to protect them from occasional light rain. Otherwise you can expect natural materials to last five to ten years at most.

History of Wicker

Wicker originated with basket weaving, an art even older than fabric weaving. (As a matter of fact, the terms *warp* and *weft* come from the craft of wicker.) Its millennia-long history is evidenced by basket remnants, including rush, reed, and papyrus from ancient Egypt. What has always been true in the art of wicker is that people around the world use materials indigenous to their location. In southern China wicker is commonly made from rattan or bamboo, while Europeans use willow and other local woods or vines.

A myriad of wicker materials grace a wicker repair shop.

Materials

Historically, wicker basketry influenced patterns in other mediums, particularly in Celtic art. The art of wicker was also used to make furniture during the Middle Ages, and much later, at the beginning of the twentieth century, basket patterns stimulated designs within the Arts and Crafts movement.

In the 1840s Cyrus Wakefield opened a factory in Massachusetts specifically for making wicker furniture from rattan. Although China was probably the first fabricator of a rattan chair, Wakefield was the first to recognize the value of the inner reed core of rattan, usually a leftover material. He discovered that this material, unlike the outer material, could also be stained or painted rather than just polished or lacquered. The Heywood-Wakefield Company, a merger between Wakefield and the Heywood Brothers, became the preeminent maker of wicker furniture in the United States during the 1890s, and this brand remains highly valued in the antique market.

An unfinished woven wicker ball makes an unusual finial for a wood post in a delightful cottage-style garden.

Because wicker is so versatile, it was frequently used in Victorian furniture. Fabricators borrowed intricate motifs from classic styles (Gothic, Rococo, classical, Renaissance, Moorish, Chinese). Wicker furniture, with all its fanciful Victorian curlicues and rolled arms, was once commonplace on American and British verandas, only to be tossed aside after the turn of the twentieth century. The Craftsman style straightened the Victorian curves, focusing on functionality and simpler design.

Fiber rush, a new product in the 1920s, became popular in the wicker industry. Since it was a paper product, it was cheaper and easier to work with but also had to be confined to the indoor environment. As machinery began to restrict the extent of design, individual expression was minimized. Tubular aluminum frames became more profitable, and wicker furniture diminished. However, comfortable wicker furniture became popular again in the 1970s as new designs were made of more durable materials.

Rattan and Rattan Reed

Several hundred species of rattan grow throughout the world, especially in Southeast Asia, China, India, Indonesia, and Africa. Although rattan is a palm, it is vinelike, growing up to 600 feet long. The best rattan seems to come from Indonesia, Malaysia, China, and the Philippines. *Calamus rotang* is widely considered the highest-quality species. Rattan colors range from pale yellow to reddish brown. You may encounter a product on the market called kubu (or kooboo) rattan, which is naturally gray. Another product, croco rattan, is made using the outside skin of rattan and is darker and more widely cut. Similar to croco rattan, natural peel rattan is bleached before use. It is a pale yellow and cut more narrowly. Thicknesses can range from less than an inch to as wide as a person's arm (with thicker pieces being used as rattan poles). The quality of rattan is determined by its hardness, color, and smoothness and by the consistency of its glossy exterior skin.

To render rattan useable, the outside skin (cane) is removed along with the thorns. Workers peel the cane from the core and cut it into long, thin strips of various sizes. These cane strips are used in weaving seats and wrapping wicker furniture joints. The remaining pithy interior of the rattan, known as reed, has a woodlike appearance and a lengthwise grain. It can snap or break if overbent. Because the glossy outer peel has been removed, rattan reed is porous and easy to stain, dye, or paint. It is also the material most closely mimicked by the synthetic all-weather wicker fabricators.

After rattan is harvested and peeled, workers sort the reed by its diameter or gauge. Eventually the material is woven onto large spools and distributed worldwide to dealers and eventually manufacturers. Most manufacturers weave reed using large automated looms that create simple webbing. Diagonal weaving to add structural

Tillandsias and a terrarium are enhanced by a backdrop of willow twigs and a small table of all-weather wicker and wood.

integrity is added physically with hand tools. Once the webbing is finished, the piece is sold to wholesalers.

Rattan and rattan reed are weather resistant, durable, and very strong, but experts recommend bringing both materials under cover for winter and protecting them throughout the year from persistent exposure to weather and UV light (the latter of which causes them to fade and degrade). A protective finish should be applied to improve longevity.

Willow

Willows come from the genus *Salix* and are common weaving materials due to their high degree of flexibility, rapid growth, and ease of weaving. They are difficult to distinguish from reed. The twigs are cut, peeled, and soaked before weaving, and allowed to thoroughly dry afterward. An impervious clear coating improves durability and water resistance. The natural colors of willows are in the range of dark green, brown, and rust.

What should you look for in quality willow furniture? For starters, cuts should be clean and sharp. Make sure frame pieces are at least 1 to 3 inches thick, tall and straight, and seasoned for at least seven days. Bender pieces should be at least ¼ to ½ inch thick. Also note whether distinguishing features such as knots or curves are used to good effect.

When it comes to attachment devices, look for galvanized ring-shank nails or bronze-colored deck screws for frame pieces and ribbed paneling nails. Look for rounded T-joints and corner joints (versus square joints), which add stability. If there are splice-joints, note their location. They are acceptable if located to complete a circle,

These graceful wicker chairs feature braided sections along the arms and backs.

but it is best to avoid them elsewhere. All joints should be glued and nailed or screwed. Nails should be staggered to prevent splitting, and nail tips should never protrude. Raw edges should be smoothed and filed if they stick out too far.

Constructed pieces should be seasoned three to six months out of direct sunlight before use; at that time, all joinery should be checked for loosened nails, or glue added where it might be needed. Make sure end pieces have rounded edges. When pieces are stacked, they should use even thicknesses for a uniform appearance, unless it is an obvious design feature. To prevent racking of larger straight pieces, curved pieces should be placed at an angle, or cross pieces should be used to maintain leg angles. Square pieces should be square (90-degree-angle joinery). Constructed pieces should be stable and not wobble on a level surface—all legs should touch the floor fully. Finally, all components should be firmly attached and not "give" if sat in or leaned on.

Fabrication

Fabrication methods for wicker derive from early basketmaking, although not all basketmaking techniques are used to make furniture. Furniture fabricators use three primary weaving methods: twining (or pairing), plaiting, and fitching (or reverse pairing). Each method is applied in a different area of a piece for a different purpose.

Twining is generally the strongest of the three methods. It involves weaving horizontal weft fibers in and out of a framework of vertical warp fibers. As with textile designs, the way in which weft fibers are woven can create patterns. A variety of knots and stitches aid in securing these elements and can add to the overall effect.

Plaiting is not braiding in the true sense, but it does mean that all of the fiber strips are active in the construction process, because they are passing over and under each other at regular distances. This type of construction forms a cohesive unit that does not require additional stitching except at the ends. Plaiting is used in lieu of twining for chair seat weaving. Braided wicker is also often found as an ornamental pattern to cover the structural portions of a piece.

Fitching is similar to twining and results in a Z-shaped twist pattern that goes in a clockwise direction.

Structural Underpinnings

A piece of woven wicker furniture, like a house, needs a structurally sound base. The methods for constructing that framework are based on simple carpentry techniques (unless there is a metal frame), and the process is similar to the construction of a frame for upholstered furniture. Pay attention to the type of joinery used to assure that whatever wicker piece you buy will hold up to its intended use.

Wicker fabricators should begin with a firm, strong attachment before beginning any wrapping or weaving. A little white glue and a minuscule nail initiate the process. For joints, screws should be used. Fabricators use white glue instead of a stronger material like Gorilla glue; if the piece ever needs repair, the white glue will dissolve more easily, making the repair a more straightforward process.

Finishes

Bamboo, willow, and the outer portion of rattan do not take stain or dye due to their low porosity. For applicable wicker materials, stain or dye should be sprayed from multiple directions so that it gets into all the nooks and crannies. If you are unsure of how well a material may absorb a stain or dye, test a small area on the underside before attempting the entire piece. Lacquering and varnishing are not recommended, since they seal wicker materials, preventing them from breathing or absorbing moisture from the air.

Although paint is not recommended for wicker because it can chip and flake, painting wicker is still common. Old pieces can find new life through refinishing. Successfully refinishing a painted piece means following a few important steps. Before painting a piece, thoroughly vacuum or hose it off (do not pressure wash) if you are positive the material will not swell (for example, do not hose off pieces built around a

Turning a chair over exposes its structural underpinnings. In this case we see an inexpensive chair with weak joinery. It would need considerable repair for continued use, and the repair costs would outweigh the value of the repair.

Painted wicker chairs set out for a summer garden party are vibrant and enticing but will need to be covered after guests leave.

wood structure). Next, allow it to dry completely in a shady location. To prevent your paint from flaking or chipping, make sure the surface is properly prepared. Once the surface is clean, apply a coat of primer in a color close to your final color. The final layer should be a glossy coat of the best spray paint recommended by your local paint dealer. High-gloss paints will repel moisture better than any other paint sheen. Although oil and epoxy paints have been used for years, many paints on the market are more sustainable and are considered equally good. Consult a reputable paint dealer to learn about the latest paint technology.

Standards

Tests for wicker furnishings tend to be performed on constructed pieces as a whole rather than on individual types of fibers. Therefore you may find test results for the flammability of a chair but not for the wicker fiber from which the chair is made. Tests are also conducted on various other components of wicker pieces, including wood materials, adhesives, fasteners, and metal products that could be used as caps for the foot of a chair leg, framework, or ornamentation.

Repairs to wicker frequently focus on joint problems, cracked posts, and weaving that has come undone, and problem areas include a chair's back, arms, and apron (a short piece across the front of a chair just below the edge of the seat). Keep this in mind when determining the quality of a new piece.

Care and Maintenance

Wicker furniture is often kept out in hot sun, which is the absolute worst environment for it, since heat causes wicker to dry and become brittle. Some wicker experts recommend protecting natural wicker from sun by coating it with a mixture of one part boiled linseed oil and one to two parts paint thinner or turpentine once per year. If you go this route, remove all dirt with a vegetable brush before applying the mixture. But again, I suggest visiting your local paint dealer to learn about the latest, most sustainable option.

To clean wicker furniture, begin by using soft brushes or small tools to thoroughly remove all dirt and fuzz. When spills occur, wipe them up immediately using a clean cloth moistened with mild detergent and water. Spray rattan reed outdoors with a hose and mild detergent. Rinse thoroughly and allow to dry completely before the next use. Avoid pressure washing or hosing too hard, which can lift a painted finish. Store furniture over the winter in an area with good air circulation and low humidity. If mold or mildew appear, gently clean the wicker with a mild bleach solution. Adding a padded seat cushion will lengthen the life of wicker.

Be very careful about cleaning natural wicker when you are unsure what material it is made from. Depending on the material, moisture or chemicals can make the

piece change color, bow, pucker, warp, or loosen. Some parts can become unglued, or the glues may soften. Chemicals can also loosen glue joints or discolor the finish.

It can be difficult to know precisely what materials were used to construct a product when you don't know its origin. Perhaps the wisest approach is to start by testing a small, less visible area. After removing as much dirt as possible with a soft brush and vacuum, move on to using water (unless your wicker is a paper product, in which case avoid water).

Always minimize the use of water and vigorous scrubbing. Use a soft, damp cloth or moistened soft-bristle brush first. Let your small test area dry before moving on to another small area. If you notice you are creating any damage, stop immediately and reevaluate your approach. If your piece is quite dirty, it is better to clean in several brief stages and allow the piece to dry in between. Too much moisture can cause warping or can get beneath paint and cause cracking in the wicker due to the different rates of expansion and contraction between the two materials. This same issue of expansion and contraction is often what causes paint to chip off of wicker.

UV light will also damage paint. Keep wicker furnishings out of extreme weather (whether painted or not painted) or cover them to prevent UV and moisture damage.

Wicker expert Cathryn Peters, also known as The Wicker Woman, recommends against using antique wicker outdoors under any circumstances. She also suggests that the shabby-chic style allows you the freedom to let a piece "chip and peel." Err on the side of the least destructive approach when caring for natural wicker.

Sustainability

Pay attention to how the natural material you choose is being harvested. Some wicker materials are overharvested in certain areas of the world, but some plantations have developed sustainable harvesting methods. Natural wicker is lightweight and transports at a reduced cost of fuel and CO_2 emissions. Consider recyclability. What are the plans for the wicker piece at the end of its useful life?

Wicker checklist

Can you identify or do you know the material from which this wicker piece is made?

Is this wicker material suited to this use?

Evaluate the structural joinery and woven components. Will it hold up to this use?

How is the wicker finished? Is the finish suited to your planned use?

What standards or tests has this wicker met?

What maintenance will be required to keep this wicker object in like-new condition?

Are there warranties from the manufacturer or retailer, and if so, what do they cover and for what period of time?

Is this item recyclable?

Ceramics

The ancient art of ceramics began when basketmakers filled the spaces between basket fibers with wet clay to improve the basket's holding ability. When a basket like this was found after a fire, the clay was still there, and the basket fibers were gone.

People have mixed dirt and water to make clay since about 24,000 BC. To transform the clay into ceramic, ancient kilns were partially dug into the earth. As communities developed around 14,000 BC, clay tiles were made in Mesopotamia and India. By around 9000 BC, clay vessels were made to contain food and water. As kilns were allowed to overheat around 8000 BC in Egypt, glasslike glazes appeared on the clay, beginning the history of glass. During the Middle Ages, as technology expanded around metals, modified kilns were able to produce higher clay firing temperatures. Higher temperatures allowed for stronger ceramics and a greater diversity of glazes.

Clay is a versatile material that can be manipulated through the imagination of the ceramic artist. An artist offers creations to the not-always-predictable kiln with high hopes that magic will occur within it. As serendipitous as clay work can be, however, success with it begins with a thorough working knowledge of the materials.

Clay for ceramics comes from good old Mother Earth. Minerals and rocks are processed into powders ready to be mixed with water. As with woods, the names of raw materials vary around the world.

No matter where you live on this planet, you should develop a basic understanding of the soil beneath your feet, whether it is sand, loam, or clay, or a combination of these. Once you recognize that all soils are not created equal, you will understand that the same goes for the materials from which ceramics are made. This is one of the most important factors when it comes to creating remarkable ceramics from plain clay.

A picturesque town in the south of France, Rousillon is known for the colors of its clay soil. Rich rust and golden ochre soils contribute to the look of finished ceramics.

A lovely garden deck is made all the more compelling by some beautifully planted pots.

Types of Clay

With hundreds of clay types available, ceramists must determine the possibilities and limitations in the choices they make. They must know what they plan to create, the properties of the clay, and the required firing temperature of that clay.

Clay is divided into five basic types: low-fired clay, terra-cotta, earthenware, stoneware, and porcelain. Selecting which clay to use is predetermined by the type of kiln the ceramist uses. Garden designers need to know how each of these clay types respond to outdoor conditions.

Low-fired clay often goes through a smoke- or pit-fired process. Raku is such a clay. I recall making a delightful raku pot in my first ceramics class in college by placing the pot inside a metal garbage bin, surrounding it with considerable amounts of newspaper, and igniting the paper. This type of clay remains porous after firing. It is a fragile ceramic not suitable outdoors in wet and freezing temperatures.

Terra-cotta is made the world round from soil high in iron, which when fired results in a characteristic pumpkin-rust color. Because of its plasticity and versatility, terra-cotta can be made into many functional items, such as garden pots, clay roof tiles, and chimney and drainage materials.

Impruneta, Italy, produces some of the world's highest-quality terra-cotta pottery. High limestone content and high firing make this pottery extremely weather resistant even in freezing temperatures.

Earthenware is a smooth, light-colored ceramic. It is fired at a higher temperature than terra-cotta but at a lower temperature than stoneware and is not impervious to water. It cannot withstand freeze and thaw cycles.

Stoneware is denser than earthenware and usually a natural, earthy or dark color. Since it is impervious to water, stoneware can be left outside during winter if it will not hold water; if it can hold water, the water could freeze and cause the piece to crack.

The translucency of porcelain is one of its defining characteristics. As a clay body it contains kaolin, otherwise known as china clay. Porcelain is impervious to water once fired due to its high density. However, kaolin has a low plasticity, which is why it

Raku is a gorgeous form of pottery that goes through a dramatic firing process. Note the unique metallic effects on the lower portion of this sculpture, very typical of raku. Such a pity this pottery is ill suited for year-round outdoor use and has limited use even indoors. It is best used as decorative ware and may be used outdoors only in nonfreezing temperatures.

must be mixed with other elements. The smooth qualities of this clay are due to the tiny particles with which the clay is comprised. During firing it can deform and crack easily because it doesn't attain its optimum density until it reaches the melting point of the clay, 2300°F, the highest firing temperature of all of the clays. To enhance the ability of porcelain to be fired at lower temperatures, some unusual ingredients must be used.

Stacks of clay pots line the yard of this Impruneta potter.

Fabrication

When ceramic artists imagine a piece they would like to make, they must also imagine how to build it. Some pieces must be entirely hand-built, while others may be best constructed using a combination of hand-built and thrown clay. Molding allows for the creation of more than one identical piece. Some ceramic artists use all of these techniques, while others focus on one or two techniques. It is helpful to designers to understand construction techniques, first of all for the sake of knowing the best way to use a piece, but particularly if they want a custom-made piece.

Hand-Building

Clay is hand-built in four ways: pinching, extruding, slab building, and coiling. Before the clay can be worked, it must be kneaded thoroughly to remove air that could otherwise create bubbles that might explode in the kiln. Pinching just means shaping the piece of clay with your thumb and fingers. Extruding involves pushing clay through a die or pattern to create a uniform long shape. Slab building requires rolling a uniform thickness of clay to be cut and assembled. This method offers a high degree of flexibility, although building a stable and uniform base can sometimes be a challenge. In coiling, flexible lengths of uniform clay are rolled between the palms of the hands and a flat surface and then joined together into a circle, often to make a bowl shape. Sagging is a weakness of this last form of construction.

Perfectly rounded pots are the result of wheel-thrown clay. On their own, containing nothing, they are a lovely foil to the beauty of these tulips.

Slip Casting and Press Molding

Molds are made from materials, like plaster, that are able to wick moisture away from the clay. Slip casting involves pouring slip (liquid clay) into a mold to create a ceramic form. Press molds make it easier to create some types of pieces and are certainly easier to use than repeatedly casting a single form, but they require the ceramicist to press clay into the mold. Building a custom mold is also time-consuming, so this can be an expensive option for only a few pieces.

Wheel and Throwing

It takes considerable practice to throw a chunk of clay onto a wheel, press your thumbs into the center of it as the wheel turns, and successfully open and form the clay. Watching a master construct a beautiful ceramic bowl, plate, or otherwise uniformly rounded shape can be awe-inspiring. Press molds can also be used on a wheel. Wheels are either manually or mechanically driven.

Greenware and Bisqueware

Clay pieces that have been formed and allowed to air-dry are called greenware. Once they are completely dry, they are placed into a kiln to be fired. After they have been fired, but before they

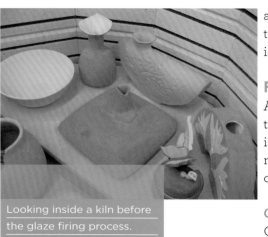

are glazed, they are called bisqueware. Sometimes artists choose to end the process here and just have a simple, earthy piece. This is the usual completed state of terra-cotta.

Finishes

A glaze finish is frequently what changes ceramics into the fantastical artistic pieces we know as ceramic art. Many other finishes are used, however, producing ceramics that are shiny or matte, smooth or textured, opaque or semitransparent, and every color of the rainbow.

Glazes and Stains

Ceramic artisans are artistic chemists who have mastered the art of mixing glazes and stains. Knowing which elements are safe to combine and their best firing temperatures is required to maintain some degree of predictability inside the kiln. Otherwise elements can react with one another to produce unwanted results.

Abundant shiny shapes, intriguing patterns, and brilliant colors characterize this ceramic artist's delightful, but not freeze-resistant, totems.

Glazes give ceramics a rich array of colors, seal the clay to assure that harmful elements such as lead will not leach out into food, enhance durability and strength, allow for a wider range of firing temperatures, and allow the artist to create textures and patterns. Glaze ingredients include a flux (to help melt the glaze at a lower temperature), stabilizer (always alumina, to expand the melting range and harden the glaze), opacifier (to increase opacity and in some cases produce a white glaze), colorant (metals, to create color), and a glass former (always silica, the main ingredient). When creating a glaze, the first step is to identify the major characteristics desired, such as sheen and texture. The colorant is the smallest part of the glaze; the ceramicist uses as little as required to create the color.

Oxides are metal elements combined with one or more atoms of oxygen. They make up the colorant within a glaze formula, whether alone or more often combined with each other or with simple metals like nickel or chrome. Chrome oxide, for example, yields a dark green glaze, while iron oxide produces colors ranging from rust to orange to ocher to gray.

Fluxes come from two sources: alkalis and alkaline earths. A glaze formula needs at least one of these, but more sources improve the balance of the glaze.

As with everything in life, glazes aren't always perfect. Small holes sometimes appear on a glazed surface, a common defect known as pinholing. The glaze may pool, leaving exposed, bare patches of clay (crawling). Glazes may also exhibit cracking that happens during the cooling process (dunting), bubbles or craters (blistering), a raised bump caused by air trapped in the clay body (bloating), or a network of fine cracks (crazing).

At left, a piece of glazed bisque before it is fired. At right, how the glaze appears after firing. You can see there is a dramatic difference!

Red-glazed containers pack a punch, especially grouped together. Since bright red glazes are extremely sensitive to variable firing conditions, they are often difficult to achieve and may be more expensive.

A rich burgundy ceramic ball plays off a rusty steel fire pit and bright chartreuse chairs.

Stains are manufactured pigments that combine oxides and ceramic material. They are fritted and ground into powder form and used to color clay and other ceramic materials. They may be used decoratively on a raw or bisque surface with a clear glaze over them. Both glazes and stains may be brushed, sponged, or sprayed on.

Basic Embellishment Techniques

After a piece is painted with slip and allowed to dry, a pattern can be scratched through the slip, revealing the base of the clay, a technique called sgraffito.

Another technique, slip trailing, involves filling a squeezable container with slip and then, much like a cake decorator decorates a cake, squeezing a trail of it atop the clay, which when dry will form a hard, raised pattern. Slip can also be sponged onto a piece, giving it the pattern of the sponge, unless the piece is carefully and completely covered with a single type of slip; it works well if using a stencil to create a pattern. Feathering involves dragging a pointed tool perpendicular through lines of different colors of slip, pulling the colors of slip into one another. Combing makes a wavy pattern by dragging a toothed instrument (or fingers) across a coat of slip.

Inlaying works just like wood inlay, with the artist creating grooves into which different colors of slip are set. Once the slip is firm, the artist scrapes away the excess to create a smooth surface.

When something like the back of a spoon is used to press and rub the dried slip over hardened clay in a circular motion, it creates a waxy surface. This technique is called burnishing and is used with specific firing methods to gain the desired effect.

Marbling involves the use of two colors of slip dripped onto a piece to create pools of color. A tool is dragged through the colors over and around the piece to create a marbleized pattern.

Agateware is pottery made by overlaying different types of clay and then pressing them into a single layer with a roller or wheel. It gets its name from agate, which when sliced has a similar appearance.

Sgrafitto is a delightful way to embellish a ceramic object. Before the ornamentation, this was most likely a molded piece.

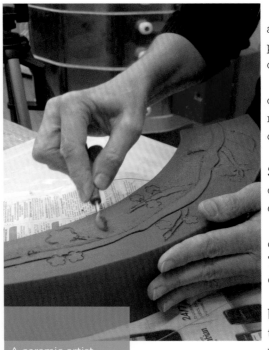

A ceramic artist enhances a piece by engraving detail onto its surface.

Relief and embossing are two opposing methods. Relief adds clay as a pattern to the surface, while embossing imprints a pattern into the surface. They can be used together to add extra depth and dimension to a clay surface.

Sometimes wax, paper, and latex are used to coat or cover an area in order to resist slip and create a pattern in the raw clay. Wax will burn off during firing, while latex and paper can be peeled off before firing. This method is known as resist.

Monoprinting involves newspaper or other printed paper. Slip is painted onto the paper and allowed to dry. The slip side of the paper is laid against the clay, and a tool is used to draw a design on top of the paper to transfer the print onto the clay.

Combustibles are organic materials such as lentils, rice, or sawdust that are soaked before being wedged into the clay. The results after firing are intriguing textures and smoky colors on the surface of the clay.

Painting styles can vary with just the use of a different brush. The brush used depends on the style of the design that the artist applies. Painting with slip can be very precise or done with abandon and freedom.

Ceramic artists can apply any of a wide variety of further embellishments before or after the glaze firing. These intriguing decorative methods can differentiate artists.

Prefiring techniques create texture and patterned interest. Engraving is used to add intricate surface detail. Sandblasting cleans or etches or creates sheen contrast. Water erosion involves the artist painting a decorative pattern onto the piece in shellac. Once it is dry, the artist wipes a damp sponge over the piece and fires it. The varnish burns away, leaving a raised design. Since water erosion is used on greenware, the artist must use caution due to the fragility of the clay.

Postfiring techniques require firing the piece again to permanently fix an additional decoration. The new element may be enamel, a malleable melting glass commonly used for hand-painted or surface design, or luster, a high-cost metal compound suspended in an oil-based resin, used to produce iridescent or metallic effects. If the artist wants to transfer a print image onto the glazed surface, a protective coating (covercoat) is applied that burns off of the piece during firing, after the image has been transferred. Additional postfiring techniques include lacquering, polishing with inks, flocking, and gilding.

Firing

Kilns fire clay to create ceramics. A variety of kilns are used, ranging from a simple electric- or gas-fired kiln for an individual artist to elongated tunnel kilns that involve a train of cars loaded with greenware or bisqueware slowly led through several stages of heating. One type known as the anagama kiln is traditionally used in the Far East

A massive anagama kiln fires hundreds of pots at a time in Vietnam.

(originating in Japan). It consists of a long chamber, bottom firebox, and chimney top. Workers stoke wood fires at intervals along the kiln, which produces a natural draft to increase heat. This is a labor-intensive firing process that can take longer than a day or sometimes several days to complete. Catenary arch kilns, top-hat kilns, raku kilns, and pit fires are less commonly used.

Other firing techniques used by ceramic artists are oxidation firing, reduction firing, and salt or soda firing. Oxidation firing involves supplying oxygen during the firing to produce reliable, predictable glazes. Reduction firing refers to the reduction of oxygen during firing. Although it is not as predictable, this method yields some rich results with charismatic texture. Toxic acid and chloride vapors from salt are released into the air while salt firing. Soda or sodium bicarbonate can be used as a substitute for salt to reduce the amount of pollution. One intriguing feature of the salt or soda method is that the clay doesn't need to be glazed or even bisque-fired first.

Firing is as much moisture reduction over time as it is simply heat. Firing temperatures for clay are expressed as cone temperatures and range from 022 to 10. Small cones are used as a visual cue inside the kiln near special viewing holes. The cones begin at an 8-degree angle. If firing is perfect, the cone leans over into a 90-degree angle. If the clay is overfired, the cone leans at a greater angle, and if it doesn't reach 90 degrees, the clay is underfired. Familiarity with cone temperatures can prove useful when discussing the water resistance capability of a ceramic piece you might be interested in. Most mid-fire and all high-fire ceramics fired to their optimum temperatures should be freeze resistant and have a low enough porosity to hold water. Firing temperatures are cone 022 to 017 (overglaze or china painting, 1087°F to 1405°F), cone 010 to 014 (glass firing, 1395°F to 1679°F), cone 06 to 1 (low-fire ceramics, 1798°F to 2109°F), cone 2 to 7 (mid-fire ceramics, 2034°F to 2295°F), and cone 8 to 10 (high-fire ceramics, 2212°F to 2381°F).

Standards

A wide variety of strength tests, chemical tests, and physical property tests are used with ceramics, but few if any apply to those used as garden furnishings. Because there are no specific tests or standards for the vast majority of ceramics one might purchase for a garden, it pays to know enough about ceramics to be able to identify defects and ask questions of the artist. A local guild with a high standard for membership may be a source for good-quality ceramic art or pots. Otherwise, check out the high-quality manufacturers listed in "Garden Furnishings Resources" at the end of this book.

Care and Maintenance

Terra-cotta and stoneware pots that have not been glazed (either inside or outside) have the most maintenance issues due to their porosity. Porosity allows mosses, mildews, and molds to grow, particularly if some remnant of soil clings to the pot. (Note, however, that mosses are sometimes desirable, depending on the client's preferences and design style.) Glazed ceramics can be simply scrubbed with sudsy water, rinsed, and allowed to dry.

Terra-cotta pots can be cleaned several ways, although the largest terra-cotta pot vendors focus more on preventive maintenance than on cleaning. Small terra-cotta pots used for starting seed should be cleaned each year to remove any possible

A beautiful, freeze resistant terra-cotta pot graces an elegant traditional garden in the Italian style.

Terra-cotta is a wonderful choice for cacti because it absorbs excess moisture. This pot's clay feet also keep the plant raised for better drainage.

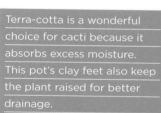

lingering disease. There may just be as many pot-cleaning solutions as there are gardeners, but most seem to agree on a solution of nine parts water, one part bleach. This same method can be used with distilled white vinegar, but note that both methods can corrode terra-cotta over time. The pots can be left outdoors for a couple of days to allow the bleach or vinegar to dissipate. Another recommendation calls for removing as much soil as possible, washing the pots inside a dishwasher, and allowing them to remain in the dishwasher until they are cool. (Terra-cotta pots are more brittle when hot.) Others advise sterilizing pots in the oven, but I do not recommend this lengthy, smelly method.

Hard-water deposits or salts can be removed by mixing baking soda and water into a paste and scrubbing the terra-cotta

with it. Steel wool can also be effective. Terra-cotta pots should also be stored empty and upside down if left outside so that water cannot collect in them (though better yet, store them indoors).

Many vendors offer excellent preventive maintenance recommendations for ceramics on their websites, beginning with the suggestion to purchase pieces with thicker walls, since thin-walled pieces are more fragile, especially for outdoor use. The biggest issue with ceramics is leaving them outside over winter. Make sure you leave out only ceramics that you know are freeze resistant. Usually you will know that a pot is freeze resistant because it will say so on the tag or a salesperson will give you this information. For all other pots, store them indoors away from moisture (a cool garage will suffice). Moving large pots can be a challenge. A hand truck is helpful, particularly one made especially for moving large pots. If a pot is too large to move or too much trouble, keep it dry over the winter by covering it. Experts recommend emptying each pot and washing in warm, soapy water with 10% bleach to kill any organisms. Once the pots are dry, they can be stacked upside down separated by a layer or two of newspaper to prevent chipping.

To care for a freeze-resistant pot, elevate it about an inch above ground to enhance drainage, particularly if it is to be left out over winter. Pot feet are available, or bricks can be used. Make sure the drainage holes do not become clogged. Do not compact the soil inside the pot, which will hinder drainage over the winter. And leave the pot full of soil rather than empty. I have done this with a large, freeze-resistant terra-cotta pot for more than fifteen years and during winters with hard freezes. I also cover the pot with a water-resistant tarp as insurance.

Sustainability

Ceramicists dedicated to sustainable practices capture excess glaze and clay waste for reuse. They are challenged to use less water, which is so much a part of the process, and may also use energy-efficient kilns.

Ceramics can be recycled by crushing for reuse in the construction industry. It is also possible to break ceramics into small pieces inside a concrete mixer and use the results as paving material.

Ceramics checklist

Can you identify or do you know the clay type from which this piece is made?

Do you know the firing temperature of this piece?

Is this ceramic material suited to this outdoor use?

Are there attached pieces? Will they hold up to the use you intend?

How is the ceramic piece finished?

What standards or tests has this ceramic material met?

What maintenance will be required to keep this ceramic object in like-new condition?

Are there warranties from the manufacturer or retailer, and if so, what do they cover and for what period of time?

Stone

"When's the last time you saw wood from Mesopotamia?" asked stone artist Matt Goddard, of Poetry in Stone. I had to admit I hadn't seen any. What we know about the ancient world is due in part to the endurance of stone. We are rich in stone, historically speaking, with examples from early Egyptian idealism, Greco-Roman expression of the human body, Michelangelo's "liberated" forms in marble, discoveries of Herculaneum and Pompeii, and centuries of classic sculpture.

A testament to the longevity of stone: classic, monumental stone and bronze sculptures ornament a public square in Florence, Italy.

Yet even with all the riches already found, scientists continue to hope that future discoveries may give us additional clues about the beginning of civilization. For example, since 1994 archeologists have been excavating a twelve-thousand-year-old site in Turkey known as Göbekli Tepe. Buried beneath sand and more than twice as old as Stonehenge or the Great Pyramid of Giza, rustically elegant carvings have been uncovered that depict an ancient menagerie of animals. Archeological finds like these seem to have inspired twentieth-century artists like Henry Moore and Isamu Noguchi to rebel against classicism and unlock new possibilities with their fresh and exceptional forms.

What is it that so fascinates us about this medium? Its permanency, its variation from piece to piece, the fact that it has developed under pressure over eons. Stone is unlike any other material available for use in a garden. Including objects made of stone gives a garden a sense of permanence.

In order to appreciate the value of any stone object, whether ornamental or functional, it is helpful to know about stone types, finishes, the degree of difficulty and effort involved in obtaining and working with stone, and the issues related to transporting and placing it. Carved stone furnishings are available but not necessarily readily. Stone is very heavy and pricey to transport. Therefore, many objects you might find on the market are cast stone, a concrete product with stone added to the mix (see the "Concrete" chapter). You will find considerable stone on the market as objet d'art and planters. You will also find stone tables and benches, but with more difficulty, since many stone furnishings are custom hewn to suit the client, locally. Often you will discover stone antiques displayed with other materials that an antique dealer or art gallery has collected.

Workers of stone identify themselves as stone carvers, stone artisans, or sculptors. I call them stone artists. Stonework is not for weaklings. This is a difficult material to manipulate, with even small pieces sometimes weighing 200 pounds, and it is expensive. Is it worth it? Given that stone has the capacity for such an extended life, it is most definitely worth it, as long as it is the right type of stone.

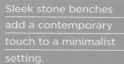

Sleek stone benches add a contemporary touch to a minimalist setting.

Stone Hardness

Theophrastus, a Greek successor to Aristotle, wrote a treatise on stones, comparing them based on their reaction to heat, their hardness, and their power of attraction. Hundreds of years later, German geologist Friedrich Mohs developed a scale to test the relative hardness of rocks based on which rock was hard enough to scratch a softer rock. The Mohs hardness scale remains in use, but it cannot be the only guideline for whether a stone is suitable for carving. For example, soapstone is a very soft, easily carved stone, but it also contains asbestos, a known carcinogen. Artists usually avoid sandstone, too, because the silicates it contains can be a health hazard during carving unless a good respirator is used. Sandstone also varies in hardness due to the amount of quartz or other minerals that bind the fine grains of sand together, and stone tends to crumble or fracture when a little quartz is present.

Stone artists prefer to work with alabaster (particularly pink alabaster from Colorado), African wonderstone, Virginia Alberene soapstone, and many marbles. Marbles come in some gorgeous colors from around the globe, as these examples will attest: white Carrara statuario, Vermont white, Rosfi rose, red alicante, Portuguese pink, Chinese gray, black marquina, and Belgian black. Some stones, like alabaster, are

Mohs hardness scale

1	Talc
2	Soapstone
3	Alabaster, wonderstone, Alberene soapstone, soft serpentine
4	Limestone, sandstone, serpentine
5	Apatite
6	Marble, travertine, onyx
7	Quartz
8	Granite
9	Corundum
10	Diamond

so beautiful that they could take the attention away from the sculpture. Henry Moore preferred French limestone, called Caen stone. Stone artists in your area will have their own preferences, often favoring local stone due to easier access. Local stone usually feels more at home in a garden, too, whether the piece is a tabletop or a sculpture.

Creating openings in a softer stone can weaken the stone and cause fractures. Limestones, marbles, or harder stones should be used, but the harder the stone, the more expert the stone artist must be. The Mohs scale rates minerals from 1 (extremely soft) to 10 (extremely hard). Limestone is rated 4, while marble is 6, on the cusp of harder stones.

Types of Stone

Geologists classify stone by its chemical composition into three primary types: igneous, sedimentary, and metamorphic. Each has its own unique characteristics, but certain stones are better for carving than others, and some make better garden art, planters, or furniture.

Igneous Rock

During the cooling of magma, crystalline solids form igneous rock. Through the process of cooling, the material transforms

Basalt columns are a classic example of igneous rock and form a complex stone water feature in this garden. The owner-artist carved rills into the stone to carry the water from the source rock to a pool beyond.

from a liquid into a solid. Igneous rocks are the primary rocks our planet is made of, and they are the most exposed to outer space. Their names are based on what they are composed of and the size of their crystals. Granite, basalt, obsidian, pumice, and quartzite are all igneous rocks.

Because igneous rocks progress from a liquid to a solid at different rates and temperatures, and because they begin with different chemical compositions, they have considerably variable characteristics.

Sedimentary Rock

A thin veneer of loose sediment covers the surface of igneous rocks. As layers of this sediment become compacted, they stick together to become sedimentary rock, which is divided into three primary types: organic, chemical, and clastic. Some sedimentary rock contains fossilized plants or animals.

Organic sedimentary rocks are an accumulation of organic debris hardened by heat and pressure. Rich in carbon, coal is such a rock.

A small, French, antique limestone planter such as this one could grace many a garden.

The most common chemical sedimentary rock is limestone. Composed mostly of calcite, limestone forms in shallow sea waters. Chalk is composed of tiny sea creature debris that dropped to the sea floor. Technically, these could also be classified as organic sedimentary rocks. Dolomite is magnesium-modified limestone, with the magnesium replacing much of limestone's calcium. Flint and agate are cherts or glassy rocks that contain a high amount of precipitated silica from water. Minerals precipitated from salt water are called evaporites and include potassium, rock salt, and gypsum. Travertine is another type of chemical sedimentary rock, formed purely by inorganic chemical changes in precipitated calcium carbonate, a process that does not require intense heat and pressure.

Limestone is one of the few sedimentary stones useful for carving, and oolitic limestones, which contain rounded concretions, are particularly favored since they are harder and more ideal for creating textures. Oolitic limestone is quarried in Indiana, while other limestones come from other parts of the United States and Europe.

Clastic sedimentary rocks, like sandstone, are sorted by the distance they travel from the source. A rock is rounded if it has traveled some distance, becoming smaller and smoother along the way, versus a larger and more angular rock that has remained closer to its source.

Metamorphic Rock

Any rock that moves from one location to another has the potential to be categorized as metamorphic. A new environment may cause it to destabilize, disrupting its equilibrium. Pressure and temperature will increase if the rock becomes buried, in which case the minerals within the rock change in the process of restoring equilibrium.

Metamorphic rock is difficult to study because of the process it undergoes, which occurs closer to the earth's core. What we do know is that there are limitless variables in the factors creating the rocks, including length of time, amount of heat and pressure, the rock's chemistry, and how much, if any, fluids may be contained within the rock. We know that limestone, through a metamorphic process, becomes marble, and that sandstone becomes quartzite. Onyx and alabaster are other metamorphic stones.

Metamorphic rocks are either foliated (with an oriented grain, as in a linear pattern), as with slate, or unfoliated (having a nonoriented grain), as with marble, quartzite, and anthracite.

Fabrication

How do we select stone from such a vast array of possibilities? What must we know about stone before using it (or asking an artist to use it) for a specific purpose? What should we know about stone in order to make knowledgeable selections?

The fabrication process applies to any stone piece made for a garden, but primarily custom pieces. Companies that offer a catalog of stone furnishings need to follow some of the same steps, but their designs generally work around the stone available to them and their perceived market's interests. Large companies also have more automated and more expensive equipment in order to make cutting and crafting stone easier and faster.

Prep

Stone projects often begin with the stone artist. A good stone artist will meet with you as well as the client to get everyone on the same page, review the budget, and agree on a timeline. A visit to the garden site is a must, even for small pieces. Evaluating where the piece will eventually live allows the artist to avoid having to move it later on. In this way he or she can also learn where water flows on the site, ascertain whether water might be pooling in the area where the stone piece will be installed, and review proportions of the garden and home. For sculptures, the artist will also need to discover the soil type and the depth to hardpan.

Stone artists frequently walk clients and garden designers through their studio or work site to explain process, geology, tools, and techniques. A clay mockup of a piece might be proposed if it is complex. They should also discuss details about payment, delivery, installation, and warranty. The warranty can vary but is commonly ten years, barring extreme weather and depending on the type of stone.

Stone is not easy to move once placed. The precise location for something as weighty as this delightful metal frame and assembled basalt must be planned well in advance.

Since we all know how long stone lasts, a warranty might seem a bit puzzling, but I know from personal experience why warranties are so important. A client of mine once selected a stone from a stone yard after I explained to the salesperson that it would be used for a water feature. Our expert stone masons installed it, and the completed water feature was gorgeous. Then winter arrived. Water froze, thawed, froze again, and a large portion of the rock broke off. Having discovered that the stone was more porous than anticipated, we returned to the stone yard and spoke to the owner, who admitted that the stone should not have been used for a water feature. He allowed us to select a new and different type of stone as a replacement, but the stone masons still had to charge for the time it took to remove the old stone and install the new one. Lesson learned: ask plenty of questions and take the time needed to assure that the stone you select fits its planned use.

This stone had to be replaced after succumbing to the freeze-thaw cycle of water during winter. Porosity is an important consideration when evaluating stone for northern climes.

During the selection process, stone artists not only measure rocks but also wet them, a technique that makes it easier to see the colors within the stone as well as any flaws. No stone is perfect. The artist inspects for fissures, vesicles, inclusions (in harder materials), and concretions. He or she also considers the logistics of acquiring the stone and getting the piece into place, as well as the cost of transportation.

Materials

Learning the back story of a stone can save future headaches. Was the stone blasted out of the quarry or rough-sawn? Was it roughly dumped or gently set onto a truck for transport to the stone yard? Reckless acquisition causes potential fractures and flaws. Artist Matt Goddard suggests that each stone be inspected at its source or initial facility and that the client and designer be involved in order to understand what issues may lie ahead. He also recommends indigenous material, which is tried and true, closer to the site, less expensive to transport, and therefore more sustainable. Stone from other climates may be problematic, leading to situations like the breakage that my client and I experienced.

Selecting from a large range of stone takes an experienced eye and a measuring tape.

Finding where small imperfections may be located is important before committing to a stone. (Once in a blue moon, an opportunity arises in the form of a surface geode or fossil.) Stone artists sometimes use a hardened steel hammer to tap the stone. If the stone produces a dull sound instead of a clear ring, it likely has a crack or color seam. If it is possible to see and remove the flaw, the artist will repeat the tapping process afterward. Stone artists often purchase more stone than they need to assure that they will be able to produce the work they have in mind.

Stone is inherently eco-friendly as a natural material and because of its longevity, but it becomes less so when it needs to be transported hundreds of miles or overseas. Stone is also labor intensive and often cost prohibitive. It doesn't need frequent repair or replacement, but it takes ten times the energy to manipulate and fashion.

Cutting

Stone carving is a slow, meticulous procedure that should never be rushed. It includes roughing out and refining the form, polishing and finishing (a lengthy and tedious task), and finally mounting the piece on a base if needed, as with sculptures. Stone artists begin the process by examining the stone, considering its size, shape, weight, and grain. Carving proceeds with caution and can take many forms, though imagination can be restricted by ability, tools, or material.

A suite of polished and beautifully crafted stone pieces should last a lifetime.

Stone artists use a wide array of tools, ranging from large electrical saws to the finest chisels. Tools are not only important for shaping a piece but also for textural treatments. The more the artist can reduce manual labor for effects, the less time will be involved and the less expensive the process will be. Each stone reacts in its own way to these methods. Some polish more easily than others.

To give a stone an artificially "natural" texture, an artist may use a propane torch (thermal treatment) to pop pieces off the surface (spall), which eliminates kerfs or marks created by quarrying. A bush-hammered texture can be produced with a pneumatic tool that looks a bit like a meat tenderizer. A unique texture created with a crandall hammer looks like a field of cat scratches or a bit like an adze was used. Frosting tools can be used to create a look similar to sandblasting or honing. A hammer and chisel can also produce heavy or light pointing, which can remove material quickly or in a more controlled manner to create a soft texture similar to needlecraft.

To keep pieces dry during the fabrication process, a controlled environment is preferred. This could be a covered area or a completely enclosed interior space. The piece may be propped up with sandbags, which also help absorb the shock of hammering. Stone artists prefer "free stones," stones with grain that allows them to be worked from any direction. The best stones are homogeneous and even-natured. Stratified stones such as basalt can be challenging, although some quarries provide better stones than others. When a stone artist is given creative leeway it is easier to develop a stone than when dimensions are fixed. For this reason also, artists prefer more unusually shaped stones, though this usually applies to sculpture pieces. If there is a predetermined shape (more common for furniture), a block or oval piece is suitable. It is always important to produce surfaces that allow water to drain off the piece as quickly as possible, even with a garden seat.

Stone can be laminated, potentially creating a very dynamic piece, but it is a very exacting process. Laminated stone should be an obvious part of the design, or the seam between two pieces should be so invisible that it is virtually impossible to tell that they are separate. This process requires an electric saw.

A beautifully pointed surface elevates this pot to the level of elegance.

Threaded steel rods attach one piece to the other. This method can also be used to repair a broken sculpture.

Stone carving and cutting produce waste. Leftover pieces, particularly the large ones, can always be used elsewhere. Spalls are jagged and angular, allowing them to compact well, and make excellent subgrade materials for concrete footings.

When evaluating a piece of sculpture, make sure that chips and nicks have been smoothed and incorporated into the flow of the work, and assure the base is level. Also note whether the surface finish is even (unless there is an obvious reason that it need not be).

Finishes

Polishing can make the difference between an acceptable stone piece and an excellent one. Stone artists can be a bit like chefs in that they all have their own recipes for finishing. Marble especially requires additional enhancement beyond the usual rigors of polishing. And since it takes more time, it is a more costly stone.

A polished stone table with intricately carved designs could be a welcome piece of furniture nestled into a garden.

Assembly

To assure that water does not sit around a piece, stone artists may improve drainage at the installation site by adding compacted gravel, with or without sand, or by pouring a rat slab (a less-than-finished slab). Rat slabs are generally used for sculptures and large planters, not for stone tables or benches.

While most sculptures are safely grounded on a base, some are suspended by cables as kinetic mobiles or to appear as if they are floating. Sculptural supply companies can provide and install bases complementary to sculptures, although it is usually better if stone artists make bases specifically for their work (which usually also adds to the sculpture's value). A base should never overpower the presence of the sculpture. As a rule of thumb, make sure the base height does not exceed 20% of the vertical elevation of the sculpture. It is probably best to err on the side of less rather than more, unless there is a compelling reason for a base to be taller. A garden seat would be an exception to the rule because it needs to be the right height for sitting, usually about 18 inches tall.

A substantial base raises this urn so that it can be seen from a distance within a large garden.

This roughly hewn, regionally native stone garden seat suits its woodland site.

When stone pieces are ready to leave the artist's studio or site, ideally they are crated to protect them from damage. Pieces are also more secure when permanently installed using a special drill. This particularly applies to sculpture, but it could also apply to a stone tabletop and base. Heavy-duty stone epoxy that sets slowly gives the installer more working time and improves the installation security.

Standards

ASTM tests stone to determine compressive strength, flexural strength (modulus of rupture), absorption, specific gravity, and abrasion resistance. These tests usually focus on building construction, not garden furnishings and ornaments, but the results are telling and may be interpreted for garden design purposes. For example, granite was about three times stronger than sandstone in a compressive strength test, five times stronger in a flexural strength test, and twelve and a half times more abrasion resistant, while sandstone was sixteen times more absorptive than granite.

A granite bench is an investment with significant durability.

Care and Maintenance

Stone artists often seal stone with an impregnator, preferring an enhancement sealer that intensifies color without making it look artificial. They tend to shy away from topical finishes that are shiny or glossy. Stone needs to breathe, too, and must not trap moisture, which can then freeze and thaw.

Sometimes old pieces need repair. Repair methods usually include the use of a stone epoxy, a catalytic hardener, and coloring paste or dry pigment. Temperatures should be on the cool side to allow more working time to complete and strengthen the repair. The catalyst is also slower to work when it is cool.

Sustainability

Stone is a natural material that lasts an extremely long time when well cared for. It is also heavy and requires considerable energy to manipulate and transport.

Stone must be quarried, which has a big impact on the local environment. Find out whether there is a plan to restore the quarry site to as close to its original condition as possible when the quarry is closed. Learn how the quarry affects the local area.

Stone dust from carving can also cause health problems. Make sure the fabricator keeps dust to a limited area and that no employees are unnecessarily exposed to it.

Stone checklist

Is this stone suited to this use?

Do you know where it was quarried and what type of stone it is?

Has the stone been carefully transported or prepared for this use?

Evaluate any joinery to other materials or to the stone. Will it hold up to this use?

How is the stone finished? Does it require any maintenance?

Are there standards or tests for this stone? If so, does this stone meet the minimum requirements?

Have third-party sustainability organizations certified this stone?

Evaluate the distance from the point of origin and the means of transport to fabrication or manufacturing and then to your site.

Does the fabricator provide any warranties? What about the stone supplier?

What will happen to this stone should it break? What happens to the stone chips from the carving process?

How difficult will it be to get the finished stone carving installed?

Glass

Luminous, hypnotic, and translucent, glass never fails to dazzle in the garden, where it appears in a variety of both practical and ornamental objects, from tabletops and light fixtures to arbor tops, privacy screens, and art pieces. The inclusion of art glass in gardens has been inspired by an upsurge in glass artists and possibly by Dale Chihuly's artistic glass displays in a few American botanical gardens.

History of Glass

Like metal and stone, glass can last thousands of years. People produced glass beads around 2500 BC in Mesopotamia. Glassmaking was a difficult process until the Syrians invented the blowpipe technique in the first century BC. Because of this technique, glass production surged throughout the Roman Empire, leading to the development of numerous techniques still used today. During the Han dynasty, third century BC, glassmaking also occurred in China.

Glass evolved over hundreds of years from the creation around 1450 of cristallo (a transparent, almost colorless glass) to lead glass, crown glass, and more recently float glass and fluoride glass. Renaissance glassmakers added more color to their work, since the Syrians had figured out much of the chemistry of glass. Venetians added hot glass bits from the furnace to a piece

Dramatic glass flowers bloom all season long, but they must come in for the winter.

in the process of being blown. During the Arts and Crafts period, techniques were debated. Those techniques used in cut glass that saved labor and produced predictable pieces were eschewed for the more creative, less perfect, character-rich pieces made by the Venetians. Louis Comfort Tiffany, whose work still influences the making of art glass, became a leading glassmaker during the late 1800s and Art Nouveau period. Corning's Steuben Glass was a famous competitor of Tiffany. During the 1930s Émile Gallé, a French glassmaker, experimented and employed numerous techniques and made what is now known as studio glass. Harvey Littleton at the University of Wisconsin began the birth of the American studio glass movement in 1953. During the Italian Memphis design movement of the 1980s, glass artists were influenced by vivid colors and angular forms.

Dale Chihuly, among the most well known contemporary glassblowing artists, learned his craft in Venice, Italy, and later began the Pilchuck Glass School in Stanwood, Washington. He and the master glassblowers he has worked with since being blinded in one eye have blown famous pieces for many locations around the world.

Types of Glass

Different types of glass are appropriate for different garden uses. Glass for outdoor tabletops can be clear, patterned, or etched on the underside. Patterned or textured glass is preferred over clear glass, which birds may try to fly through (as happens sometimes with windows). Be aware that glass for tabletops may not be tempered (treated to make it less likely to cause injury when broken). Also keep in mind that these tabletops may be marked by rain as the water evaporates from the surface.

Translucent or opaque glass screens can be very artistic but should be protected so as not to harm anyone should they

Facing:
The glass top set into this resin wicker table has a frosted back, making the glass opaque.

Materials

This piece, sited to be seen from a living room window, takes advantage of afternoon sun to show off the translucent quality of the glass.

break. Garden arbors with glass tops should be tempered glass to minimize problems from falling tree limbs, hailstones, or stray baseballs. Glass for electric or gas light fixtures should be translucent rather than clear so that the lamp inside the fixture doesn't create glare. Light fixture glass may also be merely a shade for an exposed light source. Clear glass for panels or screens may be modified by applying an adhesive film, which may provide less transparency or a pattern or both. Furthermore, adhesive films may be replaced to create different effects, if your client doesn't like the current film or simply wants a change.

Fabrication

Like ceramics, glass is made by applying heat to raw materials from the earth. However, glass has a unique structure. Most solids are crystalline solids, with a well-ordered, rigidly bound lattice structure. Glass is an amorphous solid. Without a crystalline matrix and no specific melting point, glass forms across a broad eutectic (temperature), or workable, range. The temperature range during the transition from a thick, flowing glass into a syrupy solid is what allows glass fabricators and artists the freedom to create amazing pieces of glass and glass art.

Glass artists work with many common forms of glass, including sheet glass, glass rods, noodles, stringers and sprinkles, billets or rocks for casting, and frit (crushed or powdered glass). Sometimes a combination of forms is used.

Making traditional sheet glass is a fascinating process passed down from the Middle Ages. Glass is melted in a furnace using a long-handled ladle. Different colors are measured out with different-sized ladles and combined at the rolling table after they are melted. Then the glass colors are spread and stirred using metal sticks and hand-rolled or shoved into a mechanical roller that flattens the glass into an even thickness. The glass is then annealed (heated and slowly cooled to prevent breakage), reviewed for quality, and stored.

Glassmaking techniques include bending, blowing, etching, engraving, casting, fusing, slumping, *pâte de verre* (molding and firing powdered or paste glass), stained glass, graal (a complex method that involves blowing a piece twice), sandblasting, lampworking, intaglio, and acid etching. Almost any of these can be used within a garden, but blown, fused, and stained glass tend to be used most often. Lampworking is also used, but to a lesser degree.

Glassblowing

Handblown glass is made using many traditional techniques from ancient times. For example, a wet stick (or steam stick) is used to inflate the glass.

Glassblowers use three furnaces. One is the furnace where the crucible of glass is melted and where the artist gathers the glass. The second is the "glory hole," where the glass is frequently inserted to maintain the required temperature while the artist works with it. The third furnace is usually a kiln where the glass piece anneals.

Many glassblowing techniques involve at least two people: the glassblower (or gaffer) and an assistant. A tool called a punty or pontil is used to remove the glass piece from the blowing pipe. An incredible number of punty types are used to suit any style of piece being blown.

Here is an oversimplified description of glassblowing. The gaffer gathers the glass at the end of a blowpipe and alternates between blowing short puffs down the blowpipe into the glass, rolling the piece on a steel surface for shaping (or sometimes using a form, such as thick rolls of newspaper, to roll the piece), and inserting the piece back into the glory hole. Once the piece is blown to the point where it needs to be removed from the blowpipe, the gaffer's assistant attaches a solid punty iron to the bottom of the piece and assists in transferring the piece to the punty. The gaffer

Two of the three furnaces used during the glassblowing process: the crucible furnace (left) and glory hole (right).

Ladling glass into a furnace takes steady nerves and keen recognition of the material's state.

continues to work on the piece until it is perfected. After disconnecting the piece from the punty, the gaffer has merely seconds to get the piece into the annealing oven.

Glassblowers can make both solid glass objects and blown objects. Solid glass objects rely solely on shaping the glass, which usually includes marvering, a process of rolling the hot glass on a marver or perfectly smooth, flat steel surface that quickly cools the glass when needed. Metal-bladed jacks are also used, which allow the artist to cut into the glass. Glassblowing can produce beautiful objects for the garden, including opulent finials, suspended ornamentals, luminescent flora, and even whimsical fauna.

Glassblower Alex Farnham inflates the glass at the end of her blowpipe with a quick puff of air.

Fusing

Fused-glass artists use specially manufactured glass (such as sheet glass, frit, dichroic glass, powders, or paste) in a kiln. After deciding on the general direction of the project, they select the colors and layer the glass into a pattern, taking the characteristics of each glass color into consideration. Intense heat is needed to bond each color to the other. To avoid stressing the piece, each fuse involves a lengthy heating and cooling process.

Fusing is a somewhat unpredictable process, so artists are never entirely sure what they might discover when they open the kiln once the firing is complete. The more knowledgeable they are about their materials and process, the more successful and predictable the results will be. Fused-glass artists produce garden objects such as elegant screens, colorful birdbaths, art pieces, and even small tabletops.

Fusing entails techniques known as slumping, tack fusing, and full fusing, which artists may use in combination or individually. Slumping often uses a

Fused-glass panels add a bright pop of color to the garden.

This freestanding koi screen transmits colored light from either direction, allowing it to be placed anywhere. For stability the piece has feet that can be anchored to the ground. The glass is held securely with clamps that allow for expansion or contraction from heat or cold.

ready-made mold to form the glass into a plate, bowl, or even sculpture. Custom molds can be made from fiberboard, but this obviously adds to the amount of time and cost. Tack fusing (or sintering) adds texture to a piece by melting the glass just to the point that the pieces bond and retain their shape. Full fusing melts the glass into one smooth piece, called a blank, and requires the hottest kiln temperatures.

As in any of the other glassmaking techniques, thrill or frustration awaits an artist after kiln firing. Bubbles, sharp points or sides, cracks, and other flaws sometimes cause disappointment.

Fused-glass artist Roger Thomas describes working with glass as using imagination, inspiration, and the material itself against the glass's belligerent resistance to the artist's will. It is this resistance that most appeals to him. He compares fused glass to watercolor: "The character of each brushstroke, each mark, is visible."

Stained Glass

Although stained glass was traditionally assembled with lead came (a channel made of lead the width of the glass), today it is de rigueur to wrap the edges of each piece of glass with copper foil tape to create garden art. The designer begins with a

A realistic interpretation of a butterfly in stained glass.

thoughtfully developed pattern to assure that each piece of glass to be cut will be just right. Glass is scored, then broken or nipped into shape with breaking pliers.

Once a piece of glass is cut, its edges are roughened. This helps the pieces fit the pattern and helps the copper foil adhere. After all the pieces have been wrapped with foil, they are assembled and soldered together. Common solder includes 40% to 50% lead. Lead-free solder is available but is expensive and more difficult to use. After all of the components are soldered into place, flux and stray solder beads are washed off. Then a patina in the form of acid is carefully applied to the copper and solder, followed by the application of a finishing compound (like a car wax) to seal the seams and prevent corrosion. Pieces should not be washed after sealing or they will need to be refinished.

Artists include other materials besides sheet glass in their designs. Fused glass, metals, or stone add to the complexity and unique characteristics of a design. Anything other than copper must be wrapped with copper for attachment purposes.

Some signs of a well-assembled stained-glass work are narrow, smooth, evenly soldered (or sometimes purposely bumpy) seams and curved rather than straight cuts (or if there are straight cuts, none that reach from side to side). The piece should have a pleasing relationship between shapes and sizes without looking as though it is trying to compensate for uncuttable curves. There should be no torn foil, gaps between pieces, solder stuck to glass, broken glass or hairline cracks in glass, or breaks intentionally covered with solder. Obviously the design and types of materials used factor into a quality piece as well.

Lampworking

Lampworking is the art of making glass beads, vessels, or sculptures in the flame of a torch (or historically an oil lamp, the derivation of the term).

Lampworking artists choose between soft or hard glass. Glass is separated by COE (coefficient of expansion, the measurement of glass compatibility) into hard and soft categories. Soft glass is used more by beginning glass artists because it melts quickly and is easier to use. Hard glass is often borosilicate glass. It has unpredictable color potential, making it one of the more interesting types of glass for more experienced glass artists to exploit. Artists can also create eco-friendly glass art by recycling bottle glass. The COE is not known when using recycled glass, so it is a riskier process. Recycled glass is also more difficult to cut, which is why the end product may cost more.

To make a bead, an artist heats the tip of a glass rod with a lampworking torch, then wraps the melting glass around a thin rod called a mandrel, which is coated ahead of time to allow the bead to release once it is completely cooled. Once the bead is begun, the artist shapes it and embellishes it with tiny glass strings, metal foils, or possibly enamels. The beads are flame-polished to a uniform heat, cooled briefly and evaluated for uniformity, and immediately placed inside a kiln and "soaked" at over 900°F. Alternatively some artists bury their pieces in vermiculite or lay them between fiber blankets, which anneals the glass and eliminates the stresses upon it. Finally the beads are cooled gradually overnight to prevent thermal shock. This sounds straightforward, but artists can experience a number of unexpected events, such as the bead sliding on the mandrel, unidentifiable colors, or decorations breaking off. These issues add to the cost of making glass beads. The process differs slightly for making glass sculpture but still involves melting glass with a torch and using tools to shape it. An artist might include techniques such as sandblasting and applied pigments while making a piece.

Lampworking artists make beautiful objects for outdoor use, such as artistic birdbaths and translucent sculpture.

Standards

Although quite a few tests are conducted on glass, none are used by glass artists. However, performance tests for glass are used in outdoor furniture. It is a good idea to ask what tests have been done before purchasing furniture. Tests typically rate the performance, safety aspects, and strength of various types of glass. Test methods and standards are also available for recycled glass used in manufacturing.

A glistening glass birdbath lends sparkle to a summer garden but is a potential problem in freezing weather. Bring pieces like these under cover until spring.

Facing: Inspired by fern fronds, glass artist Barbara Sanderson created a plethora of colorful, out-of-this-world "fiddlesticks," which just might be delightful enough to—dare I say it—replace the real thing. Since these pieces will not collect water, they should be fine out in the snow.

Care and Maintenance

Glass in a garden is relatively easy to maintain. Wash most glass items to keep them looking their best. Keep any pieces that can collect water during freezing weather in a sheltered area to prevent them getting broken by the freeze-thaw cycle. Also avoid getting a flame too near glass pieces, since this could cause them to break. Finally, try to locate glass items away from wheelbarrows, children, pets, and other things that move through a garden. I learned this lesson some years ago after losing a favorite Mexican glass gazing ball to a misguided length of lumber.

Sustainability

Be aware that all glass contains heavy metals. Glass is a very recyclable material, but the recovery of glass waste is still improving. It takes considerable energy to make new glass and less energy to make recycled glass. Virgin glass can be mixed with recycled glass to reduce use of raw materials.

Glass checklist

Is this glass suited to this outdoor use?

Evaluate any attachments to other pieces of glass or other materials. Will they hold up to this use?

Will any flaws in the piece's craftsmanship lead to problems in its assembly or in the garden?

Will this piece require any special or time-consuming care and maintenance?

What standards or tests has this glass met?

Are there warranties from the manufacturer, artist, or craftsperson, and if so, what do they cover and for what period of time?

Concrete

Concrete has a lot of advantages in the garden. When mixed and cured properly, it is very strong and can last thousands of years. It is inexpensive, readily available, easy to work with, extremely versatile, and recyclable. A beautifully made concrete furnishing also has a way of anchoring a garden in time—you see it capturing snow, note its relationship to spring flowers, and thanks to its texture, become aware of the quality of light during the day.

In many cities, concrete shops or yards use molds to produce inexpensive garden furnishings, which become ubiquitous in local gardens. If you must purchase through a shop, consider a custom treatment. Indeed, I was surprised by the level of expertise at my local concrete shop when investigating the possibilities beyond the pieces they generally offer. Otherwise, don't hesitate to seek out an artisan who can custom-make an original piece. Yes, custom pieces are more expensive, but they can be a touchstone in your client's garden.

Concrete works for so many items because it can be molded. Table legs, table-tops, benches, small seats, fire bowls, planters, and artistic garden focal points—the sky is the limit, although sometimes weight brings a piece back to earth. Integral color can be added to concrete as well, a very inexpensive way to customize a piece. Concrete artists can even embed materials like stone, glass, ceramic, and plastic into their unique pieces.

A brilliant wall serves as backdrop for a colored concrete leaf, Cor-Ten steel fire pit filled with recycled blue glass, and colorful chairs.

A bevy of plants in a contemporary garden superbly adorn a simple concrete urn.

History of Concrete

Concrete is often thought of as a relatively modern material, but natural deposits of cement compounds more than twelve million years old have been found in Israel. Those deposits are a result of a spontaneous combustion reaction between limestone and oil shale. More than five thousand years ago the Egyptians built pyramids using lime and gypsum mortar in addition to their normal building mixture of mud and straw. The Chinese also built the Great Wall with bamboo and cementitious materials.

By 300 BC the Romans used lime as a cementitious material. Shortly before the new millennium, Pliny the Elder's writings served up a cement recipe of one part lime to four parts sand. The Romans also used slaked lime, a volcanic ash ingredient. After the Roman Empire fell, concrete use disappeared until the 1600s, when Joseph Moxon wrote about a "hidden fire" that appears when water is added to heated lime.

During the next two centuries a series of British, French, and American concrete discoveries were patented. Additional patents were issued to cover hydraulic cements and synthesized concrete materials. By 1824, and with an increase in demand and greater complexity of components, these discoveries led Joseph Aspdin to patent what he called portland cement. He named the cement for its resemblance to a natural limestone found on the Isle of Portland in the English Channel. The United States Bureau of Standards and the ASTM established a standardized formula for portland cement by 1917.

Throughout the twentieth century, improvements in concrete construction continued, with fiber-reinforced concrete introduced in the 1970s. Experimentation continues today with additives used to strengthen, lighten, color, and otherwise improve concrete.

Types of Concrete

Simple concrete is composed of very basic materials, of which portland cement is the primary binder. Portland cement is primarily lime and silica but also contains calcium, aluminum, iron, gypsum, and other ingredients. Its production begins with a dry process, as rocks are crushed to about 3 inches in diameter or less. A wet or dry process is then used to grind the rocks into a wet slurry or dry powder while mixing with the other ingredients. The resulting mixture is preheated and then heated to 2700°F in a kiln. In the kiln the materials emit an off-gas and change into a new material that ultimately results in small, round pieces called clinker. The cooled clinker is ground to a very fine powder with gypsum (to control the setting time) and sometimes fly ash or slag (to alter other properties of the final material).

Most cements, including portland cement, are hydraulic cements, which set and harden after being combined with water. Some hydraulic cements are blended cements, meaning they blend other materials with portland cement. Cement is the binder in concrete, but it needs water to hydrate and then solidify. Water catalyzes a chemical process that interlocks crystals formed during the hydrating process and binds all of the ingredients together. The crystals need time to form, but the amount of time needed can vary depending on additives such as calcium chloride or sugar.

Air, sand, and gravel are critical ingredients for the drying process. Ballast, aggregates, or granular materials such as sand and gravel make up 60% to 75% of concrete. The properties of these materials affect the workability of soft concrete and the durability, thermal properties, and density of hardened concrete. Concrete components may need to be limited in size to manage compression and tension cracks, which are a factor of the use, dimension, and size of each piece.

Hypertufa is a more lightweight alternative to concrete. It is made with portland cement, peat moss, and sometimes perlite or vermiculite to lighten the final weight and improve porosity. Do-it-yourself gardeners enjoy using hypertufa to make pots or even ornaments like small balls.

This custom-designed, hand-carved concrete fire pit has 4-inch thick walls and reinforcing rebar to assure a long life.

Other material can be added to alter the appearance of concrete so that it looks like terrazzo (polished cementitious material that contains small pieces of marble and granite). In fact some concrete fabricators crush old building materials and recycle them into new concrete. However, the strength of the recycled concrete is a bit less than the strength of standard concrete, so it is best used for countertops or garden planters rather than building foundations.

Concrete is stronger in compression than tension. In other words, the denser the concrete, the stronger it becomes, with the caveat that reinforcement (to increase tension) is required for a longer-lasting piece. Depending upon the mix, its compression strength may range up to 50,000 psi (pounds per square inch). Chemical additives and synthetic fibers may be used to increase tensile strength. Additionally, large pieces of concrete may be reinforced with steel mesh or rebar.

Fabrication

The fabrication process is the same whether it is for a sculpture or a piece of outdoor furniture. When it comes to custom pieces,

Left:
A garden sculpture began with this little lion sketch, inspired by drawings from the Middle Ages.

Right:
The finished sculpture sits on a pedestal, bringing a corner of the garden to life.

you will usually work with a garden artist. For prefabricated pieces, the manufacturer goes through a similar process but on a larger production scale.

A concrete artist generally begins a project by discussing ideas with the client and showing photographs of their and others' work. The artist sketches various design concepts, knowing that the forthcoming three-dimensional model (if one is required) will bring new possibilities and challenges. Clients are usually asked to approve the sketch before the artist carves the model. Once the model is approved, there is no going back—the next step is having the piece cast.

Concrete mixes vary considerably depending on the needs of the fabricator or artist and can even vary from project to project. Some concrete artists carve their model and then send the piece out to mold makers and concrete fabricators. This is the method used by concrete artist Patrick Gracewood. He feels that mold making and concrete mixing and casting are best left to the experts and that the results make his pieces much better. He is then free to stain or color the concrete as he sees fit.

Precast Concrete

While concrete is a ubiquitous building material, precast concrete is frequently used for making garden furnishings. The process usually involves making a model that is

A precast concrete Ganesh sculpture creates a place of reflection and offering in a corner of the garden.

then used to make a mold, which can be made of various materials including latex rubber, silicone rubber, film-covered wood, or metal. Once the concrete mixture is poured into the mold, it may require some pushing or vibrating to fill the mold extremities and prevent voids that could weaken the cast concrete.

Concretes mixed for molds may contain a variety of chemical additives, such as those that hasten drying time to as little as twenty minutes, lighten and strengthen, increase flow, ease mixing, enhance acceptance of colorants or coatings, add fire resistance (for fire pits), augment durability, reduce odor, or improve the effectiveness of release agents. Mixes with additives that improve flow and ease mixing may not require any vibration once they have been cast. In fact excessive tapping or vibration may cause aggregates to separate from the portland cement or may cause the pour to separate into layers (when more than one pour is required to fill the mold).

Several concrete products on the market have good characteristics for precast concrete. Ductal is a high-performance concrete that uses cement, silica fume, sand, superplasticizer, water, ground quartz, mineral fibers, and other fibers. It is a good

choice for sculptures and furniture. Eco-Cement is a high-magnesium oxide concrete well suited for statuary. Syndecrete contains cement, fly ash, recycled carpet fiber, perlite, sand, water pigment, and decorative aggregates and is used for planters, tabletops, sculpture, benches, and furniture.

As an alternative to making molds, concrete artists may carve precast lightweight concrete block, such as that used for building insulation, or partially hardened concrete. The latter requires a precise plan, good use of limited time, and use of an additive that extends the time the concrete takes to harden.

Cast Stone

Cast stone is a unique form of precast concrete. Aggregates are limited to stone such as limestone and marble, and the final product should have a fine surface texture that mimics real stone. The method of casting increases the cast stone's density. Cast stone is more refined than cast concrete—and more expensive—and is typically used in garden planters and sculptures.

Concrete Armature Sculpture

Some concrete artists create an armature (or skeleton) of rebar and steel mesh as a base for building up a concrete sculpture. The complexity and stability of the sculpture depends upon the armature design. Once the armature form is securely constructed, the artist applies wet, claylike concrete. The resultant texture of the sculpture may be smooth or rough.

Finishes

Texture is not so much a finish as a result of the concrete mix or mold. But it is such a visible result that one might consider it a finish. Texture varies with the aggregate material. If the material is very fine, then the finish will be smooth. Rougher, chunkier aggregate will create a more textural surface. A chemical additive or curing agent may allow surface cement to be removed in order to expose the concrete aggregate, creating an exposed aggregate texture. A mold can be used to duplicate almost any kind of surface texture.

Color can be added to precast concrete with integral colors, concrete dyes, stains, or paint. Integral colors are powdered

This stunning, lightweight, stained concrete wall panel is highlighted with embedded glass.

pigments added to the liquid concrete mix. They tend to be fairly muted but are inexpensive. Using a sealer with integrally colored concrete can intensify the color.

Concrete dyes come in many concentrated colors that are mixed to form other colors. They are diluted with water or solvent (acetone or alcohol), then sprayed, sponged, or brushed on. Due to their dilution they penetrate the concrete and provide a transparent watercolor effect. Dyes are UV stable, dry quickly, and can be used in combination with acid stains, which work quite differently. Sealers, if needed, can be applied immediately once the dye is dry.

To get rich, vivid colors, artists frequently use concrete stains, typically acid stains. Penetrating acids chemically react with the lime in the concrete; however, the

The complementary colors of blue and orange are used to good effect to call attention to a bronze-colored concrete column in the midst of this water feature.

Materials

denser the concrete, the less the stain will penetrate. Stain colors are limited because the pigments are based on the natural colors of stone. Once the stain has been applied, it needs to set for four hours, then be washed and neutralized before a sealer is applied.

Paint can also color concrete. Because acrylic paint is nontoxic and can be cleaned up with soap and water, it is the most popular choice. When dry, acrylic paint is waterproof, making it weather resistant. It is also lightfast and able to expand and contract with the concrete (during compression, tension, or temperature changes). Due to concrete's porosity, paint penetrates it better when more water is added. For best results, a concrete- and paint-compatible primer should be applied to the very clean surface of the concrete prior to painting. This is preferable to applying expensive paint as the first coat, which will be quickly absorbed by the concrete. Because paint is a film, multiple coats may be required to assure continued coverage of rough, jagged, or protruding edges.

An artist who prefers a natural finish might lightly grind or polish stained concrete to age the appearance of a concrete piece. Alternatively the artist may add a skin of terrazzo to the concrete, either leaving that as a finish or grinding and grouting it for a terrazzo surface.

Sealers change the patina of concrete but also help keep moisture out. High-psi concretes are less in need of a sealer because they are denser and less porous. If poorly applied, sealers will cloud the work.

Standards

Because of the building industry, concrete and its construction are subject to multiple tests. Since the ingredients of concrete, particularly portland cement, are highly tested, concrete used for garden furnishings is often high quality. Some concrete fabricators manufacture both building materials and garden products. For them it is easier to use the same concrete, usually meaning that all pieces must meet the higher psi required for building products. This means that their products could be superior to those of fabricators who do not need to meet building construction standards. While the end products for building construction are tested, garden furnishings are not.

Care and Maintenance

The greatest maintenance issue for concrete furnishings is moisture and the freeze-thaw cycle. If you live in an area that freezes over the winter, cover concrete pieces so that water does not collect in their pores and then freeze, leading to damage. Once again, pieces made to a higher psi are less affected by this issue. If sealers are used, they need to be reapplied periodically, usually once every year or two or as recommended by the manufacturer.

Because concrete has some level of porosity, it often fosters the growth of moss and lichen when placed in damp, shady locations. This can add to the charm of a sculpture, and some designers even deliberately cultivate this growth using recipes that call for ingredients like buttermilk. However charming, the garden owner does need to manage the situation or the moss and lichen may engulf the sculpture, covering important or delicate details. To remove moss and lichen, pressure washing may be required.

Sustainability

Quarrying raw materials creates noise and dust and has the same issues as stone quarrying. Considerable energy and water are also consumed to make both cement and concrete; and cement making results in high carbon dioxide emissions. Both raw and manufactured materials are heavy and require a lot of energy to ship. Broken concrete can be recycled, either by using it on site or transporting it to a recycling facility.

A rolling stone may gather no moss, but a concrete sculpture does—often quite elegantly.

Facing: Reclaimed concrete decorates the site where it came from, in the midst of busy New York City, eliminating the need to transport it to a recycling facility, or worse, the city dump.

Concrete checklist

Is this concrete product suited to this use?

Has the concrete been properly prepared for this use?

Evaluate any joinery. Will it hold up to this use?

How is the concrete finished? Will it hold up to the weather?

What standards or tests has this concrete met?

Are there warranties from the fabricator, and if so, what do they cover and for what period of time?

Synthetics

The garden furnishings industry has benefitted from the use of synthetics since the mid-twentieth century, a phenomenon that has only accelerated with increasing pressure to recycle nonbiodegradable synthetic materials. Today it is commonplace to see lightweight polyresin (polymer resin) planters, knockdown seating easily assembled from what were 4-by-8-foot sheets of recycled HDPE, overhead canopies constructed of 100% solution-dyed acrylic fabric, and perhaps most popular of all, woven synthetic seating that looks like painted wicker but functions far longer outdoors.

In the lifespan of materials, synthetics are still in diapers. But this baby has had a bigger impact on our lives than any other material. We use synthetic materials in every aspect of our lives right down to our toothbrushes and cell phones. As materials for the garden, we like synthetics because they do not degrade as natural materials do. Synthetics generally resist extreme outdoor temperatures, mold, and mildew, and are less vulnerable to damage from UV light. That's the upside.

The downside is that most synthetic materials are based on petroleum or coal. To get to these natural resources, companies must drill or dig down into the earth. The raw materials are trucked to refineries, where they are transformed into a range of petrochemical products, including ethane and propane. The ethane and propane are "cracked" inside intense heat furnaces and converted to ethylene and propylene. Inside another heat furnace (or reactor), a catalyst is mixed with the ethylene or propylene, causing it to become a powdery polymer that looks a little like laundry detergent. This fluff is fed into a continuous blender and combined with additives. The resulting pliable polymer is extruded, then melted, cooled, and chopped into small plastic pellets. The pellets are sold to manufacturers who use extrusion, injection molding, and other techniques to create plastic products, including innumerable objects for the garden.

Mylar strips flap and shimmer in the wind, creating a kinetic sculpture with engaging shadows. Mylar is polyethylene terephthalate (PET), also known as polyester film.

History of Synthetics

Historically, three primary synthetic materials have been used in garden furnishings: fiberglass, resins, and plastics. Each material has a unique beginning, but each evolved to become primarily a type of plastic or resin polymer combined with glass fibers.

Fiberglass originated with the ancient Phoenicians and Egyptians, who made coarse glass fibers for decoration. But it wasn't until the 1870s that American John Player developed a way to mass-produce glass strands with a steam-jet process to make "mineral wool" for insulation. Soon after, Herman Hammesfahr obtained a patent for a flame-resistant, durable type of fiberglass cloth that was partially woven of silk. Fiberglass as we know it today was discovered accidentally in 1932 when a Corning Glass scientist tried to weld two glass blocks together—glass fibers showered him as a jet of compressed air hit the molten glass.

Made of molded plastic, the Vegetal chair by Vitra is a new classic heirloom. It is made of 100% recycled materials and is 100% recyclable—a very sustainable notion.

By the mid-1930s Owens-Corning patented "fiberglas," and soon after, DuPont received a patent for polyester resin, which could be used with fiberglass to make a composite. By the 1940s Owens-Corning's research into weaving glass fibers resulted in a suitable material for reinforcing plastic laminate. Composite fiberglass and polyester resin became more common during World War II. Today, manufacturers provide an abundant variety of products with fiberglass composite, including outdoor furnishings.

Natural resins are sticky, flammable, water-insoluble organic substances that come from plants. They were once painted on Egyptian mummies and used to seal boats, and because they cure and get very hard over time, they have long been used for glue and varnish. While natural resins are still used, in contemporary times they have mostly inspired the creation of polymer resins made with epoxy, polyester, and poly-urethane—synthetic materials found in many products, including garden furnishings.

The first known synthetic plastic was discovered in the late nineteenth century when an American inventor found an inexpensive, synthesized plastic substitute for

Painted PVC pipe creates the foundation for classic daisy pinwheels in this outdoor phenomenon.

ivory based on the plant material cellulose. He mixed cellulose nitrate with camphor, which was accidentally exposed to a catalyst: sunlight. The result, celluloid, became an important material in products like eyeglasses and photographic film for the next few decades.

Two plastics used for most synthetic products are petroleum-based polypropylene (PP) and polyethylene (PE). With these discoveries in 1951, two young Phillips Petroleum research chemists began a revolutionary industry that now produces the vast majority of the world's plastic products.

Polyvinyl chloride (PVC) or vinyl, another petroleum-based plastic, was discovered accidentally in 1838 by French chemist and physicist Henri Victor Regnault and again in 1872 by German chemist Eugen Baumann. However, it wasn't until 1913 that Friedrich Heinrich August Klatte received the first patent for the material. During the 1920s an industrial scientist at B. F. Goodrich, Waldo Semon, produced PVC while creating a substitute for natural rubber. Semon imagined a use: water-resistant fabric coating. Demand for PVC grew rapidly during World War II, as it was used for wire insulation on military ships, and skyrocketed during the 1950s and 1960s.

Now PVC is the leading plastic in Europe and second to polyethylene in the United States. Rigid PVC is often used in garden furnishings. Unlike other plastics, PVC does not emit off-gases until its temperature reaches 212°F, after which it becomes a toxic hydrochloride gas. This is a potential problem but is unlikely to occur in a garden.

Resolving sustainability issues with these materials would present many clear benefits, and research continues, with some companies attempting to reinvent plastics using more ecologically responsible methods.

Types of Synthetics

Synthetic composites are popular substitutes for metal due to their lower cost, lighter weight, excellent strength, and durability—all desirable characteristics for outdoor furnishings. Fiberglass and polymer resins are usually joined together as composites, but plastics fabrication differs according to the type of plastic used. Fiberglass-reinforced plastic (FRP), glass-reinforced plastic (GRP), and glass-fiber-reinforced polymer (GFRP) are essentially the same thing: a mix of glass fibers and plastic polymers. The glass fibers give the plastic greater tensile strength. Glass-fiber-reinforced stone (GFRS) contains alkali-resistant glass fiber, crushed stone, and polymer resin. It is used in the architectural industry and makes elegant outdoor columns for structures like gazebos and pergolas.

Because it is easily manipulated to capture small details, polyresin is often used for cast sculptures and outdoor furniture. Stone-based alabastrite and polystone are especially popular forms, and both have significant weight and a stonelike feel. No

Fiberglass polymer resin
makes an excellent lightweight
material for containers on a
city terrace.

These comfortable, white Victoria Ghost chairs are made of a polyresin. With good care they will last a lifetime.

A cast polyresin bench in the potager provides a lovely spot to rest after weeding around the lettuce.

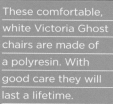

An adorable and well-made polyresin sculpture fits especially well into a traditionally styled garden.

Polyethylene terephthalate (PET)—recyclable

 High-density polyethylene (HDPE)—recyclable

 Polyvinyl chloride (PVC)—not recyclable

 Low-density polyethylene (LDPE)—recyclable

 Polypropylene (PP)—recyclable

 Polystyrene (Styrofoam)—not recyclable

 Everything else (such as polycarbonates, including highly toxic BPA)—not recyclable

heat is required in the manufacturing process, as they are cold-cast, and both require a weatherproof coating if painted.

Plastics

Plastics are also called polymers and resins, and you will often see "resin polymers" listed as a component of outdoor furniture. There are seven types of plastics, with numbers stamped on the bottom of products:

Plastics are either thermoplastic or thermoset. Thermoplastic polymers can be remelted and remolded, whereas thermoset plastics cannot typically be melted more than once.

Composites are aqueous materials that, like concrete, require a mold. Both open and closed molding are used in the manufacturing processes. In open molding, the mold is open and the material cures through exposure to ambient or warm air. A two-part mold is used in closed molding, which involves one of

The Racer Rocker is one of a number of laser-cut, recycled HDPE products.

several methods: compression, resin transfer molding, centrifugal casting, pultrusion, infusion molding, vacuum molding, or vacuum infusion molding. Composites convert to a solid due to thermosetting and cure exothermically. A catalyst is used, but excessive use of the catalyst will cause the product to fracture or become rubbery.

Composites can also be sculpted from a molded block or extruded into thin strips that mimic wicker. If woven on a lightweight frame, all-weather wicker furniture is lightweight and easy to move around a garden.

Thermoplastic and thermoset processing methods are used to create extrusion and calendaring items such as films, sheets, and pipes as well as injection-molded products like lawn chairs. Another method, rotational molding, is used to produce outdoor furniture.

This thought provoking garden, inviting the visitor to play, includes hawser balls woven of polyresin rope for marine durability.

Some garden furnishings come as knockdown (KD) components that have to be assembled. Fasteners generally accompany them. Because the automobile industry uses and assembles synthetics, many fasteners for plastics on the market are able to withstand the rigors of an automobile. Chances are they will also withstand your client's two-year-old! Some adhesives are also made especially for plastics.

Finishes

Some synthetics are capable of having finishes applied to them, but the synthetic must be mixed specifically to allow the application. Painting synthetics is best left to the experts. Composites are often painted, but for outdoor use the coating must be waterproof. If a synthetic is not painted, the colorant was included in the liquid mix. Textures are usually made as part of the molding process.

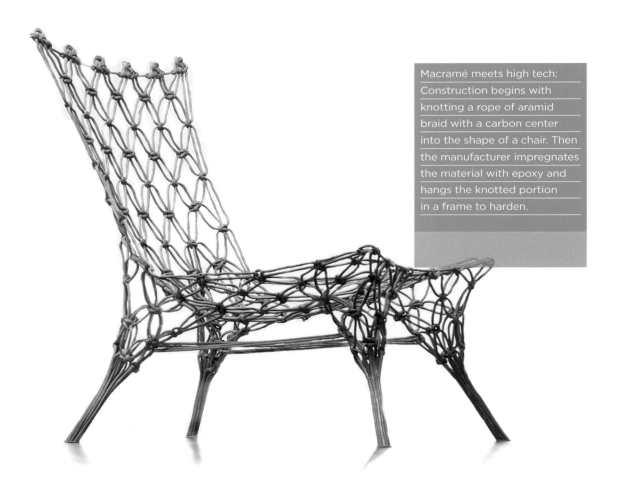

Macramé meets high tech: Construction begins with knotting a rope of aramid braid with a carbon center into the shape of a chair. Then the manufacturer impregnates the material with epoxy and hangs the knotted portion in a frame to harden.

Standards

Tests for synthetics are too numerous to mention, but suffice it to say that they cover physical properties of the materials, characterization, process chemistry, composites, additives, impact modifiers, and alloys and blends.

Care and Maintenance

The most important things you can do for synthetic products are to follow the manufacturer's instructions and keep them clean. Although all-weather wicker furniture is presumably safe in all weather, many manufacturers recommend covering it or bringing it in during extended periods of inclement weather. Although many synthetics are more UV resistant than natural materials, they are not completely invulnerable and may turn yellow when exposed. Consider selecting colors that disguise or moderate

The Wow sofa lounge, woven of polyresin, is made for relaxation and low maintenance.

Designer Claude Cormier's "Blue Tree," a diseased tree covered with recycled, plastic blue Christmas balls, became a temporary landmark at the center of a series of gardens. Before the tree was removed, visitors could see it from nearly anywhere on site.

this potential issue. Many types of plastics, such as phenolics, polyamides, some polyolefins, and styrenes, also become brittle over time. Vinyls are particularly sensitive to damage from extended sunlight exposure. Always ask if this may be an issue with any piece you purchase, because chemical formulas are ever advancing.

Sustainability

Synthetics are currently not biodegradable and literally could last forever (even if they eventually become minuscule shards). Before purchasing a product, verify that it can be reused, repurposed, or otherwise recycled. Also ask for the post-consumer waste content of the product.

Museums have found it a challenge to preserve plastics in enclosed situations. UV light, humidity, oxygen, heat, bacteria, and stress all contribute to plastic degradation. Different plastic materials can contaminate each other, too. For example, a plasticizer can migrate when a PVC object touches a polystyrene object. Researchers are studying chemical and physical polymer degradation. If these kinds of reactions aren't stopped, damage can spread to other nearby objects. Caution on the side of wrapping plastic items before you store them if you don't leave them outdoors.

The silver lining to nonbiodegradability is that the longevity of synthetic products may help us better manage our resources. If we maintain and keep synthetic products as long as they are useable, we may not need to deplete other natural resources due to planned obsolescence or frequent replacement, especially if we sell or donate unwanted products rather than throwing them away.

The resources that currently allow us to make plastics are nonrenewable. Research and development departments in many companies are looking toward alternatives to oil. Most, if not all, countries have some amount of regulatory governance over the environmental issues concerning drilling or mining for, transporting, and refining petroleum, coal, and oil shale.

Two organizations, the Plastics Institute of America and the SPE Environmental Division, are involved with assisting and some degree of monitoring in the plastics industry.

Synthetics checklist

Is this synthetic material suited to this use?

Evaluate any joinery. Will it hold up to this use?

How is the synthetic material finished? Will it hold up to the weather?

Will weatherizing add or detract from the product's value?

What standards or tests has this synthetic material met?

What maintenance will be required to keep this synthetic object in like-new condition?

Are there warranties from the manufacturer or retailer, and if so, what do they cover and for what period of time?

What will happen to this product at the end of its useful life? Can the synthetic material be reused, repurposed, or recycled?

TO THE TRADE

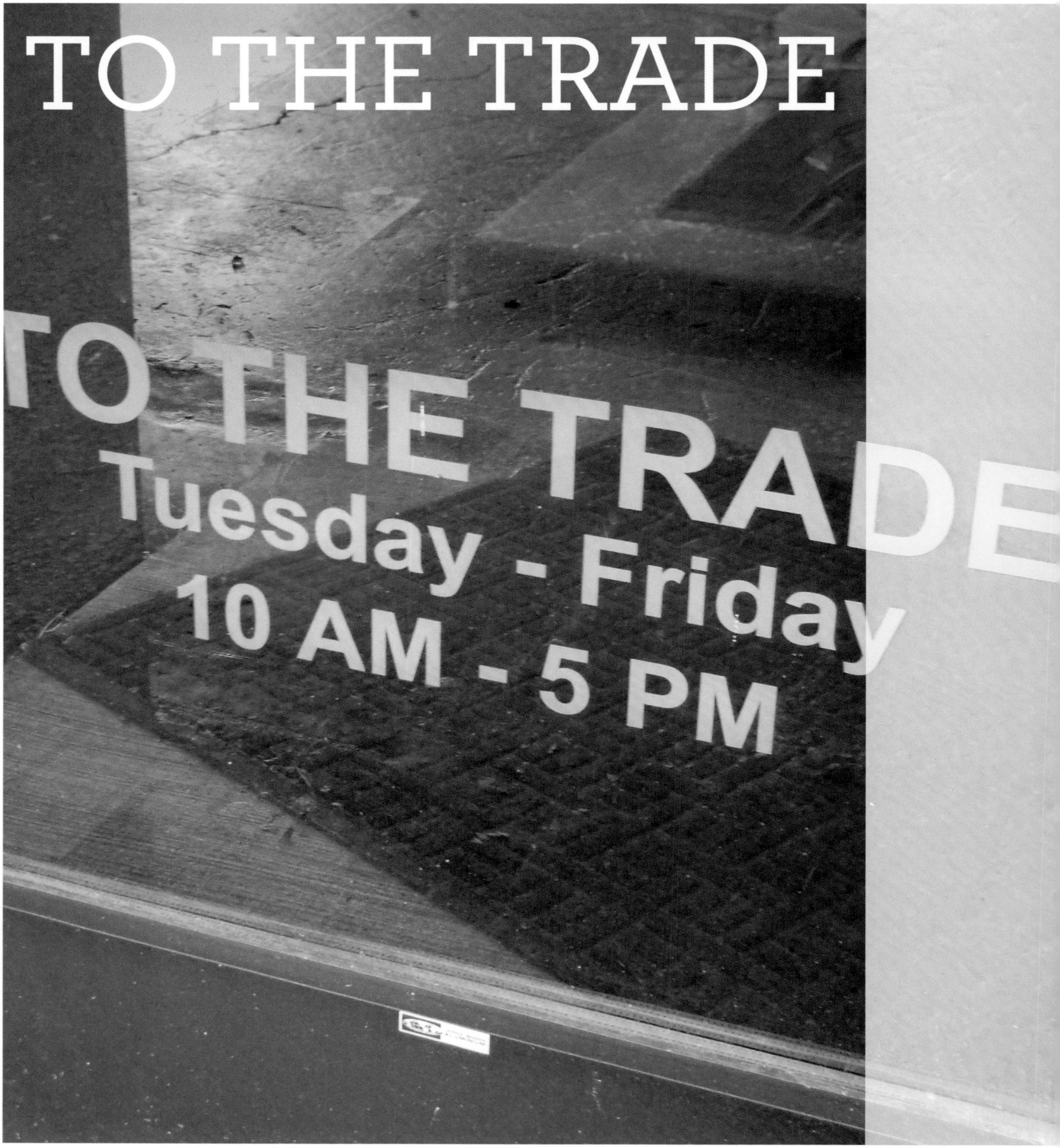

Once you have decided what kinds of furnishings the garden needs and have secured your client's approval, you enter a new phase of the process: working with artisans, fabricators, manufacturers' representatives, showroom staff, and other kinds of suppliers. These people are your resources and will contribute heavily to your success. It is vitally important to nurture these relationships, because you need these people (and they need you!). It is equally essential that you understand the trade itself, including the lingo, and feel comfortable working with it. In the end, you need to know what it means when you see a sign that reads "to the trade."

When you see "to the trade," be prepared to check in with someone as you enter the showroom. Hand them a business card so that they understand you are part of the trade.

Trade Connections

It takes considerable effort to make strong connections with tradespeople and find good resources, especially since some services and products are simply higher quality than others. An extensive list of connections and resources may take years to accumulate. If you are new to the trade, get to know some experienced designers. They will likely share a resource when you have a specific need.

Manufacturers' Representatives

Manufacturers' representatives, or reps, are among the most important groups of tradespeople with whom you will form a relationship. Reps have or can help you find the information you need about a specific product. How do you find them?

Sometimes they find you. However, much of the time the process begins when you find a product in a magazine, walk by it on the street, or see it displayed in a store or showroom. You may tip the product over to read the manufacturer's name on the underside. If you find the name but no one is available to answer your questions, try the manufacturer's website. In addition to providing product information, the website will probably point you in the direction of the representative closest to you. If not, call or email the manufacturer to find this information.

The rep will help you with product literature, material samples, photos, technical information, manufacturing schedules, lead times, pricing, and more. Get to know the reps for your favorite products really well, because you will be talking with them more than you might think. They might ask how often they may contact you to show you their latest products. Sometimes an email notice is sufficient; other times it is more helpful to meet with a rep in person to see, touch, and otherwise inspect a product. Trust me: you will want to see outdoor fabrics in person!

Dealerships and Showrooms

You may visit dealerships (dealers) or showrooms, which differ slightly. A dealership carries products from many manufacturers. Ask them for a copy of their line list, which will tell you all the manufacturers' lines they carry. Some of these lines may be "closed," and many will be "open." A closed line is one that the dealership has exclusive rights to carry in their area. For example, several dealers may serve the same manufacturer in a large city such as New York, but there may be only one dealer in a smaller city such as Albuquerque, New Mexico. With an open line, any dealer can carry the product as long as the manufacturer approves. Herman Miller is one company that restricts its number of dealerships. However, in recent years they have also made their products more available through retail stores.

Dealer reps or salespeople can be very helpful. They can often arrange for you to test-drive a chair, for example, when this isn't possible anywhere else. They also

This wholesale and retail showroom of home and garden decor begins outside its front door, with an expanse of delightful products continuing inside.

gather information for you from the manufacturer, and you can work with them to purchase products for you and your clients.

Dealerships nearly always sell to designers at a discount, so you can resell the product to your client at a profit. Much depends on how your business is set up, however. Many designers charge for their professional consulting service and time expended to arrange the purchase and then pass along the dealer's cost to their clients with a minimal markup. Some designers work with manufacturers' representatives directly to purchase products, including shipping and delivery. Others prefer not to expend the chargeable time to expedite product purchases and deliveries, which is why dealerships are so useful. Designers that do handle the entire purchase usually sell products at the manufacturers' suggested retail price (MSRP) to recoup the cost of the time spent arranging for purchase and delivery, rather than charging the client their hourly rate.

Showrooms can provide products to the trade (wholesale), dealerships, or the general public (retail). Wholesale showrooms may cluster in a certain area of town or sometimes in a single building (for example, the Merchandise Mart in Chicago, Pacific Design Center in Los Angeles, and New York Design Center in New York). Colocated

A fabric showroom provides a wealth of possibilities.

To The Trade

showrooms make it convenient for designers to check out many products in a short period of time. Wholesale-only showrooms always ask you to check in at a desk located near the entry. Showrooms allow you to bring clients along so that you can look at products together. For this reason showrooms do not post net price (discounted price) on their products, or do it in such a way that it is coded for you (in which case they explain how to interpret the code). If they display pricing it is usually the MSRP or "list" pricing. Some wholesale showrooms are devoted to only one manufacturer, while others display many products and carry multiple lines. Wholesale showroom staff can often arrange a purchase for you, too. Before you move forward with this, though, ask who will be arranging freight, delivery, and so forth. A retail showroom is open to the public, so their posted pricing is always the retail price. Since many retail stores also cater to the trade, ask the salesperson if they offer designer discounts. The showroom (or store) might even have a program you can register for to receive a card identifying you as a designer. You can show this card to receive a discount.

Fabric showrooms are full of possibilities. Take your time to go through what they offer, and write down several options for consideration—they usually offer a pad and pencil for this purpose. Show your list to the sales rep and request samples.

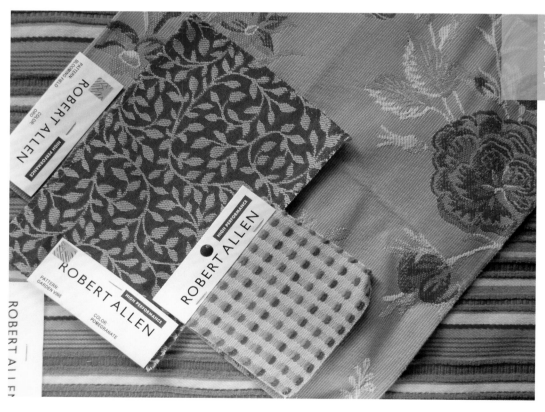

Some showrooms display different-sized fabric samples to suit the pattern or repeat.

Samples come in multiple sizes, with the two most common being card (usually about 3 by 3 inches) and memo (approximately 12 by 12 inches). If you are interested in a large pattern, you may need to ask for a larger sample. Alternatively, some fabric vendors staple cards to the samples that show the full pattern at a small scale. Always read the labels before you decide whether the fabric will work in your situation. Don't waste time and resources collecting samples that you ultimately cannot use.

Custom Fabricators

Fabricators can be custom furniture workshops, fabric workrooms, or artisans that specialize in a particular material. Designers love to work with custom fabricators because it provides the opportunity to deliver their client a unique and exceptional piece specific to their personality and intended use. Designers' ideas are just pie in the sky

A typical workroom houses busy sewing machines, many fabrics, colorful spools of thread, cushions, cutting tables, and more.

To The Trade

unless they can actually be fabricated and installed at a reasonable cost. Discussing your idea with a custom workshop, for example, and getting their advice as to whether the idea is possible or practical, can save you from spending hours developing a fruitless concept. And you may find a fabricator who can take your flimsiest ideas and turn it into something spectacular. Not all fabricators have a designer's eye, however, so be confident of their skills before they spent hours sketching ideas that you think are dreadful. Fabricators usually have a portfolio of work, some of which they have designed themselves. Reviewing it will help you discover where their talents lie, whether it is developing their own ideas, implementing other people's ideas, or both.

Fabric workrooms provide magical custom sewing or upholstery services. They can make a new outdoor umbrella cover in a custom color, cushions for the custom wood seating you designed, or draperies to create a private garden space. Talk to the workroom manager to learn what services they offer. If you don't see something you are interested in having them make, tell them about your project and ask whether it is within their capabilities. If you are replacing something that already exists, make sure to save the existing fabric piece, which will be useful for creating the new pattern.

This custom garden pillow is comprised of outdoor fabric and an outdoor cushion form that drains quickly. The cushion can be completely dry within an hour after a heavy shower.

If you are considering having cushions made, you can use standard sizes and thicknesses or have the workroom use custom sizes. Using standard sizes will save your client money. For custom sizes, give the workroom the approximate measurements in order to receive preliminary costs. Always specify that cushions will be for outdoor use! Outdoor cushions are made to drain quickly and avoid moisture buildup.

Prior to fabrication, have the workroom measure any custom piece to ensure the fabrication will fit. It is best to have them measure and take responsibility for all dimensions. If the size is off and you supplied the measurements, guess who will pay for corrections?

Other Resources

Galleries are great places to find quality garden art or decor. (Yes, there is a difference between art and decor, though it often lies in the eye of the beholder.) Garden shows most often offer decor, though you may occasionally find art as well. Sometimes garden shows also feature artists who craft furnishings entirely from recycled materials.

Found at a glass gallery, this table with a kiln-formed glass top and metal base offers possibilities for use outdoors.

In fact I first encountered one of my favorite sustainability-conscious resources, Hidden Springs Designs, at a garden show.

Sometimes Internet research yields names of possible contacts. Quality design magazines such as *Interior Design* also publish information about various resources and products, as do their websites.

Talking to other designers (or even nondesigner friends) is absolutely one of the best ways to find resources. They will often have already worked with a person or company that you haven't, and you will get the inside scoop about the fabricator's strengths and weaknesses.

Last but not least are serendipitous contacts. Once, for example, as I was visiting a designer in her store, one of her suppliers happened to walk in the door. When I saw his product, I asked for his card and gave him mine. Now I recommend his products, but through my friend's store.

Presenting to Clients

Once you have spoken with your client about their garden, you will probably begin by researching appropriate furnishings. Work with your landscape plan, determining

This beautiful table, found at a garden show, contains recycled material and was sustainably produced.

locations and sizes of seating, tables, and other furnishings, as well as other important design criteria, to make preliminary decisions about what furnishings could be included. Use manufacturers' representatives, showrooms, workrooms, or online sources to decide which furnishings are appropriate for your client's garden, personality, intended use, and budget.

Collect information on all garden furnishings being considered, and share it with your client when you discuss the overall garden design. This will prevent

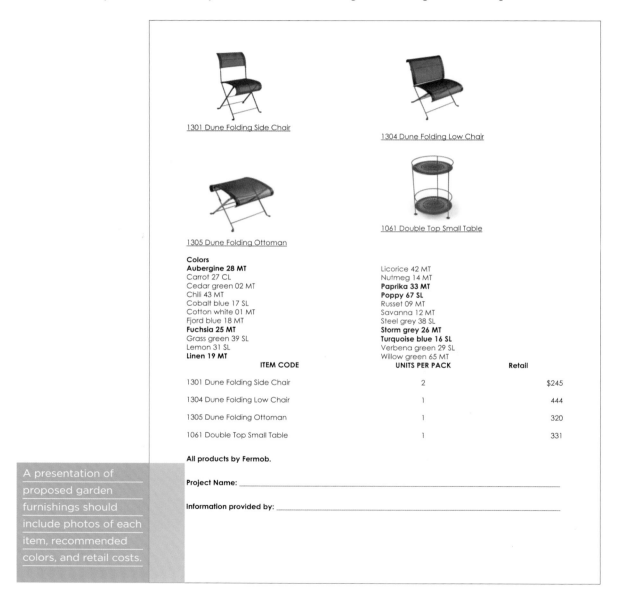

1301 Dune Folding Side Chair

1304 Dune Folding Low Chair

1305 Dune Folding Ottoman

1061 Double Top Small Table

Colors
Aubergine 28 MT
Carrot 27 CL
Cedar green 02 MT
Chili 43 MT
Cobalt blue 17 SL
Cotton white 01 MT
Fjord blue 18 MT
Fuchsia 25 MT
Grass green 39 SL
Lemon 31 SL
Linen 19 MT

Licorice 42 MT
Nutmeg 14 MT
Paprika 33 MT
Poppy 67 SL
Russet 09 MT
Savanna 12 MT
Steel grey 38 SL
Storm grey 26 MT
Turquoise blue 16 SL
Verbena green 29 SL
Willow green 65 MT

ITEM CODE	UNITS PER PACK	Retail
1301 Dune Folding Side Chair	2	$245
1304 Dune Folding Low Chair	1	444
1305 Dune Folding Ottoman	1	320
1061 Double Top Small Table	1	331

All products by Fermob.

Project Name: _____

Information provided by: _____

A presentation of proposed garden furnishings should include photos of each item, recommended colors, and retail costs.

furnishings from becoming the forgotten stepchild (or last-minute addition) and ensure they remain an integral part of the whole. In your presentation, include product photos, recommended colors, and estimated costs. Try to also include a chain-set (chain of small samples) of materials. (If the manufacturer does not provide designers with chain-sets, you will have to look at the colors online, which can be misleading, or visit a store that carries the products and has a chain-set.) Bring proposed products to your client's site to give them a better understanding of how the colors and patterns will appear in daylight. Explain whether the light in the finished garden will be direct or shaded and whether there will be outdoor night lighting.

You may wish to maintain a convenient library of sample materials. If so, be prepared to dedicate a fair amount of space to them. Companies sample their products in many different ways, and samples are not standardized, so housing them is often

Showrooms make samples available to help designers select materials and colors. You may be able to borrow samples to show your client or bring your client to the showroom.

not very space efficient. Alternatively, keep a few of your favorite samples and borrow others only when you need them.

Inform your client about the durability of each furnishing, its life expectancy compared with its cost, and whether it will continue to look good for its entire life. Discuss what the warranties cover, such as length of time and coverage during transit and product assembly on site.

Tell your client whether the proposed items are in stock or how long the lead time might be to receive all of them. Some items might be in stock and deliverable within two weeks, whereas custom orders may take twelve weeks or longer to manufacture and deliver. Always ask the manufacturer's rep or dealer salesperson to give you this information ahead of time, because the lead time can be a deal breaker. Also ask them to give you an idea of the length of time the shipping could take and estimated shipping costs. Verify whether you can purchase items in advance (to secure them and their costs) but have the sales outlet store the item at no extra cost until delivery. Note that delivery time is affected when manufacturers close their factory for a week or more, as many of them do once or twice per year. Weather can also affect delivery time.

To illustrate your design, you may show your client drawings, photos, or samples for custom items, along with cost estimates from your resources. You may, as designers often do, finalize orders with the manufacturer's rep, showroom, or workshop on behalf of the client. Sometimes the furnishing will be a standard (noncustom) item, for which you will show the client a sample with the color you have in mind. At other times it will be more complicated, and the fabricator may need to prepare (usually at a charge) shop drawings in response to your drawings, photos, or samples. These detailed drawings assure the client precisely how the item will be made.

At the end of the design process, your client will need to know how to maintain their new furnishings. Consider creating a little manual that includes all of the manufacturer product literature and recommendations. You can also include basic information for custom items and discuss the materials used. Reflect on the elements to which each item will be exposed, including wear and tear. Perhaps you can accumulate basic information in an ongoing file from which you can pull the appropriate information for each client.

Many clients will need tips on how to care for outdoor cushions. Oils from new wood can stain cushions, so advise clients to hose down new furniture (particularly if it is teak) before putting down cushions. Make sure they avoid placing cushions beneath messy trees as well, which can lead to stained fabric. Only thoroughly dry cushions should be stored over winter, and they should be placed in a location with good air circulation to avoid mold or mildew. Consider constructing a throw or cover out of the cushion material and having your client use it to cover up cushions in the rain.

This custom gate serves as the inspiration for a light fixture.

The finished light fixture reflects the original gate design and input from the garden's designer.

In a collaborative effort, the designer dictates and then the fabricator translates the gate into a light fixture as a sketch.

CRAFTSMAN MODERN w/

PENDANT

30"

MORE LESS SYM

10"

Product Specifications

Once your client has made their decisions, communicate with the purchasing agent who will order the items that are not custom fabricated. Such product specifications (specs) can be very simple or very complex, such as those used by architects, engineers, landscape architects, and interior designers who often use Construction Specifications Institute (CSI) formats. CSI formats were developed to cover seemingly every possible aspect of obtaining and installing a product. They are written to protect both client and designer from liability and faulty goods or poor installations. Generic CSI formats are updated periodically by CSI and are edited, as needed, by the designer for each specific project. A master set of CSI formats is expensive and complicated to use. Unless you or your client has the money to use them, I suggest keeping it simple. First, ask yourself how detailed your specification needs to be. What is your potential liability should there be an oversight on your part or if the purchasing company creates a problem? You may find it is useful to use portions of CSI format as a guide or checklist of items to be adapted as a simpler specification.

CSI format is divided into forty divisions (concrete, finishes, furnishings, and so on), with each division divided into sections (such as cast-in-place concrete, paint finishes, and chair furnishings). Each section is further divided into part 1, general; part 2, products; and part 3, execution. Part 1 describes procedural, administrative, and temporary requirements. Part 2 describes the materials, products, fabrications, equipment, assemblies, and more, including the level of quality you required (for example, certification or testing standards). Part 3 describes how the products will be installed or applied. This last part also covers site preparation, post-installation cleanup, and the care, maintenance, and protection of products after installation (but prior to completion) of the project.

If you give a purchasing agent the general parameters for your project, a detailed list of the products, and those manufacturing or installation requirements that are important, you will have a decent specification. Here's an example of the information you might include in part 1: submittals of samples for approval prior to purchase; mockups; shop drawings (usually for semi-custom items); instructions to the manufacturer; delivery, storage, and handling; packaging options; what the site conditions should be prior to the arrival of your product or the alternative if the site is not ready for delivery; warranty requirements; and requested maintenance information for the owner. In part 2 you might include manufacturers' products, fabrication tolerances, and finishes. Part 3 may include directions for installers, preparation for installation, special techniques, requests for verification of conditions at the site before installation, information about what to do if damages occur, and what sorts of adjustments or cleaning might be required during and after installation. You might establish a simple boilerplate that you adjust for each project as needed. The spec should say "or

268

approved substitution" (with prior written approval), not "or equal," because "or equal" clauses do not usually state the basis for what is considered equal. (Courts hate "or equal" clauses, but lawyers love them.)

A minimal furniture specification should call out the quantity of each item (unless you have the quantity shown on the plans and it can be counted by the purchasing agent, which is preferable in case there is a counting error), the model number, a description of each item, the finish for each item, optional components for each item, and, if applicable, the fabric that covers any cushions that accompany an item. If you choose to have the purchasing agent count items on a plan, make sure each item has a code that relates to the description in the specification.

You may have a couple of options for fabric. The manufacturer may have standard fabrics to choose from, or you may choose to do a COM (customer's own material) or COL (customer's own leather), which identifies custom fabric or leather for a product. If you are using the manufacturer's standard, you need only stipulate the information that the manufacturer provides to identify the fabric, but for both standard and COM fabrics it is important to specify whether the fabric will be railroaded, whether you want a "cutting for approval" (meaning that before the manufacturer cuts fabric for the entire piece, you are sent a cutting sample to assure they have the correct fabric and color), and whether you want the fabric from one dye lot (to avoid any potential mismatch) if there is enough fabric to warrant that request. For a COM or COL, state the fabric pattern and its number, the colorway name or number, the width of the fabric, the fabric content (fibers), any repeat if it applies, special finishes or tests that may be included by the manufacturer, and any other specific information that needs to be conveyed to the manufacturer, such as a "sidemark" (additional information that may identify your project, for example). If the fabric is going to a fabric workroom, specify that all cushion or pillow forms be made for outdoor use and that all items be protected from damage during shipping.

Purchasing

Once you have completed your specification, review everything with your client and then with the purchasing agent to assure they understand what you want. It is much easier to make corrections at this point than after the products are delivered or in process of fabrication. Hand the purchasing agent a check from your client for the amount required to initiate the purchase (usually the full amount). (Before you get the check from your client, don't forget to verify that you still receive a designer discount.) It typically takes purchasing agents a couple of days to enter orders into their system and submit them to the manufacturers. They will receive a confirmation of order from each manufacturer, which should include delivery schedules. They should copy you so that you can review it against your specification to assure its accuracy. Confirm with the purchasing agent that all is well. If it isn't, raise red flags and immediately tell them what is wrong. You do not want the responsibility of letting an issue go unresolved. You may hear once again from the purchasing agent when the item actually ships, so that you can anticipate delivery.

Your purchasing agent, fabricator, or workroom may have their own contract or purchase order forms. If so, read carefully (especially if there is a back side with clauses that could override your prepared specifications). You might be required to modify their agreement to avoid any conflict. The specifications should be part of the contract.

Freight, Delivery, and Installation

Products ship from an FOB (freight on board) point, meaning the location from which the shipping costs were calculated. When the products arrive, your purchasing agent should inspect them to assure that everything has arrived safely and without damage. If you are having fabric shipped directly to you for use by a fabric workroom, open the roll of fabric and inspect it for flaws. If there are flaws, notify the fabric vendor right away and follow their instructions to remedy the situation. If the fabric is being shipped to others first (for example, a finisher or fabric workroom), require that they inspect the fabric prior to finishing or cutting. Make sure it is in writing so that your client will have recourse if you receive a flawed product.

If you are handling all or part of the purchasing yourself, figure out which shipping companies you like to work with, since the companies you place your orders with will ask for this information. Alternatively you can ask the manufacturer to suggest their own preferred shipping companies.

You must decide whether deliveries will come to your office, your warehouse, your garage, or the client's site. If products are not shipped directly to the client, you need to transship to your client's site. If items you are purchasing are local, you also need to identify a delivery company. If the products go directly to your client, you need to determine who will take responsibility for unpacking. Explain to your client that if they accept this responsibility, there could be a problem if they uncover damages after the company has left the products with them and they have signed for the delivery. If possible, inspect items before the shipping or delivery people leave. Also consider at what times during the shipping and delivery process the products are insured. If they are not insured and damage occurs, what are your alternatives? Make sure no one removes tags from any products until the client has accepted and approved them.

You have probably heard stories of shipping nightmares. They do happen. Remind your client that problems sometimes occur during shipping, as this will help them feel a little less disappointed if something does go wrong.

Let's assume that everything finally arrives safely at the client's site. There may be some unwrapping to do. Were you able to arrange for the manufacturer to take back all wrapping materials if they are not recyclable? If so, the materials will return to the manufacturer for them to process, or the purchasing company may take responsibility for materials. If the materials are recyclable, will the delivery company take care of this, or will it be up to you or your client? If items are blanket-wrapped, the shipping company simply keeps the blankets and reuses them.

As the designer, you should assist in final placement of each product. If the product is a piece of art or an overhead shade structure that will require more than setting it in place, make sure the installation goes according to your specifications.

Garden Furnishings Resources

Although this directory focuses primarily on wholesalers, I also list some companies that are both wholesale and retail and some that are solely retail. Some of these businesses sell products online as well as in bricks-and-mortar stores.

I have listed preeminent, to-the-trade design centers within, or near, the United States. Some have large shows each year to show off new products and feature their vendors. The Merchandise Mart in Chicago, for example, holds an annual exposition of furnishings known as NeoCon. High Point Market in North Carolina is also famous for its large show, and the Milan Furniture Fair *(Salone Internazionale del Mobile di Milano)* may be the grandest show in the world. These exhibitions are wonderful opportunities to learn about cutting-edge products.

Flea markets, antique stores, and stores that salvage products from around the globe are great places to shop. Here you will often find something irreproducible, a furnishing that can lend something unique to a garden.

Although landscape trade shows and garden centers offer products that will be of interest to landscape designers, their focus is on plants and their care rather than garden furnishings. Expect to find planters, containers, umbrellas, garden lighting, and decor but not the expanse of possibilities that you'll find through the resources listed here.

Magazines such as *Interior Design* offer listings and articles featuring garden furnishings, and notable online resources can be found at todl.com, dezeen.com, modenus.com, and leafmag.com.

Inevitably you will find resources beyond those provided here, but I hope this list will at least provide a useful starting place.

Enjoy the hunt!

Product legend

code	product type	code	product type
	outdoor furniture		garden decor and art
	portable fire pits, fireplaces, and heaters		cabanas, arbors, trellises, pergolas, gazebos, screens
	outdoor lighting		outdoor textiles, umbrellas and fabric shading, rugs, hammocks
	containers and planters		

Resource Directory

Note the icon(s) listed with each resource.
They will tell you the range of products that each resource carries. Check
with each company to determine their wholesale or retail status.

Agua Luxury Performance Fabrics
aguafabrics.com

aK47
aK47space.com

Alexander Rose
alexander-rose.co.uk

Allegro Classics
allegroclassics.com

American Trading Company
amtradeco.com

Amerlux Exterior
amerluxexterior.com

Anacara Company
anacaracompany.com

Andrew Carson
windsculpture.com

Anthropologie
anthropologie.com

Arbors Direct
arborsdirect.com

Archie Held
archieheld.com

Architex
architex-ljh.com

Arms and Barnes Design
armsandbarnes.com

Arthur Lauer
arthurlauer.com

Auroralight
auroralight.com

Aw Pottery
awpottery.com

Axis of Hope Prayer Wheels
axisofhope.net

Backyard America
backyardamerica.com

Barlow Tyrie
teak.com

Bastille Metal Works
bastillemetalworks.com

Batyline
batyline.com

B. Berger
bberger.com

B&B Italia
bb-sf.com, bebitalia.it

Beachside Lighting
beachsidelighting.com

Bend Seating
bendseating.com

Bevara Design House
bevaradesign.com

B-K Lighting
bklighting.com

B-Line
b-line.it

BrattleWorks
brattleworks.com

Brentano Fabrics
brentanofabrics.com

Brown Jordon
brownjordan.com

Bulbeck Foundry
bulbeckfoundry.co.uk

Caluco
caluco.com

Campania International
campaniainternational.com

Capital Garden Products
capital-garden.com

Cappellini
cappellini.it,
marcelwanders.com

Carved Stone by Sam Bates
carvedstonebysambates.com

CasaBubble
casabubble.com

Cassona Living
cassona.net

Cast Lighting
cast-lighting.com

Cebu Importers
cebuimporters.com

Champa Ceramics
champaceramics.com

Charleston Gardens
charlestongardens.com

Charlie's Antiques
charliesantiques-va.com

275

CL Sterling
clsterling.com

Coalesse
coalesse.com

Codina Ceramics
lesliecodina.com

Cooke Furniture
cookefurniture.com

Coolaroo
coolaroousa.com

Costantini Design
costantinidesign.com

Country Gear Ltd.
countrygearltd.com

Cowtan and Tout
cowtan.com

Craft Fabricators
craftfabricators.com

Crate and Barrel
crateandbarrel.com

Crescent Garden
crescentgarden.com

Cumulus Studios
cumulus-studios.com

Curran Online
curranonline.com

Dabmar Lighting
dabmar.com

Dedon
dedon.us

Design Kollection
designkollection.com

Design Within Reach
dwr.com

DesignTex
dtex.com

Donghia
donghia.com

Dura Art Stone
duraartstone.com

Duralee
duralee.com

Earthcore
earthcore.co

EGO Paris
egoparis.com

Elcast Lighting
elcastltg.com

Elegant Earth
elegantearth.com

Elementa Designs
elementadesigns.com

Emeco
emeco.net

Emu
emuamericas.com

Enessentia
enessentia.com

Experienced Materials
experiencedmaterials.com

Fatboy
fatboyusa.com

Faux Iron Solutions
fauxiron.com

Fermob
fermobusa.com

Fifth Room
fifthroom.com

Flora Grubb
floragrubb.com

Frances Palmer Pottery
francespalmerpottery.com

Front Gate
frontgate.com

F. Schumacher
fschumacher.com

FX Luminaire
fxl.com

Gaia Ferro Forgiato
gaiaferroforgiato.it

Gainey Ceramics
gaineyceramics.com

Gandia Blasco
gandiablasco.com

Garden Artisans
gardenartisans.com

Garden Elements
gardenelements.net

Garden Traditions
gardentraditions.us

Gary Lee Price
garyleeprice.com

GeoBella Outdoor Fabric
plumridge.com

Giardini Veneti
giardiniveneti.it

Giati
giati.com

277

Glant Textiles
glant.com

Gloster
gloster.com

Greenbo
greenbo.co

Greenform
green-form.com

Greenscreen
greenscreen.com

Gumps
gumps.com

Haddonstone
haddonstone.com

Hanamint
hanamint.com

Hanging Gardens
randyraburndesign.com

Hart Concrete Design
hartconcretedesign.com

Henry Hall Designs
henryhalldesigns.com

Hinkley Lighting
hinkleylighting.com

Hive
hivemodern.com

Holly Hunt
hollyhunt.com

Homecrest Outdoor Living
homecrest.com

Hooks and Lattice
hooksandlattice.com

IKEA
ikea.com

Inmod
inmod.com

Innermost
innermost.net

International Art Properties
iapsf.com

Italian Terrace
italianterrace.co.uk

James Vilona
jamesvilona.com

Jane Hamley Wells
janehamleywells.com

Janus et Cie
janusetcie.com

Jay Scotts
jayscotts.com

J. Ennis Fabrics
jennisfabrics.com

Jensen Leisure Furniture
jensenleisurefurniture.com

Joan Gaspar
joangaspar.com

The Joinery
thejoinery.com

J. T. Cooper Studio
jtcooperstudio.com

Kannoa
kannoa.com

Kartell
kartell.com/louis_ghost.htm

Katy McFadden
katymcfadden.com

Kenneth Cobonpue
kennethcobonpue.com

Kenneth Lynch and Sons
klynchandsons.com

Kettal
kettal.es

Kettler
kettlerusa.com

Kichler
kichler.com

Kindle Living
kindleliving.com

Kingsley Bate
kingsleybate.com

Knoll Studio
knollstudio.com

Knoll Textiles
knolltextiles.com

Kornegay Design
kornegaydesign.com

Kova Textiles
kovatextiles.com

Koverton
koverton.com

Kravet
kravet.com

Kristalia
kristalia.it

la-Fête
lafetedesign.com

Landscape Forms
landscapeforms.com

LatticeStix
latticestix.com

Lebatex
lebatexinc.com

LED Company
LEDcohome.com

Les Jardins
teak-furniture.com

Ligne Roset
ligne-roset-usa.com

Linda Allen Designs
lindaallendesigns.com

Link Design Solutions
linkdesignsolutions.com

Liora Manné
lioramanne.com

Lithonia
lithonia.com

Little and Lewis
littleandlewis.com

Lloyd Flanders
lloydflanders.com

Loll Designs
lolldesigns.com

Longshadow Planters
longshadow.com

Louis Poulsen
louispoulsen.com

Lumière
lumiere.com

Made on the Farm
madeonthefarm.com

Madison Fielding
madisonfielding.com

Mad Mats
madmats.com

Magnolia Casual
magnoliacasual.com

Maharam
maharam.com

Maine Millstones
mainemillstones.com

Mamagreen
mamagreen.be

Manuel Canovas
manuelcanovas.com
cowtan.com

Manutti
manutti.com

Mariaflora
mariaflora.com

Mark and Efe
markandefe.com

Mary Martha Collins
marymarthacollins.com

Mason Parker
masonscreations.com

Meadow Decor
meadowdecor.com

Mind of Couture
mindofcouture.com

Mobilegro
mobilegro.com

Mode
mode.co.uk/
category-firepits.html

Modfire
modfire.com

Mohican Wind Harps
mohicanwindharps.com

Munder-Skiles
munder-skiles.com

NatureScape Lighting
naturescapelighting.com

Neil Wilkin
neilwilkin.com

New England Arbors
newenglandarbors.com

Nico Yektai
nicoyektai.com

Night Orbs
nightorbs.com

Nightscaping
nightscaping.com

**Nikita Indoor Outdoor
Convertibles**
justleanback.com

Nomi Fabrics
nomiinc.com

North Cape International
northcapeinternational.com

Not Neutral
notneutral.com

OlaVoyna
olavoyna.com

Ore
orecontainers.com

Osborne and Little
osborneandlittle.com

OW Lee
owlee.com

Oxford Garden
oxfordgarden.com

Paloform
paloform.com

Paola Lenti
paolalenti.it

Parasoleil
parasoleil.com

Patio Renaissance
patiorenaissance.com

Patrick Gracewood
gracewoodstudio.com

Pennoyer Newman
pennoyernewman.com

Perennials
perennialsfabrics.com

Perry Design
perry-design.com

Pfeifer Studio
pfeiferstudio.com

Pindler and Pindler
pindler.com

Plain Air
plainair.com

Planters Unlimited
plantersunlimited.com

Planterworx
planterworx.com

Poggi Ugo
poggiugo.it

Pollack
pollackassociates.com

Pooz Design
poozdesign.com

Pottery Barn
potterybarn.com

Proteak
proteak.com

Purcell Living
purcellliving.com

Rausch Classics
rausch-classics.de

REDI
redi.pt

Resol Group
resol.es

Restoration Hardware
restorationhardware.com

Richard Schultz
richardschultz.com

RM COCO
rmcoco.com

Robert Allen
robertallendesign.com

Robin Wade Furniture
robinwadefurniture.com

Roger Thomas Glass
rogerthomasglass.com

Romancing the Woods
rtw-inc.com

Rotoluxe
rotoluxe.com

Royal Botania
royalbotania.com

Santa Barbara Designs
sbumbrella.com

Sattler Fabrics
sattler-ag.com

Schou USA
schouusa.com

Seagull Lighting
seagulllighting.com

Seasonal Living
seasonalliving.com

Segis USA
segis-usa.com

Seibert and Rice
seibert-rice.com

Selamat Designs
selametdesigns.com

Selux
selux.us

Seóra
seora.co

ShadeFX
shadefxcanopies.com

Shade Sails
shadesails.com

ShadeScapes Americas
shadescapesamericas.com

Shade Tree
shadetreecanopies.net

S. Harris
sharris.com

Shellshock Designs
shellshockdesigns.com

SifasUSA
sifasusa.com

Silver State Fabrics
silverstatefabrics.com

Sina Pearson
sinapearson.com

Skagerak Denmark
skagerak-denmark.com

Skyline Design
skylinedesign.com

SLV Lighting
slvbyslv.com

Sofi
lovesofi.com

Soji Lanterns
sojilanterns.com

Sokul
sokul.com

Spark Modern Fires
sparkfires.com

Stastny Stone Pots
stastnystonepots.com

Stone Forest
stoneforest.com/garden

Stone Manor Lighting
stonemanorlighting.com

Stone Yard
stoneyardinc.com

Stop Spot
stopspot.com

Stua
stua.com

Summer Classics
summerclassics.com

Summit Furniture
summitfurniture.com

Sunbrella
sunbrella.com

Sunset West
sunsetwestusa.com

Sutherland
sutherlandfurniture.com

Sycamore Creek
sycamorecreek.com

Sywawa
sywawa.be

Talenti
talentisrl.it

Targetti USA
targettiusa.com

Teka Illumination
tekaillumination.com

Tenshon
tenshon.com

Tensile Shade Products
tensileshadeproducts.com

Terra Furniture
terrafurniture.com

Terra Trellis
terratrellis.com

Terrene
terreneproducts.com

Textilene
twitchellcorp.com

Thibaut
thibautdesign.com

Thos. Baker
thosbaker.com

Three Birds Casual
three-birds.com

3 Mile Imports
3mileimports.com

Torrans
torransmfgco.com

Treasure Garden
treasuregarden.com

Trellis Structures
trellisstructures.com

TropiCasual
tropi-casual.com

Tropitone
tropitone.com

T2 Site Amenities
t2-sa.com

Tucker Robbins
tuckerrobbins.com

Tuscan Garden Works
tuscangardenworks.com

Tuscan Imports
tuscanimports.com

Tuuci
tuuci.com

Ultrafabrics
ultrafabricsllc.com

United Fabrics
unitedfabrics.com

Up Country Gardens
upcountrygardens.com

Urban Fire
urbanfire.ca

Uwharrie Chair Company
uwharriechair.com

Veneman
venemanfurniture.com

Vermobil
vermobil.it

Visio Light
visiolight.com

Vista Professional Outdoor Lighting
vistapro.com

Vitra
vitra.com

Vondom
vondom.com

Walpole Woodworkers
walpolewoodworkers.com

Walters Wicker
walterswicker.com

West Elm
westelm.com

Westminster Teak
westminsterteak.com

Wicker Works
thewickerworks.com

Willow and White
willowandwhite.co.uk

Woodland Creek Furniture
woodlandcreekfurniture.com

Xtreme Leathers
xtremeleathers.com

Yard Arbors
yardarbors.com

Zuo
zuomod.com

Design Centers

AmericasMart
240 Peachtree Street NW, #2200
Atlanta, GA 30303
404 220 3000
americasmart.com

Architects and Designers Building
150 East 58th Street
New York, NY 10155
212 644 6555
adbuilding.com

Arizona Design Center
7350 North Dobson Road
Scottsdale, AZ 85256
310 697 7700
arizonadesigncenter.com

Atlanta Decorative Arts Center
351 Peachtree Hills Avenue NE, #244
Atlanta, GA 30305
404 231 1720
adacatlanta.com

Boston Design Center
One Design Center Place, #337
Boston, MA 02210
617 338 5062
bostondesign.com

Dallas Design Center
1025 North Stemmons Freeway,
#605A
Dallas, TX 75207
214 747 2411
designcenterdallas.com

Dallas Market Center
2100 Stemmons Freeway
Dallas, TX 75207
214 655 6100
dallasmarketcenter.com

Decoration and Design Building
979 Third Avenue
New York, NY 10022
212 759 5408
ddbuilding.com

Decorative Center Dallas
1400 Turtle Creek Boulevard, #141
Dallas, TX 75207
214 698 1300
decorativecenterdallas.com

Decorative Center of Houston
5120 Woodway Drive, #3002
Houston, TX 77056
713 961 9292
decorativecenter.com

Denver Design Center
595 South Broadway
Denver, CO 80209
303 733 2455
denverdesign.com

Denver Merchandise Mart
451 East 58th Avenue, #4270
Denver, CO 80216
303 292 6278
denvermart.com

Design Center of the Americas
1855 Griffin Road, #A282
Dania Beach, FL 33004
954 920 7997
dcota.com

Designers Walk
168 Bedford Road
Toronto, ON M5R 2K9
416 961 1211
designerswalk.com

Forty-One Madison
41 Madison Avenue
New York, NY 10010
212 686 1203
41madison.com

Hamilton Properties
200 and 330 North Hamilton Street
High Point, NC 27261
336 884 1884
highpointhamiltonproperties.com

Hickory Furniture Mart
2220 Highway 70 SE
Hickory, NC 28602
828 322 3510
hickoryfurniture.com

High Point Design Center
442 North Wrenn Street
High Point, NC 27260
336 885 2868
highpointdesigncenter.com

Houston Design Center
7026 Old Katy Road, #274
Houston, TX 77024
713 864 4735
thehoustondesigncenter.com

**International Home
Furnishings Center**
210 East Commerce Avenue
High Point, NC 27260
336 888 3700
ihfc.com

International Market Square
275 Market Street
Minneapolis, MN 55405
612 338 6250
imsdesigncenter.com

**International on Turtle Creek
Design Center**
150 Turtle Creek Boulevard
Dallas, TX 75207
214 741 5018
internationalonturtlecreek.com

LA Mart
1933 South Broadway, #244
Los Angeles, CA 90007
213 763 5800
lamart.com

Laguna Design Center
23811 Aliso Creek Road, #151
Laguna Niguel, CA 92677
949 643 2929
lagunadesigncenter.com

Las Vegas Design Center
495 South Grand Central Parkway
Las Vegas, NV 89106
702 599 3093
lvdesigncenter.com

Market Square and Suites
305 West High Street
High Point, NC 27260
336 821 1500
marketsquareandsuites.com

Marketplace Design Center
2400 Market Street
Philadelphia, PA 19103
215 561 5000
marketplacedc.com

Merchandise Mart
200 World Trade Center, #470
Chicago, IL 60054
800 677 6278
mmart.com

Michigan Design Center
1700 Stutz Drive, #25
Troy, MI 48084
248 649 4772
michigandesign.com

Miromar Design Center
10800 Corkscrew Road, #382
Estero, FL 33137
239 390 5111
miromardesigncenter.com

New York Design Center
200 Lexington Avenue
New York, NY 10016
212 679 9500
nydc.com

New York MarketCenter
230 Fifth Avenue
New York, NY 10001
212 689 4721
230fifthave.com

Ohio Design Centre
23533 Mercantile Road
Beachwood, OH 44122
216 831 1245
ohiodesigncentre.com

Pacific Design Center
8687 Melrose Avenue, M60
West Hollywood, CA 90069
310 657 0800
pacificdesigncenter.com

San Francisco Design Center
Two Henry Adams Street
San Francisco, CA 94103
415 490 5800
sfdesigncenter.com

Seattle Design Center
5701 Sixth Avenue South
Seattle, WA 98108
206 762 1200
seattledesigncenter.com

220 Elm
220 South Elm Street
High Point, NC 27260
336 884 8220
220elm.com

Washington Design Center
300 D Street, SW
Washington, DC 20024
202 554 5053
dcdesigncenter.com

Bibliography

Accepta Advanced Environmental Technologies. 2011. Water and chemical use in the textile industry. http://www.accepta.com/industry_water_treatment/textile-industry-water-chemicals.asp.

American Association of Textile Chemists and Colorists. 2011. AATCC test methods and evaluation procedures. http://www.aatcc.org/testing/methods/index.htm.

American Chemistry Council. 2012. Sustainability and recycling. http://plastics.americanchemistry.com/Sustainability-Recycling.

American Composites Manufacturers Association. 2012. Composites manufacturing processes. http://www.acmanet.org/resources/manufacturing-process.cfm, http://www.acmanet.org/resources/index.cfm#Materials.

Amien. 2009. Lightfast versus colorfast. http://www.amien.org/forums/showthread.php?1862-lightfast-vs-colorfast.

Architectural Woodwork Institute. 2009. *Architectural Woodwork Standards*. Potomac Falls, Virginia: Architectural Woodwork Institute.

Axel Products. 2004. Fabric testing. http://www.axelproducts.com/pages/fabrictest.html.

Azhary Antique Furniture. 2012. French furniture Louis XVI style. http://www.azharyantiques.com/louisxvistyle.html.

Baker, John Milnes. 1994. *American House Styles: A Concise Guide*. New York: Norton.

Baltimore Sun. 1993. Collection turns gallery into wicker wonderland. http://articles.baltimoresun.com/1993-03-28/features/1993087149_1_wicker-furniture-antique-wicker-wicker-furnishings.

Bennett, David. 2005. *The Art of Precast Concrete: Colour, Texture, Expression*. Basel, Switzerland: Birkhäuser.

Black, J. T., and Ronald A. Kohser. 2008. *DeGarmo's Materials and Processes in Manufacturing*. 10th ed. Hoboken, New Jersey: Wiley.

Bond, Brian. 2012. Wood use around the farm. http://web.utk.edu/~tfpc/publicat/decay.htm.

Bramwell, Martyn, ed. 1976. *International Book of Wood*. New York: Simon and Schuster.

Brimi, Marjorie A. 1965. *Electrofinishing*. New York: American Elsevier.

Bullseye Glass. 2012. Methods and ideas. http://www.bullseyeglass.com/all-methods.html.

Cameron, Brenda, and Brian Cameron. 1998. *Making Bent Willow Furniture*. Pownal, Vermont: Storey.

Cane and Wicker Furniture Restoration and Resource Site. 2012. Cane raw materials. http://wickerworks.weebly.com/cane-raw-materials.html.

Carley, Rachel. 2006. *The Visual Dictionary of American Domestic Architecture*. New York: Henry Holt

Catapa. 2011. Ecological impact of mining. http://catapa.be/en/mining/ecological.

Chapin, Mac. 2004. A challenge to conservationists. http://www.worldwatch.org/node/565.

Cheremisinoff, Nicholas P., and Paul N. Cheremisinoff. 1995. *Fiberglass Reinforced Plastics: Manufacturing Techniques and Applications*. Park Ridge, New Jersey: Noyes Publications.

Cho, Renee. 2012. What happens to all that plastic? http://blogs.ei.columbia.edu/2012/01/31/what-happens-to-all-that-plastic.

Cohen, Cecilia. 2011. *The Glass Artist's Studio Handbook: Traditional and Contemporary Techniques for Working with Glass*. Beverly, Massachusetts: Quarry Books.

Cole, Julie Christine. 2009. *Professional Sewing Techniques for Designers*. London: Fairchild Books.

Corkhill, Thomas. 1980. *The Complete Dictionary of Wood*. New York: Stein and Day.

Dollinger, André. 2003. Ancient Egyptian basketry. http://www.reshafim.org.il/ad/egypt/basketry/index.html.

Douglas and Sturgess. 2010. Which resin is right for me? http://www.douglasandsturgess.com/HowTo/Introduction-to-resins-Howto.pdf.

Ecosystem Restoration. 2004. Environmental impacts of mining. http://ecorestoration.montana.edu/mineland/guide/problem/impacts/default.htm.

Elektriska Svetsnings-Aktiebolaget (ESABNA). 2012. Weld defects: porosity. http://www.esabna.com/EUWeb/MIG_handbook/592mig10_7.htm.

Emeralds and Rainbows. 2005. Woods used for outdoor furniture. http://www.teakandcedar.com/woodinfo.htm.

Engineering Toolbox. 2011. Wood densities. http://www.engineeringtoolbox.com/wood-density-d_40.html.

ETS Intarlaken Technologies. 2011. Metal testing equipment. http://www.ets-test-equipments.com/metal-testing-equipment.html.

ETS Intarlaken Technologies. 2011. Wood testing equipment. http://www.ets-test-equipments.com/wood-testing-equipment.html.

Fisette, Paul. 2005. Wood myths: facts and fictions about wood. http://bct.eco.umass.edu/publications/by-title/wood-myths-facts-and-fictions-about-wood/.

Forest Stewardship Council. 2011. What is certification? http://www.fscus.org/faqs/what_is_certification.php.

Furniture Free. 2012. Assyrian furniture. http://furniturefree.info/assyrian_furniture.htm.

Furniture from Home. 2011. Wood furniture construction. http://furniturefromhome.com/pages/wood-furniture-construction.

Furniture Styles. 2004. English antique furniture timeline. http://www.furniturestyles.net/european/english/timeline.html.

Furniture Styles. 2012. Regency furniture. http://www.furniturestyles.net/european/english/regency.html.

Gobeklitepe. 2009. What is Gobekli Tepe? http://gobeklitepe.info/.

Greene, Joe. 2005. Commodity thermoplastics: LDPE, HDPE, PP, PVC, PS. www.csuchico.edu/~jpgreene/itec041/m41_ch06/m41_ch06.ppt.

Groover, Mikell P. 2007. *Fundamentals of Modern Manufacturing: Materials, Processes, and Systems*. 3rd ed. Hoboken, New Jersey: Wiley.

Gurr, Kim, Leon Straker, and Phillip Moore. 1998. A history of seating in the Western world. http://www.exmoorantiques.co.uk/History of Seating.htm.

Harper, Charles A., and Edward M. Petrie. 2003. *Plastics Materials and Processes: A Concise Encyclopedia*. Hoboken, New Jersey: Wiley.

Hawks, Leona. 1987. Selecting bamboo and rattan furniture. Utah State University Cooperative Extension. http://extension.usu.edu/files/publications/factsheet/hi_04.pdf.

Hooson, Duncan, and Anthony Quinn. 2012. *The Workshop Guide to Ceramics*. Hauppauge, New York: Barron's Educational Series.

Idea Connection. 2012. Environmental impacts from mining. http://www.ideaconnection.com/solutions/1430-Environmental-impacts-from-mining.html.

Kadolph, Sara J. 2007. *Textiles*. 10th ed. Upper Saddle River, New Jersey: Pearson Prentice Hall.

Knickerbocker, Eric. 2002. Byzantine, Romanesque, and Gothic: three art periods and their histories. http://www.mrrena.com/misc/art.shtml.

Landscape Design Advisor. 2011.Choosing your landscape design style. http://www.landscape-design-advisor.com/design-styles/styles-overview/choosing-styles.

Lepoutre, Priscilla. 2011. The manufacture of polyethylene. http://nzic.org.nz/ChemProcesses/polymers/10J.pdf.

Liebson, Milt. 2001. *Direct Stone Sculpture: A Guide to Technique and Creativity*. 2nd ed. Atglen, Pennsylvania: Schiffer.

Lobser, Chelsea. 2011. Prairie modern: a house and garden in Fargo, North Dakota. http://www.gardendesign.com/prairie-modern-1.

MacDonald, Alistair. 2002. Industry in transition: a profile of the North American mining sector. http://www.iisd.org/pdf/2001/mmsd_na_mining_profile.pdf.

McAlester, Virginia, and Lee McAlester. 1984. *A Field Guide to American Houses*. New York: Knopf.

McKinney, Michael. 2011. The history of fiberglass. http://www.classicglasspars.com/index.php?option=com_content&view=article&id=77:the-history-of-fiberglass.

Michigan Reach Out! 2012. How are plastics made? http://reachoutmichigan.org/funexperiments/quick/plastic.html.

Miller, Bruce W., and Jim Widess. 1991. *The Caner's Handbook: A Descriptive Guide with Step-by-Step Photographs for Restoring Cane, Rush, Splint, Danish Cord, Rawhide, and Wicker Furniture*. Asheville, North Carolina: Lark Books.

Moody, Roger. 2007. *Rocks and Hard Places: The Globalization of Mining*. New York: Zed Books.

Morley, John. 1999. *The History of Furniture: Twenty-Five Centuries of Style and Design in the Western Tradition*. Boston: Little, Brown and Company.

Museum Furniture. 2012. Thomas Chippendale style furniture. http://www.museumfurniture.com/chippendale/.

Museum Furniture. 2012. Victorian age furniture. http://www.museumfurniture.com/Victorian.

Museums of Florence. 2012. Boboli Garden. http://www.museumsinflorence.com/musei/boboli_garden.html.

NAHB Research Center. 2011. Wood exposed outdoors. http://www.toolbase.org/Best-Practices/Failure-Prevention/wood-exposed-outdoors.

National Geographic. 2009. Logging of forests and debris dumping. http://ngm.nationalgeographic.com/2009/01/gold/larmer-text/6.

National Institute for Occupational Safety and Health. 2007. Ventilation. http://www.cdc.gov/niosh/mining/topics/topicpage30.htm.

Noakes, Keith. 2003. *The Fibreglass Manual: A Practical Guide to the Use of Reinforced Plastics*. Ramsbury, England: Crowood Press.

Pacific Northwest Pollution Prevention Resource Center. 2004. Fiberglass fabrication: operations. http://pprc.org/hubs/index.cfm?page=subsection&hub_id=10&subsec_id=2.

Panero, Julius, and Martin Zelnik. 1979. *Human Dimension and Interior Space: A Source Book of Design Reference Standards*. New York: Whitney Library of Design.

Plastipedia. 2012. A history of plastics. http://www.bpf.co.uk/plastipedia/plastics_history/default.aspx.

Powder-Coater. 2012. Powder coating manual. http://www.powder-coater.com.

Quality Logo Products. 2012. The different types of plastics and classification. www.qualitylogoproducts.com/lib/different-types-of-plastic.htm.

Queensland Government, Department of Agriculture, Fisheries and Forestry. 2012. Wood properties and uses of Australian timbers. http://www.daff.qld.gov.au/26_5509.htm.

Rainforest Relief. 2006. Patio and garden furniture. http://www.rainforestrelief.org/What_to_Avoid_and_Alternatives/Rainforest_Wood/What_to_Avoid_What_to_Choose/By_Product/Furniture/Outdoor_Furniture/Patio_and_Garden_Furniture.html.

Rattanland. 2011. Furniture materials. http://www.rattanland.com/rtl_material.php.

Shaw, Ian, ed. 2000. *The Oxford History of Ancient Egypt*. New York: Oxford University Press.

Shrager, Arthur M. 1969. *Elementary Metallurgy and Metallography*. New York: Dover.

Singer, Ruth. 2009. *The Sewing Bible: A Modern Manual of Practical and Decorative Sewing Techniques*. New York: Potter Craft.

Smithsonian Science. 2009. Problem plastics in museum collections have conservators on alert. http://smithsonianscience.org/2009/08/problem-plastics-in-museum-collections-have-conservators-on-alert/.

Stephens, Mark. 2008. Outdoor woods: Woodworkers Source's guide to choosing hardwoods for your exterior woodworking projects. http://www.woodworkerssource.com/outdoor_woods.php.

Strickler, Mike. 2012. Glossary of geological terms. Index to mineral and rock identification. http://jersey.uoregon.edu/~mstrick.

Stromberg Architectural. 2012. GFRP—glass fiber reinforced polymer. http://www.stromberg architectural.com/materials/gfrp.

Stromberg Architectural. 2012. GFRS—glass fiber reinforced stone. http://www.stromberg architectural.com/materials/gfrs.

T. H. Dick. 2011. The metallurgy of cast iron. http://thdick.co.uk/index.php/process/the_metallurgy_of_cast_iron.

Taylor, Louisa. 2011. *The Ceramics Bible: The Complete Guide to Materials and Techniques*. San Francisco: Chronicle Books.

Tikkurila. 2011. Visible wood knots and resinous bleeding through paint. http://www.tikkurila.com/decorative_paints/instructions/common_errors_in_surface_treatment/problems_in_exterior_paintingvisible_wood_knots_and_resinous_bleeding_through_paint.

Tylecote, R. F. 2012. *A History of Metallurgy*. 2nd ed. London: Maney Materials Science.

United Nations Environment Programme, International Resource Panel. 2010. The recycling rates of metals: a status report. http://www.unep.org/resourcepanel/Portals/24102/PDFs/Metals_Recycling_Rates_110412-1.pdf.

United States Department of Agriculture Forest Service. 1984. Tropical timbers of the world. Agriculture Handbook 607, Forest Products Laboratory, Madison, Wisconsin.

United States Department of Agriculture Forest Service. 1999. Wood handbook: wood as an engineering material. General Technical Report FPL-GTR-113, Forest Products Laboratory, Madison, Wisconsin.

Wall Street Journal. 2007. *Wall Street Journal* exposes FSC policy chaos. http://www.fsc-watch.org/archives/2007/10/30/Wall_Street_Journal.

Warm Glass. 2012. Pate de verre. http://www.warmglass.com/pate_de_verre.htm.

Washington State Department of Archaeology and Historic Preservation. 2012. Architectural style guide. http://www.dahp.wa.gov/learn-and-research/architectural-style-guide.

Williams, R. Sam, and William C. Feist. 1999. Water repellents and water-repellent preservatives for wood. General Technical Report FPL-GTR-109, United States Department of Agriculture Forest Service, Forest Products Laboratory, Madison, Wisconsin.

Woodworking Network. 2012. Wood species. http://www.woodworkingnetwork.com/wood/hardwood-softwood-species.

Your Antique Furniture Guide. 2008. Furniture timeline. http://www.efi-costarica.com/Furniture-Timeline.html.

Photography Credits

Sketches and photos not listed, or listed without a photographer credit, are by the author.

page 2: photo courtesy of Gloster

page 9: garden of J. J. DeSouza, Portland, OR

page 12: garden of J. J. DeSouza, Portland, OR

page 45: garden of Jim Rondone and Ky Dehlinger, Portland, OR

page 47: home of Curtis Holyk, La Center, WA

page 48: garden of Lucy and Fred Hardiman, Portland, OR

page 49: Shafa chairs; photo courtesy of Design Kollection

page 50: garden of Margaret Stapenhorst and Peter Menza, Vancouver, WA

page 51: ornaments by Wall Play; photo courtesy of Flora Grubb Gardens

page 51: design by Seasons Garden Design, Vancouver, WA, and Williams Landscape Lighting Design, Portland, OR

page 52: Star Lily chandelier by Lance Lindsay; photo courtesy of Stone Manor Lighting

page 53: landscape design by Grace Design Associates, Santa Barbara, CA; photo by Douglas Hill

page 53: photo courtesy of the Bulbeck Foundry through Elements International, Portland, OR

page 54: photo courtesy of Parasoleil

page 55: photo courtesy of Walpole Woodworkers

page 56: photo courtesy of Modfire

page 56: photo courtesy of Westminster Teak

page 57: photo courtesy of TropiCasual

page 58: landscape design by and photo courtesy of Allworth Design, Seattle, WA

page 61: garden of Geoff Beasley and Jim Sampson, Sherwood, OR

page 62: Bulldozer Lounge chair; photo courtesy of Mark Goetz and Efe Buluc; photo by Grace E. Chen

page 63: photo courtesy of Westminster Teak

page 64: garden of Linda Ernst and Greg Dermer, Portland, OR

page 64: chair by NIPpaysage; photo by permission of Cornerstone Gardens, Sonoma, CA

page 65: Bulldozer Lounge chair; photo courtesy of Mark Goetz and Efe Buluc; photo by Grace E. Chen

page 65: photo courtesy of Innermost

page 67: QT chairs and table by Royal Botania; photo courtesy of Royal Botania

page 69: photo by permission of Artefact Design and Salvage, Sonoma, CA

page 70: Golden Gate Park outside the Japanese Tea Garden, San Francisco, CA

page 71: photo by permission of Filoli, Woodside, CA

page 72: sculpture by Simon Allison; photo by David Rodal, by permission of Kiftsgate Court Gardens, Chipping Campden, Gloucestershire, England

page 73: photo by permission of Sleeping Lady Mountain Resort, Leavenworth, WA

page 74: garden of Pat Collins, Portland, OR

page 75: photo by permission of the Ruth Bancroft Garden, Walnut Creek, CA

page 151: garden design by Kristy Ditmore and Jamie McAuliffe for the 2012 Northwest Flower and Garden Show

page 152: outdoor leathers by Xtreme Leathers

page 154: fabrics by Sunbrella

page 155: design by Alexander Purcell; photo courtesy of Purcell Living

page 156: Castillo chair by Giati

page 158: garden of Susan Fries and Lew Bowers, Portland, OR

page 160: fabric by Thibaut

page 160: Pavilion IV fabrics by Duralee

page 162: fabric by S. Harris

page 163: Aqua Velvet fabrics by Holly Hunt

page 163: fabric by Nomi Fabrics

page 167: fabric by Sina Pearson and Sunbrella

page 168: garden of Michael and Maryellen McCullough, Portland, OR

page 170: fabric by Comtrex

page 173: the author's garden

page 174: photo by permission of The Wicker Fixer, Tigard, OR

page 175: photo by permission of the Bellevue Botanical Garden, Bellevue, WA

page 177: garden of Laura Crockett, Hillsboro, OR

page 178: photo by permission of Chanticleer Garden, Wayne, PA

page 180: Bella Madrona, garden of Geof Beasley and Jim Sampson, Aurora, OR

page 182: garden of Mort and Judy Levin, Shaker Heights, OH

page 186: garden of Joanne Fuller and Paul Pierce, Portland, OR

page 189: photo by permission of Filoli, Woodside, CA

page 190: ceramics by Linda Kliewer, Clay Art Botanica

page 190: photo by permission of Codina Ceramics

page 191: ceramics by Linda Kliewer, Clay Art Botanica

page 192: ceramics by Gainey Ceramics; photo by Caitlin Atkinson, courtesy of Flora Grubb Gardens

page 192: garden of Linda Ernst and Greg Dermer, Portland, OR; chairs by Fermob

page 193: garden of Kym Pokorny, Portland, OR

page 194: ceramics by Linda Kliewer, Clay Art Botanica

page 195: photo courtesy of Aw Pottery

page 197: design by Lamberts, Dallas, TX

page 197: garden of Tom Koster, Berkeley, CA

page 198: planting design by Karen Chapman, Le Jardinet Designs

page 198: Bangle garden seat; photo courtesy of Tucker Robbins

page 202: photo courtesy of Stone Forest

page 203: Chanticleer Garden, Wayne, PA; sculpture by Marcia Donahue

page 204: garden of Greg Lueck and Rebecca Seymour, Vancouver, WA; design by Seasons Garden Design, Vancouver, WA

page 205: photo courtesy of Charlie's Antiques

page 206: photo by permission of the Boboli Gardens, Florence, Italy

page 207: garden of Lisa Wence and Dan Partin, Hillsboro, OR

page 208: garden of Francis and Sharri LaPierre, Battle Ground, WA

page 209: photo courtesy of Matt Goddard, Poetry in Stone

page 210: photo courtesy of Stone Forest

page 211: garden design by Anthony Fajarillo, Redwood Builders Landscaping and Puget Sound Bonsai Association, for the 2012 Northwest Flower and Garden Show

page 212: stone table by Sam Bates

page 213: garden of Francis and Sharri LaPierre, Battle Ground, WA; design by Seasons Garden Design, Vancouver, WA

page 213: photo taken at the Dallas Arboretum, Dallas, TX

page 214: garden of Susan Fries and Lew Bowers, Portland, OR

page 217: garden of Joanne Fuller and Paul Pierce, Portland, OR

page 218: garden of Craig Quirk and Larry Neill, Portland, OR; landscape design by Laura Crockett

page 219: photo courtesy of Zuo

page 220: garden of Bonnie Bruce and Michael Peterson, Portland, OR; photo by Bonnie Bruce, glass art by Roger Thomas

page 221: photo courtesy of Uroboros Glass

pages 221, 222: Gorge Glashaus, McMenamins Edgefield, Troutdale, OR

page 223: art by Roger Thomas; photo by Bill Bachhuber, courtesy of Roger Thomas Glass

page 223: garden of Linda Ernst and Greg Dermer, Portland, OR

page 224: art by Mason Parker

page 226: garden of Joanne Fuller and Paul Pierce, Portland, OR

page 227: art by Barbara Sanderson, Glass Gardens Northwest

page 229: garden of Craig Quirk and Larry Neill, Portland, OR; landscape design by Laura Crockett; concrete leaf by Little and Lewis; fire pit by Experienced Materials

page 229: garden of Jim Rondone and Ky Dehlinger, Portland, OR

page 231: photo courtesy of Stastny Stone Pots

page 232: sketch by Patrick Gracewood

page 232: sculpture by and garden of Patrick Gracewood, Portland, OR

page 233: garden of Lisa Wence and Dan Partin, Hillsboro, OR

page 234: mold design by Patrick Gracewood

page 234: sculpture by and garden of Patrick Gracewood, Portland, OR

page 235: panel by and photo courtesy of Hidden Springs Designs

page 236: garden of Craig Quirk and Larry Neill, Portland, OR; landscape design by Laura Crockett; concrete column art by Little and Lewis

page 238: garden of Michael Schultz and Will Goodman, Portland, OR

page 239: Queens Plaza, New York; design by Margie Ruddick; photo by Robert Khazzam

page 241: photo courtesy of Gloster

page 242: Cornerstone Gardens, Sonoma, CA; design by Rios Clementi Hale

page 243: photo courtesy of Vitra

page 244: "Daisy Border" by Ken Smith; Cornerstone Gardens, Sonoma, CA

page 246: photo courtesy of Jay Scotts

page 247: garden of J. J. DeSouza, Portland, OR; chairs by Kartell

page 247: garden of Jim Rondone and Ky Dehlinger, Portland, OR

page 247: sculpture by Orlandi Statuary; design by Wight's Home and Garden for the 2011 Northwest Flower and Garden Show

page 248: photo courtesy of Loll Design

page 249: garden design by Topher Delaney and Seam Studio; Cornerstone Gardens, Sonoma, CA

page 250: Cappellini Knotted chair; design by Marcel Wanders

page 251: Normand Couture design from Couture Jardin; photo courtesy of TropiCasual

page 252: Cornerstone Gardens, Sonoma, CA

page 257: Elements International, Portland, OR

page 258: photo by permission of NEST, Portland, OR

page 259: photo by permission of Robert Allen

page 260: Nip and Tuck, Portland, OR

page 261: fabric by Sunbrella

page 262: table by Bullseye studio team; photo courtesy of Bullseye Gallery

page 263: table by Hidden Springs Designs

page 265: Elements International, Portland, OR

page 267: gate design by Seasons Garden Design, Vancouver, WA

page 267: sketch by Experienced Materials

page 267: design and light fixture by Experienced Materials

Index